# Already To Harvest

## Marjory Fullmer

ISBN: 978-0-6152-0429-1

# Chapter 1

It was a cold morning near Nevada City, California, that January 2nd, 1858. John L. Blythe left his warm comfortable cottage as soon as he could find an excuse to leave his wife and small sons. He had to leave to keep from saying things that would hurt his precious wife. He must think, must work it all out in his own mind.

The snow rhythmically snapped and crunched under John's feet, as the crust on the thin layer of snow broke, making jigsaw puzzles of pieces about twice the size of his boots. He walked unhurried, lost in his own unhappy thoughts.

Herds, the nearest neighbor, lived just a good distance when a man wanted to think. John pulled the ends of his coat collar tightly together. The cold he felt wasn't from the penetrating canyon breeze, but the cold that stems from a frozen heart, chilled by death, the death of a newborn babe. He had tried everything! His prayers of faith and even the Priesthood of God did not save this tiny baby boy whose life span had been twenty minutes. Only time to be named and given a father's blessing and start a prayer that he might be spared.

"Dear Lord," John now asked fervently, "help me to understand." His wife Margaret's superior knowledge of these things irritated him. She had belonged to the Church of Jesus Christ four years before he joined it. He still had much to learn of God's commandments, what was to be expected in this new, yet ancient covenant. He was now part of God's Church, one of the Latter-day Saints.

Margaret and John had their future all planned. They would have a large family and raise all of their children in the true Church, teaching them to know and love God. He must settle his business affairs and leave for Utah where they would live among the Saints. They had a firm belief that no better influence could be found in which to raise their children than among God's chosen people who were united in worshipping a known Heavenly Father and Son as revealed to Joseph Smith. This was the Blythe's constant motivation for working towards going to Utah. Their plan was in righteousness, after God's own plan, 'to multiply and replenish the earth.' But their second-born was now dead.

"Then why," wondered John, "did God let this baby die?"

He thought of this religion he had accepted less than a year before and the priesthood that George Q. Cannon had conferred upon him. "If it is of God, why wasn't the power of the Priesthood sufficient to keep this baby alive?" He asked himself. "Yes, why didn't it work?"

He remembered the stories he had heard of the Saints, how they were driven from their homes in the dead of winter. How they were insulted, beaten, and killed but found no comfort there. Where was God when they needed his help?

"God chastens those He loves." he could hear Margaret quote. The thought only made his resentment grow.

Yes, before he was baptized in the San Francisco Bay, he was sure. There had been no doubt. He tried to keep all of God's commandments, as he understood them, but the law of tithing he could not accept. To give one tenth of all the gold he had gleaned from his mines and one tenth of his rents as he received them seemed more than God should ask.

"John, our Heavenly Father has given us every thing we own. To give back one tenth will show our gratitude for all we have." Margaret reasoned.

One day Margaret jokingly said, "If you don't pay a full tenth of all the money you get, God might take his tenth from you." John shook his head, thinking what funny ideas Margaret had at times.

He had been generous with his money. $625 given to George Q. Cannon for aiding and establishing a printing press for the missionaries on the Sandwich Islands and had given the Church $4000 in gold for the benefit of the work of God. Even after this, Margaret was not satisfied.

"But John, you added 'or for my own benefit' and had Elder Cannon bind himself to render a full account of those funds whenever you required him to do so. I tell you tithes and offerings can't be given in that spirit."

The neighbor's door rattled as John's firm knock echoed in the still wintry morning. The door opened little more than a crack. Mrs. Herd peered through it and asked in a cool manner, "Yes?"

John was surprised and wondered why the sudden change. The Herds had always been so friendly. Mrs. Herd had even offered to act as mid-wife when Margaret was confined. John waited for her to invite him in, but the door didn't move. "What do you want?" she asked.

"The baby---" John's voice faded away. He found it hard to say the word.

Mrs. Herd's dark eyes lit up, "Oh it's her time!" she exclaimed. She was about to swing the door open and let him in when a male voice

4

from the back of the room called her name sharply, and just as quickly the door resumed its former position.

"No," John answered, watching her face redden, "the baby is dead. We thought you would like to come and lay it out for us."

"Oh, what a shame!" Mrs. Herd's face knotted in sympathy. Then stepping out of the cabin, she closed the door behind her. "I would come, but my husband won't let me," she confided. "He says you are Mormons."

"Oh," John said understanding the reason for his unfriendly reception. But he asked anyway. "Then you read the book 'The Voice of Warning' I left with you?"

"No, I didn't get a chance to. My husband burned it Christmas Day."

"Edith! Edith! Get in here!" came a demanding voice from inside the cabin and Mrs. Herd slipped back into the house without saying another word. John stood at the closed door for a moment, then huddled up against the cold and turned, going back to his own home.

Margaret put both pillows behind her and leaned her tired, aching back on them. This way she could see out the bedroom window. It was uncomfortable sitting in bed like this. The added discomfort would be worthwhile if it helped get her mind off of this subject that was haunting her. If little Johnny had awakened and needed a word of comfort from her, she believed this would help, but there hadn't been a sound from that room. He was such a good sleeper.

Looking out the window, Margaret could see the dark green pine trees growing among the partly naked boulders. The snow that had completely covered the red earth, which was waiting patiently for her green dress of spring, had only started to dress the large rocks in a white petticoat. Margaret looked the other way and saw the level spots she and her husband had laboriously prepared for seed and garden. Mount Pleasant was a beautiful place. Each year it became dearer to her. "If we don't leave to go to Utah soon," she thought, "the love for this place will keep us here."

She saw John coming without Mrs. Herd. "He mustn't see I've been crying," she said aloud, and sliding down under the covers she wiped her eyes with the end of the pillowcase.

"She couldn't come?" Margaret asked as John entered the room.

"No, and try and guess the reason why."

"She had bread to bake?" Margaret offered gaily, but her talk and smile couldn't hide from John the many tears she had shed in his absence. The growth on her right eye always looked much worse when she had been crying.

"No. We are Mormons!" John managed to laugh trying to hide his true feeling.

"Well, I didn't expect that from them!"

Margaret was disappointed, but looking at John's solemn face she added, "We can expect a great deal of that, dear." When John's expression didn't change she continued, "I thank God every day that you were converted and baptized. How nice it is to have you believing as I do and how much easier it is living with another Mormon who will stand up for the truth."

John smiled and squeezed her hand, but Margaret was solemn now. Her eyes flooded over and she was crying again, this time in gratitude. She shouldn't have allowed herself to start, for after once releasing her damned up tears she couldn't find a way to stop them. Try as she would.

Sitting on the bed by her, John patted her hand and smoothed her silky auburn-brown hair.

"My darling," he comforted, "I know how disappointed you feel. Still we did our part and God said 'No', but we won't give up. We shall have our family yet! Now, don't grieve any more for tiny Daniel. He has returned home to his Father in Heaven."

Margaret reacted strangely to this. Pulling away from him, she turned over and cried as though her heart would break.

"What did I say wrong?" John wondered as he continued to try to comfort her without success. Getting nowhere, he gave up trying and went into the kitchen where he prepared a simple meal of milk and mush for the three of them. He was so lost in his own thoughts that he completely forgot the ham and eggs and other fancy foods he had obtained for this special day.

As soon as John left the room Margaret let herself go completely. "It's not John's fault!" She sobbed bitterly trying to drown the sound in the pillow. "It's mine! I was not worthy to keep this baby! I've tried. Oh, how I've tried to forget Mathew and his clever, cunning ways, but I can't! I just can't! Why am I constantly comparing everything John does with the way he would do it? John is so good to me. He is such a sincere man then why do I long for Mathew and our family?"

She thought of her five children she left behind with Mathew after the divorce and felt she would give almost anything if she could just see and hug and hold them and know that they were all right.

She couldn't tell John these thoughts that had possessed her since their marriage. She had no intention of hurting him by sharing them. Her folks had shown they hadn't completely disowned her when they asked John to find her and see how she was faring when they heard he was leaving for California. Margaret often wondered what her father said when he heard from her letter that John not only found and married her, but also joined her Church.

She hoped and prayed to forget the life she had with Mathew Stubbart, but found she longed for his presence at the most unexpected times and he entered her dreams much too often. No mother could be expected to forget the children to whom she gave life, but she couldn't remember them without remembering the love she had for their father. This futile love she held made her a captive of the past. It was self-destructive and would have consumed her if she hadn't found strength and a reason for living in the Faith she had accepted.

Now she had a home with a son and a loving husband. Yet her heart had an odd way of clinging to what she felt her life could have been with her first husband, if he hadn't changed.

Margaret had every reason to hate Mathew. He had been more than cruel hurting her as only a loved one could.

Since the day they met, he acted as though he worshipped the ground she walked on. She was the center of his universe. The fall from the pedestal had been hard and sudden. From the day she was baptized it seemed some evil spirit took over the body of her lawyer husband and substituted hate and deceit for the love and tenderness he had given her so abundantly before. He looked the same. Her heart filled with love and pride whenever she saw him for he was a handsome man, straight in stature and clean-cut in feature, carrying an air of importance that made men as well as women admire and respect him. Now, only the shell was left like an over-ripe apple that had fallen from a tree. He looked desirable, but was rotten inside.

Margaret felt a tightening in her stomach as she remembered the first time she and Mathew met the Mormon missionaries. Mathew was as impressed as she was, when he heard of the restored Church of Jesus Christ. The more they heard and studied, the more she felt it was indeed the true Church restored in these latter days, while Mathew, influenced by the rumors and unpopularity of the Mormons became poisoned against it. Partly against his wishes Margaret had been baptized.

Hoping that someday he would see the light, she prayed nightly that he would come to see and accept the truth. Instead of improving, conditions became worse. She was careful how she mentioned her church to him trying to keep peace. Another child was added to the family – baby James, their third boy.

One night when Mathew told her the current stories of the terrible Mormons, Margaret could stay quiet no longer.

"Oh, Mathew," she cried, "These things you hear aren't true!"

"They really have you fooled, haven't they, Margaret?" Mathew replied, his voice full of disgust. "I tell you this right now, it won't be long before we will wipe this evil out and your Church will be completely destroyed. Then where will you be? It's a sinking ship you have joined, Margaret. Get out of it while you can!"

"Get out of it!" Margaret echoed. "If I were to say I didn't believe it to be the true Church of Christ, I would be lying. I would be denying the knowledge the Holy Ghost has given me."

"And if you don't, you will be denying your love for me. Now which is the more important, a ghost or a real live flesh and blood man?"

"You don't understand. I can love both you and God, just as I can love both you and the children." She only added fuel to the fire.

"Margaret, I'm telling you I refuse to be humiliated like this. Twice today I had people say, 'Your wife's a Mormon, isn't she?' I had to find excuses for you."

"I'm not ashamed of it!"

"Well, I am! And if you don't do something about it, we're through!"

Margaret was taken unaware and gasped, "What do you mean, Mathew?"

"If you don't love me enough to do this for me, I don't want you as a wife."

"What are you saying, Mathew? Surely you don't mean that!"

"I mean exactly that. Choose between your Church and me." His words cut deep, but this was only the beginning of the heartache her firm belief caused before Mathew was through.

She fasted all the next day and prayed all night desiring to know what to do. Early in the morning little James started crying for his milk. Margaret picked him up lovingly and held him tightly in her arms until he was satisfied. Instead of weariness from the last twenty-four hours, she felt a strength sweep through her whole body. It was felt as definitely as the tingling feeling her milk made as it filled her breasts. All uncertainty was gone. Margaret knew what she must do.

Now years later in her bed thinking about this, she asked herself, "Was I right? Has this testimony been worth the price I had to pay for it?"

Once more Margaret saw the painful picture of the courtroom. "He was already sure of a divorce. He did it to hurt me." She sobbed to the pillow. "He told the judge to look at my eye--that I had an evil power obtained when I became a member of the Devil's Church and was using it to ruin his law practice. He knew I was sensitive about my eye and he lied! This growth on my eye started to grow before I was baptized. He went with me when I saw Dr. Alden and was told it was some kind of cancer. The doctor gave me a salve to put on it, but it kept growing. We were both worried for fear I would lose the sight in that eye, and gradually I did.

"He knew, yet he said that! It hurt almost as much as when the judge said a Mormon was not a fit mother and that I was not to have or see my children again. Poor James! He was such a little baby, still nursing when they tore him from my arms." How often she thought of him and prayed for the well being of all her children.

She must forget the past. Worrying about the children wouldn't help them any and it wasn't fair to her husband and little John. Once again Margaret tried desperately to stop crying. The palms of her hands were sore from the pressure of her fingernails because of the many times she had doubled up her fists in an effort to control herself.

"I will! I will! I will!" She determined through gritted teeth, not realizing John was coming through the doorway with her breakfast. Hearing the tinkling of dishes, Margaret looked up and saw the worry in John's eyes.

There was a silence as John placed the food before her. Then with a shamed expression Margaret asked in a small voice full of humility, "John, will you anoint my head with this oil?"

John's heart filled with tenderness and love as he took the small bottle of consecrated olive oil. It was part of an ordinance 'to be used for sickness in a household of faith' that his new priesthood gave him. He would administer to her as the apostles of old. When he finished praying, she smiled and he knew she felt much better.

He kissed her lightly as he handed back the bottle of oil. She used this oil daily in a little ritual all her own. Each night she rubbed it on the growth above her sightless eye while saying a prayer to her Father in Heaven.

Margaret stared at the bottle a long time, fingering it nervously. She had the faith. "Then why wasn't the growth going away?" She felt her eye once again. "At least," she consoled herself "it doesn't seem to be growing very fast."

Late afternoon came before John was able to leave Margaret and his little son. John was amazed at the many chores his wife had been doing and wondered how she found time in one day to get them all done. He only did the things that needed his immediate attention and wondered how he could make such a mess doing a little job. He spilt the new milk when he was straining it before setting it out in pans. While he was cleaning up the mess he made, he let part of his dinner boil over, the meat had burned, and little John sensing something was wrong, had been so demanding.

Before leaving, John made sure they were both asleep. His son looked so small in the new bed. He had radiated with pride at the thought of being big enough for a big bed, not realizing his little bed was intended for a newcomer. The little bed was not needed after all, but John knew his son would refuse to return to it. Although only 16 months old, John Jr. had a mind of his own.

Going into the hall, John passed the tiny bundle in the cradle. He had taken it from the bedroom early that morning and put it in this unheated part of the house. Glancing at it now, he wondered if he should have packed snow around the wee little fellow.

Bending down, John uncovered the baby's head. "A beautiful child," he thought. "Looks as though he is just sleeping." Then it happened! John thought he saw the blanket move up and down with the rhythm of breathing. "The baby is alive!" he exclaimed aloud and quickly knelt and felt the baby's head, then his arms. No, his imagination was playing tricks on him. The little baby was cold and lifeless.

John slumped wearily into a chair where he could watch this still little form, hoping to see the blanket move again or see some other sign of life. He was looking for a miracle to prove that he did have the power of God through the priesthood he held. He waited and stared. Nothing happened. The little bundle stayed so still, so terribly still.

The Sabbath came on the third morning of the year. That was to be his son's funeral. At nine o'clock only two persons attended the funeral of Daniel Blythe, the sexton and his father. Solemnly he was lowered in a tiny grave in a cemetery on a pine-covered hill. Many years collection of pine needles kept the earth from being frozen solid. After the box was carefully covered, the two men walked in silence over the crest of the hill to the road. Here John paid the sexton the prearranged fee.

"Can I take you home?" asked the sexton, motioning to the wagon he used as a hearse.

John shook his head. The sexton shrugged his shoulders, climbed up on the seat of his wagon, clicked to his horses and was soon out of sight. John listened as the wind made mourners of the pines who wailed their sad song. Then picking his way to avoid stepping on the new graves, he returned to the newest one of all. Here he felt hidden among the pines at the head of Daniel's grave. John went to his knees and poured out his troubled heart to his Maker.

Death was no stranger to John. He had seen its handiwork many times. Violent death in the coal- mine tragedies at Pittston, Pennsylvania and among feuding California miners and death after years of suffering, accepted almost with thankfulness for this act of mercy. But this baby's death was different. It always is when it takes your own flesh and blood, especially for the first time.

Walking back home John wondered why he felt as he did about a little one who only lived a few minutes.

# Chapter 2

The next morning, after caring for the comforts of his wife and small son, John went to town to take care of his affairs. Much had to be done before the Blythe family could leave for Zion. First he went to see his lawyer, Francis Dunn. He had previously employed him to defend his rights to a piece of ditch property at Red Dog. As yet, nothing had been done about it. John anxious to get the matter settled made a very liberal proposition and asked his lawyer to settle it amiably if possible.

"I'll have my clerk take care of the matter tomorrow for sure." Dunn promised. "I know the other parties will agree to these terms."

He next went to see a Mr. Thomas Anderson hoping to sell him some mining claims. In the course of their conversation, before the papers were signed, Mr. Anderson asked, "Is your wife a Mormon?"

John automatically came to her defense, "And none ashamed of it."

Smiling at John's attitude, Mr. Anderson confided, "I wouldn't tell this to everyone, but I was a Mormon too, for several years."

"You were?" John was surprised for he often saw him at the Methodist Church where both of them usually went to worship on Sunday.

"Yes. In England I was even ordained a Priest by Brigham Young."

"And what happened that you fell away?" asked John.

"Oh, I was wandering about in California with none of the Saints to speak to, so I joined the Methodists. It being the more popular."

John asked sternly, "And when you joined the Mormons you knew the Church of Jesus Christ of Latter-Day-Saints was the true Church?"

"I suppose so, at least I thought so at the time," Mr. Anderson paused, and then continued, "But now I wouldn't change. I'm a Methodist, same as you."

"I am not a Methodist. I am an Elder in the Mormon Church!" John declared emphatically. "Well, I see you at services all the time."

"Only because I have no Mormon Church to go to."

Mr. Anderson laughed, "Be a Mormon when you are with Mormons but a Methodist with Methodists. That's my way. I see you are not so different."

John never cared for Mr. Anderson with his aggressive, boastful ways and resented being accused of having any of Mr. Anderson's same characteristics.

"I am not denying I am a member of Christ's only true Church." John stressed the 'only' and showed his irritation by adding, "That makes me different!"

His resentment amused Mr. Anderson and he said, "If the men at the Methodist Church knew that, I wonder how friendly they would be!"

"I would not be afraid to stand up and announce it!"

"You won't have to. I shall pass the word along." He teased.

John felt his anger hard to control and answered hotly, "You go right ahead!"

That is just the kind of thing this man would do, John decided, but even in this atmosphere of antagonism he felt a little responsible for this ex-Mormon.

He must try to reach him. Although still angry, he added, "But let me ask you, or better still, ask yourself. Are you enjoying the same blessings now that you did while you belonged to the true Church of Christ, clothed with the Priesthood?" John's face was red, but he had controlled his voice.

This question annoyed Thomas Anderson, and he answered quickly, "Yes, I am! You can see I have been blessed of God. Don't I have money? Position? I am the District Attorney of Nevada City and you came to sell your mining claims to me, knowing I had the money to buy them."

"But the thing you have lost, money cannot buy." John was now calm and sincere. "I feel sorry for you, Thomas. You have lost your testimony."

"A testimony is a cheap price for all I have," he bragged.

"Then I tell you, it would have been better had you never joined the Church of Jesus Christ in the first place, for once knowing the truth, greater will be your condemnation for denying your Savior."

For the first time Mr. Anderson showed his anger as he shouted, "I do not deny Him! I worship Him! I belong to the Church I attend! I am no hypocrite like you!"

"A hypocrite for standing by the truth?"

"A Mormon," Thomas said the word with disdain. "Making people think you are a Methodist! Wait until Herd, your neighbor hears about this!"

That did it. John's anger was kindled again. "He knows I am a Mormon!"

"He does?" Mr. Anderson raised his eyebrows in surprise. "Man, I would hate to be in your shoes!"

With this information Mr. Anderson thought of an easier way for obtaining John's claims and announced, "No, Mr. Blythe, I am not interested in your mining claims after all. If I wait a little while I will be able to pick them up dirt cheap, and since our business is completed, good day and good-luck. You'll need it!"

Mixed emotions branched out from John's main purpose, like the many twigs on an unpruned tree, confused him until he dared not speak as he gathered up his papers and walked out.

As he reached the door, Anderson called, "See you at Church, Brother Blythe." Then he roared with laughter.

The sound rang in John's ears as he slammed the door after him. Soon he regretted showing his temper. Once again his firm belief and lack of self-control had cost him the results he had desired. He must get his mining claims and property sold before he could hope to leave for Great Salt Lake.

When he made further attempts to sell his claims, John found word had been spread through the town that Mr. Blythe was trying to sell all of his worthless mining claims to any poor sucker who was foolish enough to buy them. It was reported he had the nerve to try and push them off on even the eminent District Attorney who had really put him in his place.

Mr. Anderson's influence had also affected Mr. Dunn. Although the lawyer was pleasant enough when John found him home and sober and after repeated promises to take care of John's business, he never followed through. As an incentive John offered him a bonus of one hundred dollars if he would settle and collect his money on the Red Dog ditch property. Dunn gave him another empty promise. When he received a suit against him, John went to Dunn's office and sat there most of the day until he actually saw the completing of a counter suit made out by his lawyer and filed in the County Clerk's office. Too late, Dunn's negligence cost his client two thousand five hundred dollars.

Sunday, John Blythe was not found in the Methodist Church. "Not because I am afraid to go," he told his wife. "It is this feeling I get, so unbefitting the Sabbath Day when I see that cocky Mr. Anderson."

The Blythes held their own Sunday services. Margaret who

seldom left the protection of her home, was delighted and suggested they have a meeting every Sunday in their home whether John went to other meetings or not. They had prayers and songs and reading of the scriptures and a discussion about the first four principles of the Gospel: faith in the Lord Jesus Christ; repentance; baptism by immersion for the remission of sins and the laying on of hands for the gift of the Holy Ghost.

Often part of Sunday was spent writing letters. John usually wrote to his favorite brother, Daniel, who had chosen Australia instead of America to seek his fortune. Since his conversion, the letters John wrote were of a preaching nature, for John desired that Daniel should also receive the light of the true Church.

John took this chance to start rereading The Book of Mormon. He was surprised at how much better he understood it and how much more there seemed to be in it of God's word than he had remembered. When he came to the words of the Savior, the prayers to be used for the blessing on the bread and wine, he desired that he and his family should partake of the sacrament. Since he was an Elder he had the authority to prepare it, but his wife in her sweet way suggested he wait.

"Until your heart is free of this feeling towards Mr. Anderson," she urged.

John told Margaret what Mr. Anderson said about Mr. Herd. They wondered what he meant. Some months ago, John had helped Mr. Herd fix up his house in readiness for his wife's arrival from back East. "They were so friendly until they knew we were Mormons," John reminded his wife.

"Mrs. Herd hasn't been after butter and milk lately," Margaret said.

"So they're unfriendly. We won't worry about it. Mr. Herd is too nice a man and too civilized to do harm to his neighbors simply because they believe differently than he." John suspected the talk he and his wife had before they went to bed about the Herds was the reason for the vivid dream she related to him in the morning. Margaret believed differently. She insisted it was a warning.

"I saw a man about to hit you on the head with a large rock while you were working on your Austimah Hill claims, but seeing him come upon you, I was able to call to you just as he was going to strike."

"And what happened? Did he hit me?" John asked smiling.

"I don't know. I woke up before I found out."

"Then I wasn't hurt, was I?" John laughed.

"I'm serious, John. I'm telling you, I know this dream was a warning. Once before I dreamed you were lying with your head near a fire, but you were not burned. I pleaded with my Maker to let me understand and I feel this dream is the interpretation of that one and definitely a warning. Oh, John! Do be careful. Don't let anything happen to you!"

"Now, don't worry your bonny little head. I'11 be careful." He assured her as he set his course toward his Austimah Hill claim. The air was not too cold, just invigorating. John found the earth soft enough to dig and soon had his sluice box filled with promising soil. He devised an interesting way for the water to reach his box and today just enough water was slipping through the icy fingers of winter to do a good job.

The day had turned out rather pleasant. John enjoyed his own company. He could plan and dream as he worked. How different this mining was compared to the coal mining he did in Scotland and Coaldale, Pennsylvania. Yet the experience he had in these mines made it possible for him to become a man of some means. He had been among the first to tunnel into the earth to find gold at another claim.

John's thoughts were far from Margaret's dream. He hadn't consciously seen anything or heard anyone. But suddenly it happened. John wheeled around just in time to see gleaming metal -- the end of a shovel. It cut the air where his head had been. It crashed into the side of the sluice, breaking it up. John sprang up and grabbed the coat of his attacker. "What are you trying to do? Kill me?" John was breathing hard. He looked up into the coarse-featured face of the man.

Instead of answering, the man wrestled out of his coat and ran down the hill. John gave chase. Down the hillside they went at breakneck speed. A cabin came into view. Before John could catch the man, he reached his cabin, slammed the door closed and bolted it. Since the door looked flimsy, John flung himself at this barrier but it did not give. Next he hammered on it with his fist and shouted, "What are you afraid of, you big bully! Come out! And fight like a man!"

He listened for an answer but all he could hear was his own heavy breathing. After he had calmed down, John quit knocking. Nearby a large rock made a good resting place and John could see the only door of the cabin from there. He waited for some time to see if the man would come out. He wanted to find out if he could, why he wanted to kill him. He wondered if this was one of Mr. Anderson's men. Perhaps this was how Anderson intended to get his claims. Or was he simply a Mormon-hater?

After waiting quite a while, John gave up, for the man never even unlocked the door. John asked himself why he was waiting. Of course the man would never tell him why he wanted to kill him. He didn't even come out to fight. As John left to go home and tell Margaret about his experience, he remembered her dream and a feeling of thankfulness came over him. God had spared his life. Next time he wouldn't take her dreams so lightly.

About four inches of snow fell during the night and John found it necessary to hunt for their cow that had strayed away the day before. He heard she was seen two miles away. John hunted all morning for her without success. Coming home at noon, he and his wife made it a matter of prayer that he might find her soon. After he went out again, the first man he met told him where she was.

"Yes, God does answer prayers," Margaret said, "and someday He will answer another prayer and cure my cancer."

The snow fell steadily the next two days. However, John managed to build a corral for his cow and go to town for the mail. A letter from Brother Evelith gave him an account of the departure of Brother George Q. Cannon and his company of Saints for the Valley. He also stated that there were still about fifteen or twenty of the Saints in San Francisco and that they held regular meetings, but all were desirous to gather home. Home to 'Zion'– the name for the place of the Saints. John liked the idea, where every man was his brother and every woman his sister.

Now Elder Cannon was gone. How he loved that man! He had baptized John and explained the Gospel to him. He would miss him. But it would not be too long before they would be joining him and the rest of the Saints in Zion.

The next Sunday morning when John went to town to mail two letters, he noticed a handbill posted up on the wall of the Post Office. In large letters it read, To the Rescue! Ho! For Salt Lake! Ho! For Salt Lake! It requested all that were willing to shed their blood in favor of the Stars and Stripes to come forward with their name. John decided to go to the Methodist meeting and see to what extent this handbill and Mr. Anderson had incited the people of the town.

Nothing unusual happened at meeting. He neither felt tongues wagging behind his back nor any uncommon hostility. Those who ordinarily spoke to him, spoke, those who didn't were silent.

The text of the sermon was "On the resurrection of Christ depend all the hopes and beliefs of Christianity". The minister's preaching was good, he admitted to himself. The preacher asked the audience to secure an inheritance with God in Eternity and stated that all that was necessary to obtain an inheritance was to give themselves and the world to God, but he failed to tell them how to do this. John was thankful that his Church taught him how.

As he left the church, he was told the mail from the East had arrived. Back he went to the Post Office. The center of town swarmed with the largest part of the population of Nevada City. The main attraction was the sun. It drew more people than Jenny Lind would have brought to the Nevada City Theater. As it warmed the wintry air both coarsely dressed miners and people in their church finery gathered in groups to talk. The loud laughter accompanying vulgar talk, which John heard as he passed these groups, churned in John's head. He was glad Margaret wasn't there to hear it as some of it concerned the posted handbill and the Mormons.

John waited in the line that had formed in front of the Post Office window. He heard two men talking in front of him. "They finally caught that stage robber that gave them the slip for so long."

"Yeah," the other man answered, "But we're still not safe. Two men were shot through the head and apparently robbed. They were just found on the road leading to Dry Gulch."

Robbing, killing, drinking, cheating and vulgar talk seemed the natural way of life in the Gold Kingdom, John thought. A place where ideals were forgotten and passions ran a wild race with life and money.

Nevada City was one of the most refined and gentle of all of the towns that mushroomed into existence during the rule of gold fever. To John it had become an undesirable and wicked city. His soul yearned for perfection that he thought would be found in God's Kingdom.

John went home and pulled down his rifle. He cleaned and reloaded his revolver as well. He kept them for the protection of his family and property, since he lived in a lonely place and had the reputation of keeping a large amount of money in his home. He fervently prayed that he would never be compelled to use them.

Winter reclaimed the Sierras. Between storms and even during storms, John worked on his claims at Sugar Loaf and the one on

Austimah Hill. But one day he found two men living in his cabin at the Sugar Loaf claim who claimed the right to live in it. "A log cabin cannot be held as property unless it is occupied," they declared and John knew they were within their rights. He also found a window had been stolen from his board cabin and a prospect pan taken from within.

Each time he passed the big man's cabin on the way to his Austimah Hill claim; he hoped he might see him and maybe he could talk to him. He had about decided the handbill against the Mormons had aroused the man's actions when he had another encounter with the man.

One day a particularly heavy storm came that turned into rain in the afternoon. John was informed water flowing down the hillside in Nevada City had flooded his lower building on Broad Street, sending mud and water into it. He rushed into town to assess the damage.

While he was making ditches to lead the water from the building, a man came up to him. John stopped digging for a minute and leaned on his shovel. The old man spit tobacco into the ditch. "You John Blythe?"

"Yes."

"Is Brandy Point your claim?"

"Why, yes, it is."

"I just come to tell you that I saw three men workin' on it yesterday. Probably still up there."

John hired the man to go with him as a witness. When they reached Brandy Point, John saw that one of them was the same man who tried to kill him on Austimah Hill. He was the biggest of the three, and when he turned towards John, his heavy face had the same look of hatred.

John rushed up to them. The old man who was his witness stood nearby. "This is my claim!" John shouted. "You can't work my claim!"

The big ugly man lunged toward John, raising his shovel above his head. Just then the other men grabbed the shovel and held him.

"Get out of here you dirty son-of a bitch, or I'll kill you!" the ugly man snarled. John backed away. This man meant business. His life was more valuable than any claim. John and his witness left.

John stayed near home the next day. Although many of his ideas changed since he had accepted the Gospel, John was not the kind of man to let any one get the best of him if he could help it. His Brandy

Point claim suddenly seemed not only worth keeping but also worth working. He reasoned that if a man had been willing to kill him for this claim, it must be paying good money.

Going to town next morning, he went by way of Brandy Point. The shovel-wielding man was not there. John talked to the other two men busy working John's claim. They told him Sam Disdun was John's attacker. As John reasoned with them, they finally agreed to quit working on his claim, but asked permission to clean up the gold they had washed. John consented. He felt he owed them that much for restraining the big man who had tried to kill him twice. They also explained why he had. "Sam? He's crazy for gold!" John understood.

Just as some become addicted to alcohol, there are those who become addicted to finding gold. Not for the material things this gold could bring them, but to satisfy a craving to find it, to see it, to hold it. No amount of hardship, or suffering reduced this craving. Neither did the big strike reduce it. Their greedy craving was never satisfied. Sam Disdun was such a man.

Afterwards, John had an offer on his Sugar Loaf claims. He accepted it. Selling it was worth not causing trouble with the men who had taken over his cabin on these claims. He sold his interest to the Public Administrator, F. H. Nickleson for two hundred ninety-five dollars and fifty cents. This was the amount he figured was due him for the material and work he had put in on these claims.

After his business was finished, John passed a man from Folsom selling fruit trees. "They look like real nice trees. What kind are they?" he asked.

"Mostly peach," the man replied. "I've sold the largest part of them. All but these peach. I have about three-dozen left. Wish I could get them sold so I could start back home."

"If I took all of them, how much would they be?"

"I'll give them to you for thirty cents each."

"Make it twenty cents and you'll have a sale."

"Sold!" exclaimed the man as he started lifting the trees off of his wagon and handing them down to John.

When he pulled away, John found himself surrounded by forty small trees. Already he began to regret making this bargain, for now he had to borrow a wagon to transport them. Worse than this, what would Margaret say when he brought forty trees home? There was something permanent about planting trees. Margaret would be so disappointed because she would think he didn't have any intention of

20

leaving for Salt Lake. That he wasn't even trying to get his business settled. "But a man couldn't pass up a bargain like this," he justified himself. "Imagine only twenty cents for one of those magnificent trees."

John envisioned the fragrant blossoms and the tasty peaches these barren sticks would someday produce. Forty trees, enough for a nice sized orchard. But Margaret would not understand. He decided he would have to get rid of most of them before he got home.

Up ahead, John saw a man fixing his fence. Pulling up along side of him he called, "Say, Mister, how would you like to buy some nice peach trees to plant around your place?"

"Hell, no!" the man replied, "I've been digging holes all day and I don't aim to dig any more for any old trees."

John went on and glancing back again at his trees decided that that man wouldn't have appreciated his trees anyway.

A pretty little cottage was near by. He saw a man come out of the door. John stopped his horses again and went up to him.

"I have some lovely little trees out here that I'm practically giving away. Would you like some?"

"What kind are they?" the man asked.

"Peach." John replied.

"Peach! Ugh! Take them away. I never could stand peach fuzz. Now if they were apple---."

John continued trying to sell them, then to give them away, but he met one objection after another as he was getting closer and closer to home. He even tried Herds, but no one came to the door. When he came to his own driveway, he was still carrying all forty little peach trees.

As the wagon rattled toward the house, John was glad night was falling. Perhaps Margaret would not see what was in the bed of the wagon, but apparently she had heard him coming for she was waiting at the side of the house.

No, it wasn't dark enough to hide forty little twigs all waving "Hello," he decided as he looked back and saw how the bumpy road animated each tree.

## Chapter 3

Margaret heard the wagon and pulling the curtain back, she strained to see who was coming toward the house. As the wagon rattled nearer, she was surprised to see her husband driving the team, for she knew he had walked to town and was more surprised when she made out in the growing dusk the load he was carrying in the bed of the wagon. She went outdoors to get a better look.

"What kind are they?" She asked in greeting, wondering what he was doing with this strange load.

"Peach."

"Are they for us?"

John nodded. Margaret stared at the little trees, then at John and sighed.

John knew what she was thinking. "Oh, Margaret," he said, "Surely you don't think I have it in my heart to stay here----and they will improve the place."

Margaret nodded her head in agreement then sighed again in disappointment but didn't say a word.

"They were just such a bargain I couldn't pass them up." He went on to explain and with these words Margaret's concern changed to understanding. She knew her husband could never resist a bargain. John seeing her relieved smile started up the wagon, knowing he would be planting all forty little trees around the place.

The next day was mild and John planted out a row of his trees on the west side of the garden walk leading to the spring. Margaret took over the job that afternoon while John went up to Austimah Hill and cleaned up the gold in his ripple-box.

The warm, pleasant air gave new life to Margaret's energy. After shoveling a hole nearly large enough to take the sod-laden roots of a little peach tree, Margaret enjoyed scooping up the rest of the dirt with her hands. The ground was a little too wet for planting, but the clean, earthy odor was perfume to Margaret.

"My ancestors must have been farmers," Margaret thought as she felt the contentment that came over her as her hands worked with the dirt. She loved to see green things grow and laughed at herself when she remembered the regret she felt as she destroyed weeds, shrubs and wild blackberry bushes while helping her husband clear this land between the house and the spring for a vegetable garden.

After she had planted four trees, she stood up and surveyed her handiwork.

The garden, a tiny part of her domain, was wrapped in beauty. Snow lay heavy on the north but had almost disappeared on the south side except in the winter-permanent shadows and on the peaks of the mountains.

Over by the house she saw John Jr. throwing muddy handfuls of dirt at Browny, the dog, who was sitting there taking it. Browny was so gentle with little John. Margaret knew her son was as safe with Browny as he would be with a nurse who was constantly watching him. To strangers, Browny showed an entirely different side. Because of his eagerness to bite any guest, when one was expected, they found it necessary to keep him chained. Browny wasn't much to look at but for their needs Browny was the ideal dog.

Margaret suggested her husband take the dog with him while he worked on his Austimah claim. John answered he would feel safer if Browny stayed home protecting the family.

The next day John planted ten fruit trees without the help of Margaret, for the day was cold and cloudy. The day after was still cold and threatening. John and Margaret worked together to plant the remaining little peach trees. John had a load of manure hauled from town, part of which he worked around the peach trees and then spread the rest over the garden plot.

"Now, it smells like spring," he laughed when he saw Margaret hold her nose as she passed on her way to get a bucket of water.

It rained nearly all of the next week and part of the time the wind whipped the rain against the windows. A small crack made an entrance for the rainwater to trickle down the walls in the house. This did real damage to the parlor walls. When Margaret saw they could do nothing to prevent this damage, and John had become discourage trying, she said, "Let's not worry about it but feel thankful."

"Thankful!" John asked in surprise.

"Yes, thankful. Thankful that we were unable to get that beautiful red satin brocade I wanted so badly on my parlor walls, for it would have been ruined and I would have felt sick, but these walls can be patched and white-washed again and look as bright as new."

The Blythes had some visitors during the rain. One man came to buy quicksilver. John sold him seventy-seven pounds at eighty-five cents a pound, which the man was able to carry away in bottles. A Mr. Cunningham called on John to see if he would help him get some money owed him for work on the Eureka ditch before John bought the water company. He needed it to stake a claim at Scott's Flat. John promised he would try to help him get his money, for Mr. Cunningham was a brother-in-law to Mr. Colburn, a friend and co-owner of one of John's mining claims.

The rain and high wind was responsible for Mr. Cunningham's invitation to dinner, then for his staying all night. John took this opportunity to tell him of their religion. He seemed quite receptive. He prayed with them and promised to read the copy of The Book of Mormon that John loaned him. He later became John's first convert.

Margaret dreaded company and being conscious of her eye, tried to stay out of Mr. Cunningham's sight, but John insisted she eat with the rest of them. Margaret found a small scarf and pinned it in her hair letting it fall over the right side of her face, covering the growth.

How good it was to talk to an outsider and hear about his sister, Mrs. Colburn. Mr. Cunningham was an interesting, friendly man. It wasn't long before Margaret felt she had known him for many years.

That night Margaret had an impressive dream, which she related to her husband. "My eye was cured of cancer. I saw a little girl all dressed in white and newly baptized in the Church of Jesus Christ. She put a cabbage leaf on my head and I could see in my blind eye! A voice filled the room and said, "You have been cured by the power of God through your faith." I reached up and felt my face and it was smooth and free of all cancer. I walked up, thanking God for curing my eye. I saw my father standing there and threw my arms around his neck, but he stood there as though he hadn't seen this miracle and I pleaded with him to write a letter to my kindred and tell them of my cure that they might know and believe."

After Mr. Cunningham left, Margaret and John fasted and prayed the rest of the day that her dream might be fully realized. Shortly after, Margaret took courage and wrote to her father on the principles of the gospel. She had written once before after she married John, telling her folks of her experiences since she was disowned. This letter was never answered.

"Don't you think it's a bit strong?" John asked when she let him read it.

"No, I have only written the truth and if he reads it, it might make him see that there is something to this Church I have joined, after all. Isn't the teachings of Christ a blessing to share, not a thing to hide?"

John agreed.

When he went to mail her letter, John received three issues of

The Deseret News, which had been printed in December in Fillmore, a small town south of Salt Lake City,  John couldn't understand why.

"I also received a letter from Mr. Evelith," he told Margaret after returning home. "I can't understand a man like that. He said that a large company of Saints was going to start for the Valley from San Mateo and Santa Clara Counties. Mr. Evelith was offered a wagon to take him through but he declined the offer. And for what reason? Money! He said right now he has less than two hundred dollars to his name." John shook his head in disgust. He had heard that Mr. Evelith, a fellow Saint, was now receiving a salary of a hundred dollars a month! Although he had been in California about seven years and had received between eight and nine thousand dollars in wages during that time, he hadn't saved any money.

"Oh, what a shame he can't go!"

"He could, Margaret, if he were willing to give up his hundred dollars a month. The Gospel doesn't mean as much to him as the money. He is--"

Margaret broke in, "Oh, John, here is our chance! Couldn't we go with them?"

"How? Margaret, how?"

"Leave everything! Take the money we have and buy what we need." Margaret's heart danced with the idea.

"Leave everything as it is? We couldn't possibly!" and seeing Margaret's keen disappointment, he explained, "I have obligations. I have another suit coming up. This one is against two buildings of my Broad Street property. I have also signed notes for which I am responsible."

"Oh, John!" Margaret begged, not wanting to give up the idea, "But we do have the money we need now!"

"Trust me, Margaret," he answered, "It is more than money."

"You know best." Margaret conceded and wondered if they were not very much like Brother Evelith. It sounded so simple to pick up and leave. However in her heart she knew it would not be easy even for her to leave their fine home and the security they had here.

When the ground was ready, John planted peas.

"Not with a desire to remain here and enjoy the produce of our garden," he repeated to Margaret what he had told himself, "but for the purpose of improving the looks of our place. I'll get this ground planted and if something should happen that we don't get away, we will have a few vegetables to eat."

A little later, carrots, turnips, and onions were planted. Then corn. Fields of oats and hay were planted on the ranch and a man helped John clear a field near the corral that was also planted in alfalfa. This man, Appleton Plumley, plowed and sowed the seed for the privilege of taking sixty-four cords of oak wood from John's ranch.

John paid to have most of his planting done, leaving him free to work on his Brandy Point claim. The more he heard of the character of the big man, Sam Disdun, the more alert he grew to the danger of being attacked. He admitted some relief when he heard that Sam was working a claim over near Scott's Flat and warned Mr. Cunningham, who was also working there, against him the next time he came to visit them.

Reports of claim-jumping made it impossible for John to spend all of his time on Brandy Hill so he found it necessary to work each of his major claims, Austimah Hill, Sugar Loaf in the cut where he worked underground and one in Buck-eye Ravine. Yet all the gold he washed was so little it did not pay the men for the work they were doing on his places.

Usually mining for John was solitary work, but he had a number of visitors on the 26th of February. That day most of Nevada City was attending a hanging held within the sight of his dwelling. A man named Butler was being hung. John, not relishing this type of entertainment, spent the day working on a claim, stripping off top dirt. After the hanging, every man that passed him had to tell him something about it. They couldn't understand how he came to miss it. "Yes, I read about it in The Nevada Journal. Yes, it was held within walking distance. Yes, it should be a lesson to all the robbers and murders here about," he found himself agreeing with the men who passed.

"Nothing could have kept me away from it, neither the storms of nature nor the force of man. I like to see a man get what he justly deserves," one man said. "You really missed a sight!"

A few days later, John heard more about the hanging when he went to see his lawyer, Mr. Dunn, who he found sober for a change.

"I didn't see you at the execution," Mr. Dunn remarked.

"No, I didn't go. I was busy."

"What a shame you missed all that excitement. It was better than a parade, all those horses and uniforms and things. I would say it was even better than a play. This was real life, no acting like you see at our theater. When he was declared dead, you knew he wouldn't get up again and start bowing." Mr. Dunn dramatized. "I'm surprised you didn't go see it. He was hung on a hill over by your place. Didn't you know about it?"

"Yes, I knew. I didn't want to go."

"What a shame you missed all that excitement," Mr. Dunn repeated not believing anyone would want to miss such a spectacular event. "Here is a paper I bought at the hanging. It tells all about the life of Butler. One thing I will say about the man, he died bravely. Here- read this while I am working on these papers."

John felt obliged to read the newspaper whether he wanted to or not and found the details of the life of Major Boling alias M. Butler fascinating, yet depressing to think such an able man had wasted his life robbing and killing.

"This Butler surely suffered worse than death fleeing from it," was John's comment to Mr. Dunn when he finished reading the biography. A hanging still wasn't his idea of entertainment, but after knowing more about Butler, he could understand why the execution drew such a large crowd.

John didn't have to look at the March sun to know it was noon. When he was doing hard labor like shoveling dirt, as he was this Monday morning on his Austimah Hill claim, his stomach was a better timekeeper than the sun. With his stomach feeling hollow and his appetite keen, John started down the hill to his home and dinner.

When he came in sight of big Sam Disdun's cabin he saw the roof near the chimney was on fire. John ran to the cabin door since the smoke coming out of the chimney showed the cabin was occupied, and pounded with his might to give the alarm in case Sam or some other person was inside. "Fire! Your house is on fire!" John yelled and was about to stop knocking to try and drown the fire when he heard someone coughing.

John tried the door. It was locked. John kicked at the door with even more energy than the time before when Sam had threatened his life and was able to knock it open.

The smoke overcame Sam, who had been sleeping, and it was with great effort that John dragged the heavy man from the burning cabin. Then he set to work extinguishing the fire. The fresh air revived Sam and he sat staring, unbelieving at John.

"You must be crazy!" Sam called in his deep husky voice, the closest he could come to expressing his thanks. He later sneered, "Well, the fire's out. What are you waiting around for, a reward?"

John chuckled to himself as he continued down the hill. Yes, he had his reward. His heart was filled with the joy of saving this man who had tried to kill him twice.

The next Sabbath was one John remembered vividly for many years. He and Margaret fasted and prayed, asking God to teach them His will and their duty in all things both spiritual and temporal. How fervently they prayed to be able to arrange their affairs and soon gather with the Saints in Zion.

The climax came when John partook of the sacrament he prepared for the first time. The Lord's Supper or the sacrament was not new to Margaret, having been taught its purpose by the Elders who baptized her and she agreed John was ready to renew the covenants he made with his Maker when he was baptized. John, using his authority, having been ordained an Elder by George Q. Cannon, prepared and blessed the sacrament. They both ate in remembrance of Christ's body, which He gave for them, and drank in remembrance of His blood, which he shed for them, in a thoughtful, solemn, and repentant way.

After which being filled with the Holy Ghost, they testified to each other that they knew Jesus was the Christ and the Son of the living God and that their Heavenly Father heard and answered their prayers. They thanked Him for restoring His Church in these latter days and for sending the missionaries to their homes, allowing them to be 'one of a family, one of a City' to belong to His Kingdom. After expressing themselves by these testimonies, the peace and contentment they felt went beyond any previous experience either had ever had and they reveled in the love, respect, and appreciation they had for God and for each other. Even little John seemed filled with the same beautiful spirit.

John woke from a dream that night, and the next morning he left his house with renewed energy, determined to get his business cleared up and his claims sold. Before he reached town, a big part of his enthusiasm was taken from him in the form of Sheriff Samuel Boreing who asked him, "Are you John Law Blythe?"

John laughed, "Of course I am John Blythe and you know it!"

"Yes, but I had to make this formal." He answered as he handed John a subpoena, another suit to test ownership of a building and lot on his Broad Street property. This was a boundary dispute.

After seeing his lawyer, John obtained two bondsmen as security, and he was also advised that in order to recover the money he loaned on the Red Dog ditch property, he would have to carry his suit to the California Supreme Court.

The next day he traveled seven miles to subpoena a witness, Mr. Jenkins, to appear on the 23 of March to testify to the title of two houses and lots that he, A. R. Jenkins, sold John for $1 700. Mr. Jenkins refused to go until John paid him a fee of $5 and $2.50 for the mileage he would have to travel. John wondered at his reluctance if the title was free and clear as Mr. Jenkins had told him at the time of the sale.

Although the next day turned cold and threatened to storm and the warmth of his home appeared so inviting, John went to town again and by the request of his lawyer, gave the Sheriff $20 as redemption money for the H. R. Forbes ditch. It was also sold by Sheriff's sale while John was down in San Francisco taking money to George Q. Cannon. However, John had discovered the Sheriff had deeded away the property sixteen days before the time specified by law.

"I'll leave the money in your hands until tested." He insisted when the Sheriff told him it would do no good.

Instead of being relieved of his material problems, every way John turned new problems were added and the more he struggled to clean up his affairs, the more they seemed to cave in on him. He was trying as hard as he could to get ready to leave for Utah, but it seemed his prayers were far from being answered. John could not understand why and was becoming discouraged.

Then one evening Margaret became ill. In the middle of the night she woke John saying she was suffering very much from a headache. "Will you please administer to me?" she requested. John anointed her head with oil and then laying his hands upon her head asked in the name of Jesus Christ that the pain would be removed. Because of his discouragement, there was some doubt in his mind that this prayer would be answered, but the Lord did grant his request and the pain was gone within half an hour and Margaret slept well.

It was John who tossed and turned the remainder of the night and the short time he did sleep his dreams were wild. Once he heard the alarm of fire. He jumped out of bed, checked through his house, and out in the yard. Relieved at finding no fire and seeing all was well, he soon went back to bed, yet he could not return to sleep.

A letter came from Brother Young, a relative of the Church

President Brigham Young, from his home in Grass Valley. This member of the Church was new to John. He had never heard of him before. Brother Young had sold his place preparatory to leaving for the Great Salt Lake Valley in about ten days. He wanted the Blythes to travel with them.

John laughed and Margaret sighed when John read Brother Young's letter to her.

"I don't know how I have managed to get things so complicated." John exclaimed when he finished reading the letter. "Even when I went to see if my trial would come off on the 23$^{rd}$ as scheduled, I was told by Judge Niles that he had a murder case to try and after that he would try no more cases this term of court. That means the $7.50 I paid to a witness was just wasted."

"I know how unfavorable things look, but you will keep trying, won't you?"

"You know I will, Margaret. We will leave for the Valley as soon as we can."

Because the sluice boxes in the Ravine needed cleaning and John's business kept him busy, it was the last day in March before John could leave to go to Grass Valley to see Brother Young. The boundary suit, which had been filed against him, was settled out of court. Through a flaw in the title John lost one fine board building and one third of the land he had bought in good faith.

"Yes, I know you lost $900 worth of your Broad Street property," Margaret comforted, "but look at it this way. The two buildings you have left are worth more than you paid for the three of them. When you sell them, you will make a nice profit."

Leaving the stage that brought him from Nevada City to Grass Valley, John walked directly to the Orleans Quarts Mill where he found his friends, members of the Church. Brother Morgan, Brother Baxter, and Brother Stackhouse who were all in good health and Brother Morgan was especially happy. He saw a good prospect of realizing considerable wealth from his quartz mining.

"Yes," he told John, "I think I shall have quite a fortune by June, and then I am going to sell my quartz mine and leave for the Valley."

"Wish I could get my business settled by then." John said wistfully.

"Oh, I thought you were going with the Youngs. They have been waiting to hear from you."

"No, I can't possibly make it. I came to tell Brother Young as soon as I could get away, but I don't know the man or where he lives. His letter took me by surprise. I didn't know we had another member here in Grass Valley."

"Oh, yes, they are members, a whole family and Grandma, too." Brother Baxter, who was listening to John's and Brother Morgan's conversation broke in. "He's a very likeable person, a relative to President Brigham Young, you know."

"But not very active. He doesn't come to any meetings." Brother Stackhouse explained, "His wife feeling the way she does."

"How's that?"

"She's bitter. Went through a lot in Nauvoo. Felt that God had deserted the Saints. Well, that may well be, but the Holy Ghost deserted her. That's for sure! She can't say a nice thing about the Church or anyone in it." Brother Stackhouse answered.

"Then why are they going back to Zion?" John asked.

"He wants to go back." Brother Morgan explained, "He has family there and his mother-in-law has been pleading to go back ever since they came. I guess that's why. He hasn't struck it rich here, either."

"Oh, I see, but how do I get to his place?"

"I'll take you," Brother Baxter offered. "They call their place Primrose Cottage. It's rather nice."

When they reached the Youngs, Grandma Jolley came to the door and told them Mr. and Mrs. Young were not at home that they were out on business. When she heard John Blythe was the stranger with Brother Baxter, she insisted they come in.

Grandmother Jolley's name was deceiving. Her wrinkled, frowning face advertised her misery. She was a very unhappy, complaining woman who made it a habit to tell anyone who would listen, her tale of woe. The men barely stepped over the threshold when she started with her current aches and pains. Then she said she hadn't been at all well since she came to California and after numerating her many past illness and tragedies she said, "If I had only known they were bringing me to California, I would have never come! I keep telling them, this is not the place we should be, we who gave up so much for our Faith. We should be with the Saints and if they don't take me back soon; I'm going to start walking! Even if I have to go all by myself."

On and on she talked of how miserable she was here in California. Since it was noon, she did stop complaining long enough to insist the men sit down and eat with her and the children. The men accepted and soon she was repeating all her troubles and her desire to get back to the Valley, never giving the men a chance to say anything except a sympathetic "That's too bad, or an understanding "Oh".

The table was neatly set. Hot bread, fresh butter, honey, cheese and pitchers of rich, cold milk were placed on the table. The children were very polite and didn't say a word during the entire meal. John wondered if they were shy because of the company or if they never had a chance to be heard above Grandma's constant, complaining chatter.

She had repeated herself about five times before John was able to break in to compliment her on the meal and added, "With all this milk, butter and cheese, you must have some fine cows."

"Yes," she replied. "We have two and a calf that my son-in-law wants to sell. But why he wants to sell them, I can't understand. We shall never find cows like these in Great Salt Lake. But, will he listen to me? No! I don't think he ever hears a word I say."

After lunch Brother Baxter learned the Youngs had gone to visit friends in town who had spent the winter with the Saints in Salt Lake the year before and as soon as they could get away from Grandma Jolley, he took John to their house.

Once again John was disappointed for Brother Young had just stepped out with the man of the house but Sister Young was here. After being introduced to Mrs. Young and her friend, Mrs. Jones, John felt this would be a good opportunity to find out more about Great Salt Lake and the conditions he would meet when he traveled to the Valley. He was pleased when Brother Baxter suggested he stay there in case the men returned while he went out to look for them.

John was soon to regret this decision. Mrs. Jones didn't want to talk about that "terrible trip" nor did she appreciate that "awful Mormon City."

"She agrees with me," Sister Young said bitterly, "Great Salt Lake is no place to live. She and her family got out of there as soon as the weather would permit."

"It was cold and the people were cold." She answered to his persistent questioning. "They were the most miserable and unfriendly persons I have ever met. If you weren't one of them, they ignored you completely. Oh, they had their good times, all right. They were always having a social or party of some kind, but do you think they would ever ask an outsider to one? Heaven forbid!"

"It wasn't as if they were ordinary emigrants. The Jones are refined and wealthy people," Sister Young offered in her defense.

"Her husband was the mayor of their home town and her ancestors came over on the Mayflower. Oh, Mr. Blythe, you ought to see the beautiful wardrobe she brought with her. She has two dresses I would give my eye-teeth to have."

"Would you show them to him?" she asked Mrs. Jones. "I bet he never saw anything like them in his whole life."

Mrs. Jones quickly went to a trunk and brought out two beautiful dresses.

"Look at this red silk one," Mrs. Young exclaimed. "The lace is exactly the same color. I can just see this dress on me. It would show up my dark hair and dark eyes." Then touching the other one she asked, "But now, Mr. Blythe, did you ever see anything as regal as this brocaded one? All this embroidery was done by a craftsman's hand."

"It took my dressmaker over a year to do that and to sew these beads on the skirt and bodice. Yet, to get the real elegance of these dresses, you must see them on."

"Why don't you put them on and show him? Put this one on first." Mrs. Young held up the red gown. "It is my favorite." Mrs. Jones laughed at Mrs. Young's enthusiasm and said, "Would you like to put it on? And I'11 wear the other one and we can show him the latest fashions from back East."

"Oh, I'd love to!" Sister Young exclaimed, hugging the dress to her.

"Please, no. Oh, no!" John begged. "That won't be necessary! I can see how lovely these dresses are without trying them on. It is true. I have never seen finer material or better workmanship. So don't put them on for me. Save them for some grand affair."

"I have little occasion to wear them in Grass Valley," Mrs. Jones sighed.

"We are going to put them on!" Mrs. Young insisted, determined to take Mrs. Jones up on her offer, "and you are going to sit right there so you can tell us how grand we look. Promise?"

As he heard the giggling and loud exclamations of the women dressing in the next room, John sat on the edge of the sofa twisting uneasily, hoping the men, Mr. Young and Mr. Jones, wouldn't show up. If they came through the door he wondered how he could explain what was going on.

This was a new situation for John and he did not like it. It seemed an eternity since they had gone into the next room and thinking better of his promise, John picked up his hat and was about to escape through the front door when the women, flushed with excitement, made their entrance.

"Mr. Blythe, you weren't going to go!" Mrs. Young pouted. "You promised." John came back and sat down on the sofa. Mrs. Young tossed his hat on the table and each in turn gracefully pivoted in front of him showing off their lovely dresses and figures.

"Now you must choose," Mrs. Jones insisted. "Which dress is the most beautiful?"

"You are both lovely. I could not possibly choose." John stammered, as his face grew red.

When the women were satisfied that he would not commit himself, they grew tired of their game and they decided to walk through the town showing off their pretty dresses.

"We may see someone we know!" exclaimed Mrs. Jones.

"We better see someone we know," Mrs. Young answered.

As the women stood in front of the mirror, primping and getting ready to go to town, John excused himself and slipped out the door. He walked the streets until time to leave by the four o'clock stage, but he saw no one he knew except the two beautifully dressed ladies walking some distance in front of him. He was careful not to catch up with them and noticed they were apparently having a great time talking to almost every one they met unconscious of how out of place they looked in their finery.

Disappointed, John climbed into the stage and thought how useless the whole trip had been.

# Chapter 4

A few days later, Margaret suggested it. She thought John should go back to Grass Valley and talk to Brother Young. He thought so too, and insisted Margaret and little John go with him. He never told Margaret of his experience with the ladies, but insisted she accompany him. He did not intend to be cornered by them again. Margaret wondered why he was so determined that she go but found herself anticipating the trip with a feeling of excitement as she dressed in her finest clothes. To conceal the growth on her eye, she chose a bonnet trimmed with a graceful ostrich plume and, a heavy veil.

They took their buggy to Nevada City then the stagecoach on to Grass Valley. John felt the stagecoach would be safer explaining to his wife, "Usually the passengers on the stage get through with their lives, while one or two persons traveling alone often don't have the same protection. One never knows where the robbers might be hiding ready to attack."

As they traveled the five miles, John pointed out the favorite haunts of the road agents. A little hollow where the underbrush was thick and very high and darkened by a grove of spreading oak trees, was one of these and it didn't take much imagination to see why bandits frequently used this beautiful spot. "Not long ago," John told her, "two men were riding here. One was robbed of seventy-five cents and the other of eight dollars. One was shot through his head. The other through his hat and he escaped to tell about it." Their trip was uneventful.

This time, both Brother and Sister Young were home and very hospitable, but disappointed that the Blythes would not he going to the Valley with them. An adoring ten-year-old took little Johnny outside to play with the other children. Grandmother Jolley was in bed with one of her illnesses and Margaret did not get to meet her.

Margaret enjoyed the visit very much, but wondered what Mrs. Young meant when she was showing her the beautiful red dress she had recently acquired and turning so John could see the dress she held up in front of her and said, "Look what I have. It's all mine! She let me buy it! Did you ever imagine she would part with it?"

The Blythes agreed to buy the two cows and the calf for $160. Two milk crocks went with the deal. John was to raise the money and get the cows April 22nd unless Brother Young sent his oldest son to

Nevada City to tell John they would be leaving before or after this date.

As before, Mrs. Young didn't have a good word to say about going back to Salt Lake, but apparently had come to accept the fact they would be leaving soon. On the other hand, Brother Young's conversation showed the warm affection he held for the Church and the Saints.

"Today is the 6th of April. How I wish I were in the Valley today!" he sighed. "The Saints will be gathered for a great Church Conference." Then seeing the lack of understanding expressed on John's face he explained, "You see, they always meet on this day for it is the anniversary of the organization of the Church. Of course we met together at other times too, when important issues came up or when we dedicated the temple. And you know April 6th is also the true birthday of our Savior, Brother Blythe?"

"No, I didn't know that, but it sounds reasonable. I often wondered what the shepherds were doing out in the fields watching their sheep in December. But what is this conference you are talking about, Brother Young?"

"It is a time when the whole Church meets together to take care of Church business, like sustaining the First Presidency. That means through your vote you are saying you agree to support and follow those who are in leadership of the Church. At this time men are also called on missions to go out and teach the gospel to the Indians and all people who will listen to the Word of God.

"Then too, there will be much counsel and inspiration given to the people by President Young. The twelve apostles and other men are called on to talk, too. It was at such a conference that Brigham Young was called to be President. I knew he was going to be the next President of the Church long before the Quorum of the Twelve chose him. Now, that was one meeting I shall never forget!"

"Why is that?" John asked.

"Our first President, Joseph Smith, as you probably know had been shot by a mob at Carthage Jail. Most of the Quorum of the Twelve was not in Nauvoo at the time. Some were on missions. Some were helping to bring the new Saints to Nauvoo. I guess you never heard of Sidney Rigdon? Well, he was one of the First Presidency but he became dissatisfied with the Church and went to Pittsburgh to live until he heard of the Prophet's death. He then returned to Nauvoo and put himself up as the Guardian of the Church. Telling the people he would hold this office "to build up the Church unto Joseph." At a meeting he convinced many of the members of his right to be Guardian.

"Then it happened! Brigham Young, the President of the Quorum of the Twelve, called for a meeting at two in the afternoon. Many of us came to that meeting and while Brigham was speaking to us his countenance changed and he appeared to be, not Brigham, but Joseph Smith who was speaking to us."

"You saw this and others saw it, too?"

"Oh, most of the congregation saw this transformation! Not only his face changed, his voice was that of Joseph's, too."

"Oh, what a wonderful thing to witness!"

"Yes, I saw this as a manifestation from God. Those of us in the meeting knew beyond a shadow of a doubt that Brigham Young was to be our next President. Yes, I saw this revelation and I cannot deny it!"

"After seeing something like that, why didn't you stay with the Saints? What are you doing way out here?"

"My wife was so unhappy there. Oh, now, don't misjudge her. She has put up with many hardships and sorrows since we joined the Church."

"You are talking about me, aren't you?" Mrs. Young asked as she walked over to where the men were sitting. Then she sat down by her husband and motioned for Margaret to come and sit in a chair near her.

"Was he telling you about Nauvoo?" she asked John. "Did he tell you of the rotten, dirty, filthy men who made up the mobs that drove us out of our homes? Who beat men, women and children alike? Stole our livestock and burned our fields? Oh, we saw so many pitiful things and we were so helpless! We couldn't do a thing about it! No, there has been nothing wonderful about being a member of the 'true' Church!" she exclaimed bitterly. "It was full of fear and horror and we came here to try and forget those tragic, unhappy years. And now, since my husband insists, we are foolishly going back with the Saints to be hounded and molested again."

"Oh, surely it will be different now." Margaret remarked soothingly.

"Oh no! Mark my words! The Saints are not through being persecuted yet. The next time the mobs will probably he dressed in soldier's uniforms, but they will still beat, kill, burn and steal. I have seen more than one man who was beaten by a mob for no reason other than he was a Mormon. Our neighbor, Brother Boyce, was whipped until his back was shredded and he was mangled from his shoulders to his knees."

"And so was Brother Rogers." Her husband added. "They were kidnapped by a mob of twelve men and taken to Tully, Missouri. That night they were beaten then thrown in jail, where they were left in irons for a month and a half. Then through the kindness of God they escaped. So Brother Boyce said."

"Couldn't the members get help from the government or from those who have political power in the state? Why did they stand for such inhumane treatment?" John asked.

Brother Young laughed and slapping John on the leg said, "Brother Blythe, I can see you have never had much experience with our government and the way they feel about us Mormons. You see, men in high positions were influenced by the devilish lies that were spread. Didn't you know they believe us to be the Church of the Devil? Joseph Smith was supposed to be reincarnated Lucifer and we as members start to grow horns after we are baptized? Do you mean to say you have been cheated and don't have any horns?" As they all laughed, he continued seriously, "What public figure could afford to give help to such an unpopular cause? Yes, many times our grievances were taken to those in charge, President of the States to the local lawyers and judges but all were found hostile to our cause."

To this, Margaret exclaimed, "I can believe that, as my first husband was a lawyer, and he divorced me because I was a Mormon."

The Youngs waited for her to continue. Instead, being embarrassed for blurting out a family secret, she bowed her head and felt the red creep into her cheeks. Now they knew she was a divorced woman.

Brother Young understanding her embarrassment changed the subject, "Now, take these beatings we were talking about. Two members, Wells and Miller took a petition to Governor Carlin of Illinois, asking him for the release of these men and for the offenders who were the real criminals to be punished for their brutal deeds. When they told the Governor and his wife of the capture and torturing of these men who were being held in irons in a jail in Tully, he assured them that he would help. The Governor's wife wept when she heard of their pitiful and painful condition but no action was ever taken to release the prisoners or bring the guilty men to justice."

"That's hard to believe."

"It wouldn't be hard to believe, Brother Blythe, if you had lived in Nauvoo when we did. After Governor Ford replaced Governor Carlin, we thought we might get some help from him but he proved to be worse than Governor Carlin was. We were given promises and assurances on condition we move out of Nauvoo and the State, yet even when we agreed to their unreasonable terms, they were not satisfied and did not keep any promises.

"At one time we had to actually blockade and defend Nauvoo but the siege of the mob was too strong for us since most of the members had already left the city and there were few of us left who were not sick or bad off in some other way. We improvised a cannon from some steamboat shafts, but we were no match for the mob and their arms. The two Andersons were killed, a father and a son and another young man was killed and quite a few were wounded and a number of the houses were destroyed on the eastern side of town from their cannons. We therefore decided rather than to have more blood shed, we would surrender."

John asked, "When did all of this happen, Brother Young?"

"In September, '46. We had a real battle going there for about six days and we repulsed the enemy four times, but they would come back stronger than ever so we finally made a treaty with them. We agreed to surrender the city of Nauvoo and deliver our arms up to the Quincy Committee that was made up of citizens of the town of Quincy. We knew they were in sympathy with the mob but thought that would be better than surrendering to the leader of the mob, Thomas Brockman. Now, there was an evil man!"

"We were to get our guns back as soon as we crossed the river and were out of Illinois. The citizens and their property were to be protected from all violence and those who were sick or helpless were to be treated with dignity and humanity and five members of the Church were to remain in the city to dispose of the property. There had been a number of non-members that had come to the city by then. Some had bought our lands and houses. Some even helped us with our fight. They were to be unmolested and allowed to live in their homes in peace. That was the 17th of September when they took over and immediately they started driving us out of the city, member and non-member alike. They absolutely disregarded the Treaty."

"Mother was very sick. We thought she was on her death bed," Sister Young added. "We had to leave everything that we couldn't put in one wagon in less than an hour's time. I had dinner on the table, but we couldn't stop to eat. We knew the men who were watching over us with pointed guns and gleaming bayonets meant business when they threatened to kill us."

"They had been drinking so you couldn't reason with them." Brother Young continued, "And when we reached the banks of the river, other half-drunken men made all of us get out of the wagon. They took the things they wanted then scattered our flour and other supplies all over the ground. When our oldest son objected, they beat him up until his nose and head was bleeding badly. Oh, yes, we were lucky to get out of there with our lives." Brother Young shuddered, remembering the events of that awful day.

"Our family was one of many who were abused. You can't imagine how horrible it was unless you were there. It was like the Devil himself had taken over the city. Even our temple was desecrated! Those fiends! We could hear them yelling and screaming in hellish delight as they defaced and tore up the sacred parts of the Temple. They went up into the tower and kept ringing the bell."

"Oh, the bell!" his wife exclaimed. "We could hear it even when we got on the other side of the river. It almost drove us crazy!"

Remembering, Brother Young closed his eyes and painfully shook his head and said, "Oh, it was a beautiful temple. We worked day and night to finish it. But we DID finish it as we had been commanded!" he said defiantly. Then his eyes plead for understanding as he continued, "But the thing that hurts me the most, is to think that I was the one on guard at the temple when the mob came and took over the city. When they threatened to kill me, I gave them the keys to our beautiful temple," he confessed as tears ran down his cheeks.

"And Mother, we almost lost her three times that night," Sister Young began, "Two elders administered to her and she got out of her sick-bed and went about nursing and caring for others. There were many sick and dying in the camp we set up just over on the other side of the river. You never saw such misery."

"Oh, you witnessed another miracle!" Margaret exclaimed. "Your mother raised from a death-bed!"

"Yes, she lived. It was our baby who died. I guess she caught the fever from Mother. We tried everything we could to save the sweet little thing, but nothing helped."

Tears streamed down Margaret's face. The pain of her own recent loss returned as she shared this woman's suffering.

"I misjudged that woman." John said as they walked to the

stagecoach.

Living outside of the City Corporation, John was not allowed to enter the April Shoot as it was called, which was held April 10th. This annoyed John as he felt he was pretty good with his gun and would like to have entered the competition. John watched as more than forty men missed hitting the bulls-eye. He was itching to have a try. Mr. Van Hagen won the gold medal and Mr. Anderson, the District Attorney, won the silver one. When the competition was over, John congratulated Mr. Anderson then complained, "I'd hate to have my life depend on the accuracy of some of those crack-marksmen. No one hit the bulls-eye."

"And I suppose you could have done better?"

"I hope so. I couldn't do much worse."

"Ha! Mr. Blythe, we'll see! Say, hear this," Mr. Anderson called to the men who were standing about. "Mr. Blythe doesn't think we are very good marksmen. He says he can do much better than any of us here today."

"Then why didn't he enter the match?" one man called. "Then he could have proved it."

"He couldn't. He doesn't live within the city limits," was the answer.

"Well now, let's not let that stop him from showing us what he can do." Mr. Anderson continued to shout. "Let's see if he can shoot as good as he can talk."

"Sorry, but I don't have my gun with me."

"That needn't stop you. Here, you can borrow mine," Mr. Van Hagen offered.

"Let's have a match between the two of us," Mr. Anderson suggested.

"And I'll tell you what I will do. If you are as good as you say you are and if you hit the bull's-eye more times than I do, I'11 give you my silver medal." As he said this, his voice grew louder and louder until everyone could hear.

This pleased John and when they drew numbers, Mr. Anderson was to shoot first. Mr. Anderson did well this time, much better than during the April Shoot. The crowd was with him, cheering him on. During his five chances he made one bulls-eye, but John made four out of five tries.

"I agree," Mr. Anderson shouted, "He's the better marksman." And taking the silver medal off his coat lapel, he pinned it on John's coat.

The crowd was shouting, not only for John's good marksmanship but also for Mr. Anderson's good sportsmanship.

When he returned home Margaret asked him where he got the silver medal he was so proudly displaying, knowing he was unable to join in the April Shoot although she knew how much he wanted to. He just laughed and kept her guessing. The more questions she asked the less he would say which amounted to nothing. However, she noticed he wore the medal wherever he went.

A few days later Brother Young came up from Grass Valley to see if John had heard of anyone who wanted to go to Salt Lake with him, as he did not want to go alone. John had written to Brother Evelith but had received no answer. Brother Young seemed desperate to find a suitable company to go with him. His mind appeared dark and clouded with a fear and foreboding of being robbed and of having serious trouble on his journey to the Valley.

John felt sorry for him that he did not have enough faith to trust in the protection of his Father in Heaven and consented to travel with him the first day. The Youngs were planning to leave on the 23rd. John had been successful in collecting money from rents and a debt owed him and was able to pay him for the cows.

"Why don't you go back home with me?" Brother Young suggested, "And tomorrow I will have my son, Brigham, help you drive the cows back here."

On the way to Grass Valley, the men exchanged all the things they had heard and read about the trouble the Saints in Salt Lake were having with the U. S. Government. John told Brother Young what he read in The Cincinnati Dollar Times.

"It said General Scott was to come by steamer to command an army in Utah to exterminate the Mormons!" and asked, "Don't you think it would be wise to stay in California until we hear how the Saints are faring?"

"No, Brother Blythe. We are on our way at last and I finally have my wife willing to go, and Grandma Jolley--she would start walking if I told her we weren't going. Oh, no! I don't want to go through all that again. Anyway, if I believed every rumor I heard we would never leave for the Valley. Promise me you won't mention any of this to my wife."

Early on the morning of the 23rd, John rode his horse to Grass Valley. He found the Youngs had left the day before. Remembering his promise to travel with them for a day, he followed the road to Indian Springs and found them camped in Penn Valley.

"We thought it would be wise to leave a day early to get a head start on any robbers that might have heard of our leaving and might plan to lay in wait to rob us as we pass by," Brother Young explained.

The fear of being followed and robbed still hung heavy in camp as the Youngs prepared for sleep. John stayed all night with them and in the fore part stood guard over the wagons and stock. Then Brother Young who could not sleep relieved him. John went to bed and slept soundly.

About eight o'clock in the morning the wagons were all repacked. They started moving again and went as far as Indian Springs with John traveling along with them. Here they stopped to get some chains fixed and John wishing them a safe journey bid them good-bye and returned home by way of Grass Valley picking up the milk crocks Sister Young had left for him at Primrose Cottage.

John felt left out again when he was not allowed to vote in the Nevada City May 3rd election because he lived out of the City Corporation. He laughed at the methods the supporters used to try to get votes for their candidates.

He was offered many things from a drink to a five dollar gold piece if he would vote for their man. How disgusted these eager beavers became when they found out that they had wasted their efforts on a man who had no vote. Some became violent. John could take care of himself and his little scrapes were few among the many that were fought on that voting day.

While reading the outcome of the election in The Nevada Journal, John read about the holdup of the Auburn Stagecoach that had taken place the day before. It was just outside Nevada City when five bandits stepped out into the road. The stage was stopped and the passengers were made to get out and were prepared for a thorough fleecing. One passenger wouldn't cooperate. He was a Nevada City bank messenger carrying a sizable amount of gold dust. He drew his pistol with no other effect than to bring a comment from one of the bandits, "Be careful."

When he saw the robber's attitude, the bank messenger calmly agreed there was nothing worth fighting over and remarked, "Isn't it a shame that you stopped this stage instead of the one following which is carrying the Wells Fargo shipment. After all, the little valuables we have are nothing compared to the treasure in that chest."

The robbers talked together for a few minutes. Made a quick search of the stage to make sure there was no Wells Fargo chest in it and let the first stage go with the passengers still in possession of their valuables and the Bank messenger with his dust.

They robbed stage #2 of $21,000. The Journal said, "The clever bank agent felt bad about getting off at Wells Fargo's expense, but after all business is business."

May was a warm beautiful month. The vegetable garden and the weeds were growing luxuriantly. John told Margaret he could put off working on the Eureka Ditch no longer. "I hate to leave you alone with all this work to be done."

"Now stop your worrying. I'll do what I can and let the rest go. Don't worry, your cows will be milked. I'll see to that."

John found the ditches in worse shape than he expected and was grateful to get two Colored men to work along with him. They were hard workers. Well worth the ten dollars he paid them a day.

Margaret had her own problems while he was gone. Milking three cows wasn't the same as milking just Cherry. Neither could she let all the extra milk and cream go to waste nor keep from working in the garden pulling weeds. She made cheese and butter to sell. She was glad John had found buyers for the calf and heifer.

The third day that John was away, Margaret decided after milking the cows to let them graze on the grass just outside of the corral and save her the chore of carrying hay to them. Little John was delighted at watching them feed and Margaret wondered at the wisdom of letting him be so close. Cherry was gentle and would never hurt him but she didn't know about the new cows. After warning him not to get too close, she carried the milk to the house leaving Johnny with faithful Browny and the cows.

She strained the milk and poured some of it into the new crocks that had belonged to the Youngs. These Margaret didn't like. They were heavy and the milk splashed over the sides at the slightest movement. She carried the new milk to the vegetable pit, a distance much shorter than the Springhouse. Not wanting to spill the milk she walked so smoothly her skirt appeared to be drawn by a rope attached to a pulley. Down the dirt slope she went not spilling a drop, which wasn't easy to do when she reached the door and had to open it.

Once again the spider that nightly made a new web across the cellar entrance irritated her. A chill ran down her spine as her face caught the web. She quickly put the milk down, spilling part of it, and wiped the cobweb off her face. She hated spiders and spent a few minutes looking for it without any luck. She heard Joseph Smith would never kill a spider and wondered how he could feel that way about them.

After taking care of the milk, Margaret went to work on the weeds in the vegetable garden. She could see little John, Browny and the cows. All was well.

Margaret became involved in her garden and felt good at her accomplishment. She knew it was getting late and finally decided to call Johnny and go in for a late noon meal. She looked where she had seen him last. Neither he or Browny nor the cows were there. She called but there was no answer. She walked to the corral. He was no place around there. It seemed such a short time since she saw him. "Surely he couldn't be far away." She decided. However, he wasn't near by.

After searching for some time down through the fields and timber, she finally heard an answer when she called, "Johnny". Much relieved she ran and found little John and Brownie in the lucerne field. The cows were there too and apparently had been for a number of hours. Her feeling of relief when finding John soon turned to concern for the cows. They were so bloated they reminded her of a snake that had swallowed an animal three times its own size. She had only seen cows in this condition once before and knew that they could soon die.

Margaret dropped Johnny and ran to the cows trying to decide what to do. Cherry was worse off than the new ones. First she thought of running to Herds and see if Mr. Herd would help her. No, she couldn't do that. Even if he would help that would take time and the cows needed help right now.

She started running towards the house trying to remember what she had seen done before. As she ran past Johnny, he looked up and asked, "What's the matter, Mama?" When she didn't answer and kept running John began to cry. Margaret ran on to the house not daring to stop.

"Now which side?" She asked herself as she ran. She had heard an old sailor say a cow's stomach was supposed to be pierced on the starboard side. The cow's right or left, she wondered, not able to think clearly, but knowing what had to be done.

Running through the kitchen door she grabbed a pointed butcher knife and went almost flying back to the lucerne field. John was still crying and reached for her as she passed. She didn't stop. When she came to the first cow she hesitated only a moment to decide which was the starboard side then plunged the knife in the cow's swollen stomach. The air rushed out as she pulled the knife from the cow's flesh. With the same feeling of urgency, she was able to relieve the second cow but her courage failed her when she reached Cherry. She raised the knife up. Her arm fell to her side. How could she hurt Cherry? This patient, beloved cow!

Looking at her, Margaret knew that if she didn't help her soon it would be too late and convincing herself, she mustered up the courage and the strength to plunge the knife deep into Cherry's side. As the air rushed out making spitting noises, Margaret slumped to the ground exhausted and started to cry. Little Johnny who had been running after her finally caught up with her. She laid the bloody knife down, took him in her arms and rocked him to and fro until both of their sobs ceased. Then they slowly walked back to the house.

Because of her actions, the new cows both lived. Cherry was not so fortunate. To Margaret's distress, she died.

## Chapter 5

Mr. Herd, John's nearest neighbor had been killed. He and some other men were raising his house intending to move it within the Nevada City limits when some timbers gave way crushing Mr. Herd's head between the house and a large rock. Mrs. Herd had fainted seven times having witnessed this terrible accident. John went to Mr. Herd's funeral held in the Methodist Church.

After the funeral, Mr. Anderson, who had also attended, walked over to where John was standing and said, "I'm surprised to see you here."

"This is the least I could do, him being my neighbor."

"Yes, and that's exactly what killed him."

Thinking that surely Mr. Anderson was joking, John demanded, "What do you mean?"

"Have you talked to his wife?"

"I tried to. She being too distraught was unable to see me."

"Right, and she won't ever see you. She blames you for the accident."

"Now, how could that possibly be?" John asked unbelieving.

"Then you didn't know the only reason he was moving was to move away from you?"

"From me? Why would he want to do that?"

"He was a Mormon-hater, that's why! Oh, how he hated the Mormons! Said he had already killed some of them. In fact, he boasted about being one of those men at Carthage jail when Joe Smith was shot and also said he helped drive the Mormons out of Nauvoo. He told me lots of other things he did to annoy them. Believe me; he had no use for a Mormon."

"You're just saying this. He never bothered me!"

"Oh, no, I'm not." he teased. "He really hated you. You are lucky to be alive!"

"That's hard to believe. I helped him white- wash his house and get it ready when his wife was coming to join him."

"And that is probably what saved you. Remember those posters they had in the Post Office a while ago? He said when he read them he would love to go to Great Salt Lake with General Scott to kill all the damn Mormons—and he would have, too, if he didn't have to leave his wife. I can understand that. If I had been in his shoes, I wouldn't leave her either. She is a beautiful woman. Of course she doesn't look her best at present. By the way, what does your wife look like? I have never seen her and I don't know anyone who has."

"I think she is beautiful. She doesn't get out very often with her babies and all." John avoided any mention of Margaret's eye, the real reason she stayed so close to home.

"I thought you only had one child."

"We lost one in January. Mrs. Herd's husband wouldn't let her come and lay the baby out for us, but I didn't realize he hated us that much."

"Well, count yourself lucky he was killed before he killed you."

As John took leave of Mr. Anderson, his heart was heavy and he wondered if he did have any part in the death of his neighbor. "No, that wasn't so," he decided. "That was just Mr. Anderson's way of annoying and belittling me." Yet if it could possibly be so, he reasoned, wasn't this a perfect example of how hate destroys the hater.

He would go and talk to Mrs. Herd and surely she would tell him if this were true. However, Mrs. Herd never came back to the house. She returned to her folks back East and the house was taken off the blocks that were partly holding it up, bringing it back from its tilted position.

John heard it was sold to some Germans. This made him unhappy. Not that he had anything against Germans, but he understood they could speak no English and he could speak no German.

In answer to the letter John sent to Brother Evelith, Elder Naylor came from San Francisco to go through with the Youngs and was very disappointed when he learned he had missed them. John tried to get him work with the Nevada Water Company without success. Brother Naylor was still staying with the Blythes when Brother Baxter came up from Grass Valley to tell John what he heard about the Saints evacuating Salt Lake City.

From a letter written by George Q. Cannon he had received the news. The Saints had left Great Salt Lake and had moved south to Prove City. He said the reason for this was the government was going to spend some ten to fifteen million dollars in building and establishing post routes to and from this country. They were going to put military posts along the same routes. As Mormons are looked upon as blocking up this great thoroughfare of the nation, the Saints deemed it wisdom to move way south of the route so there would be no excuse for harassing them or exterminating them. As generals and other men sent from the nations headquarters had threatened to do.

For the first time, Elder Naylor felt glad he had missed going to Salt Lake with the Youngs. Brother Baxter took him to Grass Valley where he knew Brother Morgan would give him work. John spent the rest of the week working on his claims on Austima Hill and Brandy Point.

On Sunday, May 23rd, Brother Naylor and Brother Baxter came to spend the day with the Blythes. They had more news about the Saints to share with John, and John had received a letter from Brother Evelith during the week. The greatest item of interest was the newspaper press had been moved to Fillmore, a small town more than a hundred and fifty miles south of "The Great Salt Lake City of the Great Basin of North America". The original name of this city suggested by Pres. Brigham Young and accepted by the members of the Church.

Margaret had prepared a large Sunday dinner for the men after which they found the comfortable sofa and chairs in the parlor where they were relaxing and talking before Brother Naylor and Baxter had to take the stage back to Grass Valley.

Brother Naylor saw it first. As he was looking out the window, a cloud of smoke started pouring into the sky. "Isn't that Nevada City?" he exclaimed, pointing in the direction of the smoke.

By the time the other men reached the window, the flames had caught up with the smoke, pinpointing the inferno they were making of Nevada City.

John didn't stop to saddle his horse. He threw a bridle that was hanging near by over the horse's neck, jumped on his back, heeled him into a gallop and hurried off to his property, leaving the two men running after him.

Margaret who was clearing up after dinner heard the excitement and understood Nevada City was on fire. From the parlor window she could see the flames leaping high into the afternoon sky, seeming to engulf the whole horizon. The sun looked blood red behind the smoke. Fear gripped her heart. "Is this the end of the world as the Bible predicted?" she wondered. She found her frightened son who had been upset at his father's action of pushing him aside as he ran through the kitchen on his way to the barn. Margaret holding the sobbing child in her arms returned to the window.

"In the last days the sun will turn to blood and the wicked will burn as stubble." she thought. "Well, this is the Great and Terrible Day of the Lord!" she sighed aloud. "No, it's not the end of the world." she told herself. "It is only Nevada City burning." Yet, it could be the end of their world, their dreams of leaving for Salt Lake soon.

When John reached Broad Street, his buildings were on fire like the rest of Nevada City and finding it impossible to save his buildings, he saved the doors and windows and the lining and petition boards. This was made possible through the help of Brother Baxter and Brother Naylor and Mr. McDonald. The four men worked fast and hard and saved quite a large pile of lumber and hardware before the flames took over. They worked right up to the last minute before the heat and smoke drove them away.

John's thanks couldn't express the gratitude he felt in his heart for the help that these men gave him. His gratitude cemented their friendships for a lifetime.

After the brethren found a ride to Grass Valley, a tired and discouraged John talked to other victims of the fire. Then he slowly rode his horse home.

"As long as I live in Babylon," John told his wife, "I must naturally expect to share in her plagues--and believe me, Nevada City is Babylon. All during the evening and into the night, you could hear many of the men whooping and yelling and acting more like demons than civilized men.

"How I pray for deliverance! May the Lord speedily open up our way so we can leave this place and join the Saints."

"That is my prayer, too." Margaret answered but she knew in her heart the fire would set back their starting date rather than bring it about sooner.

On Monday, John went to the place where the town stood before four o'clock the day before. How changed it was! Nearly all of the wooden buildings in the main part of the city were in ashes. He saw two brick buildings standing at the end of the street and wished his building had been brick.

Then he started checking and found that about half of his doors and all of the windows they had worked so hard to save had been carried away.

"What kind of people am I living among," he wondered. "When a man has a misfortune they would rob him of the little he has been able to save!"

He kicked at the ashes and felt like shouting his anger and would have if a number of people had not been within hearing distance. Many less fortunate than he were sifting through the ashes to see what they could find. It was their homes that burned. Some of their household goods and furniture had been saved since there was little wind during the fire. It lay scattered and piled in the middle of the streets, making the city look like a giant junkyard.

During the week that followed, John deciding not to rebuild his buildings and tried to sell the doors, lumber and hardware saved from the fire but found little success, still his pile of goods dwindled day after day, until it was entirely gone,

John bought an extra edition of The Nevada Journal telling about the fire. It stated John's loss as $2,500 and the total amount of property destroyed as $230,000.

"That is about a tenth of all I own." John sighed when he read this to Margaret.

"One tenth? That would have paid your tithing." Margaret laughingly suggested.

"I was thinking the same thing." John said solemnly. "Oh Margaret, I have been neglectful, expecting blessings from God without being willing to keep the commandment on which these blessings are based. Believe me, I won't have to be reminded so painfully again. I shall set aside $2,500 worth of gold as tithing to be sent to the Church as soon as I can find a suitable person to take it to the Valley for me if I can find such a man before we go to Salt Lake ourselves."

Immediately John went to his gold cache before he changed his mind and carefully measured out his tithing, putting it in a separate bag. Knowing his own weakness, he gave the bag to Margaret and said, "You take care of this. Hide it, so I will be able to keep it separate from my money." Margaret smiled as she took the tithing, pleased that John had accepted another part of the Gospel, the law of tithing.

One beautiful day John worked outside the house catching up on the many little jobs that needed his attention. Margaret had been playing with little John out in front of the house while his father was working nearby. She was enjoying the warm fragrant air, the blue skies and the fun she was having and hated going back into the house, but her unfinished household chores were calling her. She had just gone through the front door when she heard Browny barking. Since she had seen no one near the place, she opened the door to see what was the matter. There standing at the foot of the stairs was one of the German men who lived in Herds old place. Conscious of her eye,

Margaret felt flustered. Not wanting to be rude to their new neighbor, she fought the desire to quickly close the door and instead amiably greeted him.

He finally made her understand that he wanted to buy a pound of butter. Margaret feeling upset anyway and with the dog continuing his barking and growling, this hadn't been easy. To make matters worse she could see John laughing at her. She could see him though he was not in sight of their neighbor. This burned Margaret. Why didn't he come to her rescue? She would tell him what she thought as soon as she got the butter.

Seeing Johnny near by, the German went over to him to try and make friends, but little Johnny not understanding his strange talk and seeing his mother leave to go to the Spring House, felt frightened and deserted and began to cry. That did it! Loyal Browny pulled the stake he was chained to and barking even louder started chasing this threatening stranger. Catching up with him, he knocked him down and bit him on the shoulder before John, who saw the dog take after the German, could reach them and pull Browny off.

After locking the dog up, John brought the injured man into the parlor where he cleaned and dressed the wound, liberally using Margaret's consecrated oil on the bite then he set the oil on the mantle over the fireplace. The Blythes insisted he take the butter without paying for it. John saying, "This should not have happened. How can we make up for our dog biting you?" He could see the German didn't know what he was saying. Finally the man understood he was to take the butter without paying for it and he left.

As soon as he went out the door, Margaret found a mirror she kept hidden away and looked at the ugly growth on her eye. In the reflection she saw the witch her first husband accused her of being. She shuddered and wondered what her neighbor thought when she opened the door. Why hadn't she covered it? "Oh," she sighed, "I didn't remember how horrible it looked! It has grown and is getting so much larger."

The repulsive effect she thought she had on others was magnified many times in her mind caused partly by the blindness of her affected eye and partly by her own self pity. She couldn't see herself as her husband saw her, beautiful brown hair with auburn highlights, her beautiful blue eye, her disarming smile, the grace in her walk, her happy cheerful-spirit nor the eager child-like enthusiasm she had for the every day things around her. This beauty her husband saw and loved.

In late afternoon, John came in the front door calling, "Margaret, Margaret, we have company!" There was excitement in his voice. Margaret knew it was someone important.

This time before she answered, she ran to her bedroom and pinned the scarf in her hair that hung down over her eye. The important company was two miserable-looking men. Their clothes were dusty and worn. One looked pale and so sick he could hardly walk.

"These are two Elders!" John exclaimed, "Just returning from the Sandwich Islands where they were missionaries. Now they are trying to make their way back to Salt Lake."

"Yes," the more healthy of the two agreed, "Brother Evelith in San Francisco believed you would be going to the Valley about now and thought you would be good enough to take us with you. And Brother Blythe tells us you aren't going." he sighed.

The other Elder joined in "We walked nearly all the way from San Francisco hoping we would catch you before you left."

"I told them we hadn't planned to leave for Utah right now." John explained to Margaret. "Perhaps not this year, with all the problems the Saints are having in Salt Lake. I don't think it would be wise to go. I wonder where Brother Evelith ever got that idea?"

"We just about killed ourselves trying to get up here in time." the sick Elder lamented and looking at his companion asked, "Oh dear, what shall we do now?"

Margaret's heart was touched and she said, "I know what you are going to do right now. You wash up while I get supper. I'm sure you will feel much better after you have had something to eat."

And John said, "Plan on spending the night with us and tomorrow I will take you to Grass Valley where more of the Saints are. Maybe they can find you a way to the Valley." Then he asked, "Are you sure you want to go into all that trouble? Why don't you stay here and work for awhile?"

"We have our families there. We must get home as fast as we can."

John led them to the soap and water and brought out linen towels for them to dry on, while Margaret busied herself in the kitchen.

One Elder's feet were giving him a great deal of trouble. His shoes, which apparently had never been a good fit, were worn out and his feet had developed painful bleeding blisters, corns, and calluses. Margaret poured warm water into a pan so he could bath his feet.

Then John had him try on his new twelve-dollar boots. They fit as though they were made for him.

"They're yours," he said and after supper he took the other Elder's shoes to Nathan Hemmingway, the shoemaker, and had them half-soled.

John filled an empty tick with fresh hay and Margaret added a feather bed as a mattress and a bedroom was made ready for these distinguished visitors right in the parlor. John felt the bedroom that had housed many other visitors was not good enough for them, especially after one Elder told him about using the printing press John's money bought and sent to the Sandwich Islands.

John was sleeping and Margaret lay at his side wide-awake. Looking in the mirror and seeing the growth on her eye had shocked her. How she prayed that somehow she could get it removed. She reached for the consecrated oil to rub it on the growth, but it was not there. Oh, yes, she remembered, her husband had left it on the mantle in the parlor after he dressed the German's shoulder. The Elders were sleeping in there. She would have to forget the oil tonight. She tried to go to sleep and forget about her eye, but each time she closed her eyes she could see the ugly growth just as she saw it when she looked into the mirror. She knew before she could go to sleep she had to get the oil and put some of it on her eye.

The tired Elders were surely asleep by now. She knew just where the oil was and could creep in there and get it without bothering anyone. She got up out of bed, walked down the hall and opened the parlor door. She could hear both men snoring and although it was so dark in the parlor she couldn't see a thing, she had no trouble finding the bottle on the mantle.

Not waiting to leave the room, she pulled the cork and poured a few drops of the liquid on the large warty-looking growth. Instead of soothing her eye it started burning like fire and Margaret began screaming, the pain was so intense and so unexpected.

The Elders jumped straight up out of their bed, wearing nothing but their underwear and started feeling for their pants. John came running down the hall and through the door to the parlor. There was much confusion until John was able to get a candle lit.

Margaret was sobbing and screaming with pain having poured more of the liquid on her eye believing it was the consecrated oil and it would sooth the pain, but it only became worse.

"Oh!" exclaimed one of the Elders. "She has our foot medicine in her eye! Last night we stayed in an Indian camp and one of the Indians gave me this medicine when he saw my sore feet. It was to remove my corns and calluses. I didn't use it for he said not to use it full strength and I forgot about it until we were getting ready for bed and when I found it, I put it on the mantle so I could remember to use it tomorrow."

Margaret sat in a chair still sobbing and moaning with pain. John saw the bottle of consecrated oil on the mantle that was about the same size and shape as the bottle Margaret was holding. He grabbed it, pulled the cork and poured oil on her eye and growth until it ran down her face. This took some of the stabbing pain away.

The other Elder asked Margaret if she would like to be administered to and Margaret sobbed, "Please!"

The Elder who sealed the blessing, besides asking the Lord to remove the pain, promised Margaret her eye would be healed and she would be able to see in her blind eye and her sight would not fail her all the rest of her life.

As the prayer was finished, the pain did leave as quickly as it had come.

Margaret thanked the Elders and went quietly to her room and climbed into bed wondering what John would have to say to her. But John's concern was for Margaret and he said to the Elder who had just administered to her, "You promised her she would be able to see in her blind eye. She will believe it and it will break her heart if she finds she can't see out of her eye. I think you should have been more careful what you promised her."

"I did not promise her anything." The Elder answered quietly. "I did not know she was blind in that eye. I only said what the Spirit told me to say."

John apologized. The Elders returned to their bed and John holding the candle as he walked down the hall thought of the blessing that had been given to his wife. Could he dare hope her eye would be healed and this great wish of her heart could be realized? The excitement of the idea kept him awake long after Margaret had fallen asleep.

He was disappointed when he got up the next morning and saw the growth was still there. It looked sore and much redder than usual. Maybe, he told himself, she can see, anyway. His doubts were confirmed when Margaret woke up. No miracle had taken place, the growth was still there and she was still blind in her bad eye.

Margaret read John's thoughts and said, "The miracle was the relief I had from that terrible pain. Oh, what a vain and foolish woman I am."

John hugged her and said, "And I love every bonny bit of her, even her sore eye."

John didn't have to take the Elders to Grass Valley. Before breakfast he went to town and found them a way to Salt Lake and what's more they would be paid for their trip as drivers of a freight wagon leaving that very day from Nevada City.

Margaret felt embarrassed as she prepared their breakfast and put together some food for them to take on their trip. The happy, deeply spiritual and appreciative Elders who graced her table soon put her at ease.

Sharing the experience of the night before made them very special to her. They were indeed important company. She never remembered their names, yet she was constantly reminded of the debt of gratitude she owed them the rest of her life.

This miracle didn't come about suddenly. In fact, it was a month before she could see through her eye again. Gradually the growth shriveled and through a painful operation she performed on herself, more painful than the times John cleaned out her teeth and filled them with silver, she removed it all together. Then she had a bleeding running sore which did not heal for sometime. It looked worse, she thought than the old growth. She kept it bandaged not wanting it seen by anyone. Yet her faith was strong. Daily, in strictest privacy, she applied consecrated oil on the sore. As it slowly healed her sight slowly returned. Rejoicing over this blessing, Margaret brought her mirror out of its hiding place. The growth was gone! Only a scar remained. And she could see! The promise had been fulfilled.

Then on the first of January 1859 she had another wish fulfilled -- the birth of a darling baby girl who they called Elizabeth.

# Chapter 6

"Have you heard of a young girl named Hannah Marie living with a family in Nevada City?" John asked as he came in through the door holding up a letter.

"Hardly!" Margaret laughed. "I know she doesn't live in Pleasant Valley.

"Brother Evelith thought she might be living with us. He writes her folks left her there in San Francisco with the Bowers to help Sister Bower with her children and household duties. In exchange, her folks received some help outfitting them so the rest of the family could go to Great Salt Lake. She was 14 years old and their oldest daughter. The Bowers were to bring her with them when they went to Zion, which was to be as soon as they could arrange their affairs. But that was two years ago. The Bowers just arrived in the city and when her father met them, Hannah Marie wasn't with them. Of course her father and mother are upset. The Bowers said they thought she was living in Nevada City."

"I'm sorry." Margaret replied. "They must be mistaken. We are the only members in Nevada City."

Hannah Marie was promptly forgotten until John received a letter from her father pleading with the Blythes to locate his daughter.

"How do you go about finding a 16-year-old girl in Nevada City?" John asked Margaret.

"Ask around. The people you know. You must try, John." Margaret replied.

Searching in Nevada City, the postmaster gave John his first lead. He said she was in Rough and Ready the last he heard.

"If they think I'm going to Rough and Ready chasing after a young lady, they can think again." John told Margaret.

"But what if she were your daughter, left behind so the rest of the family could go? Wouldn't you do everything you could to find her and bring her back with the family? I can imagine how her mother feels. I know she must be worried sick."

John still refused to go even though Jack Cunningham was now working a claim in Rough and Ready. Before Margaret could get him to change his mind, an accident happened. John was bringing a load of wood ashes from the ranch to put on his garden when the wagon capsized. As it was tipping over, he jumped out, but the horses and wagon rolled over on top of him, fracturing his jaw, cutting his mouth and lips. His body was cut and bruised, sore and tender to the touch but miraculously no other bones were broken.

Three men saw the accident happen, his two German neighbors and Jack Cunningham. Jack happened to be on his way to visit the Blythes. They had to upright the wagon and horses before they could rescue John.

When they brought him home his appearance so distressed Margaret she stood horrified and transfixed thinking he was dead. When she saw him move, she still stood paralyzed with her arms folded across her chest, afraid to start treating his wounds for fear she would add to his pain, believing he was dying.

One of the Germans with the skill of a physician set his jaw in place and the three men dressed his wounds and made him as comfortable as they could. Jack stayed to help Margaret with his care until he could get up and take care of himself.

About as soon as he could talk so they could understand him, John asked about the horses. Neither of the horses was seriously hurt, he was told.

"But it's a wonder you are alive! No one can understand how you kept from being killed! " Jack Cunningham exclaimed. "You should be so lucky!"

While staying with them, Margaret asked him about Hannah Marie. Yes, he knew her. "She is living with a man over there. Why do you ask?"

She explained to him, "Her folks left her with a Mormon family in San Francisco when they went to the Valley two years ago. This family didn't go to Zion until this year but they came without bringing Hannah Marie with them, as it was originally planned."

"Don't tell me she's a Mormon!" Jack exclaimed.

"Why? What's the matter?"

"Well, she's not too careful about the company she keeps, or I should say the men who keep her. If you know what I mean."

Margaret sighed. "Then you know where I can find her?"

"Yes, right now she's living with a fellow called Slim, in a little board cabin near the creek which is quite close to mine. I don't know how long she will be there, though. I hear Slim's wife plans to join him shortly. She's a pretty little thing."

"Would you go see her and tell her to write to her folks? They are so worried about her."

"No! No!" he protested, shaking his head. "I stay away from situations like that!"

"All she would have to do is let her father know she is alive." Margaret suggested.

"Well, I won't tell her." When it came to Hannah Marie, Margaret could see she would get no help from him.

The next time Jack Cunningham came to visit, Margaret asked about Hannah Marie. Was she still in Rough and Ready? Yes, Jack thought so and he asked Margaret, "Why don't you go and talk to her? I'11 show you where she lives."

John was up and getting around and offered to take care of the little ones so when Brother Cunningham left, Margaret followed him on horseback. Stopping in front of a small cabin, Jack helped her down off her horse, tethered it, then jumped on his horse and quickly rode away.

Standing on the wooden step, she knocked on a sturdy plank door. Quickly the lock was lifted and there stood Hannah Marie quite as pretty as Margaret imagined. She was well developed for a 16-year-old, yet slender and her skin was smooth and white.

At first she looked frightened when she saw Margaret standing there. Her big brown eyes reminded Margaret of a hurt fawn. Then her jaw became set and her eyes narrowed. "Well, what do you want?" she demanded.

"I'm Mrs. Blythe. I have a letter from your father and I want to talk to you about it. May I come in?" Margaret replied.

Hannah's attitude softened a little. She stepped back letting Margaret pass by and motioned for her to sit in a hand-made willow chair, while she sat on the bed.

After looking around the room, Margaret complimented, "You are a good housekeeper. Every thing looks so nice and clean."

Immediately Hannah was on the defensive. "So that's why you're here! You want me to be your housekeeper! I thought you said you had a letter from my father."

"Oh, no, not that." Margaret replied, holding up the letter which Hannah Marie grabbed from her hand, tore it open, and started reading it.

"Your father and mother are so worried about you. Why didn't you write to them and let them know you weren't coming? You can write, can't you?"

She finished reading the letter before she answered. "Yes, Mother taught me. But why bother? For two years I've been kicked around and thrown out of these righteous Mormon homes. Yes, I mean the Bowers and the Calders, too. I worked like a dog trying to please these women. No matter what I did, I could never satisfy them. And when Mrs. Bower's husband praised and complemented me for what I was doing, she became so jealous she found fault with every thing I did and when he took my side she got rid of me."

"Yeah, she sold me like a slave to the Calders and that's the way they treated me and when Mr. Calder showed a little interest in me, she literally threw me out the back door with nothing but a few belongings. If my folks love me like they say, why didn't they worry about me then? No, I was forgotten as soon as they left me behind!"

"You're wrong, Hannah Marie. They do love you. I know how they feel! I'm so worried about my children, the ones I left behind. You must let them know that you are all right. Wouldn't you like to be with your family again? See your mother and father and your bothers and sisters? I'm sure they miss you."

"Who cares?" Hannah shrugged. "Anyway how would I yet there? Walk?"

"We could take you." She offered without thinking what John would say.

"We plan to leave for the Valley soon. I'm sure we could find room for you."

"No. Anyway, I wouldn't leave Slim. He's such a good husband."

"Oh, that's different! I didn't know you were married. I heard he was already married."

"Well maybe he is. I don't care! Anyway it's none of your business!"

"You are such a pretty girl. You are throwing your life away, Hannah. This is no way to be happy. Come and go with us."

"No! You Mormons make me sick!"

The way she said "Mormons" disturbed Margaret. "Oh, Hannah, you're a Mormon or I should say a member of the only true Church of Jesus Christ. Doesn't that mean anything to you?"

"Yes, it means I've been cheated! I remember the home we left. It was more beautiful than yours. We were happy there until my parents became obsessed with joining the Saints. Ha! I've had my fill of Mormons. And don't accuse me of being one of them."

"Is that all the Church means to you?" Margaret asked in surprise. "Don't you remember anything about the Gospel being restored by

Joseph Smith? It's Christ's own Church, Hannah, don't you remember anything about it at all?"

"Yes, I remember how cold it was when I was baptized in the river."

"Didn't your folks tell you why you were baptized and why they wanted to go to Zion? Did they own a Book of Mormon?"

"I don't know. My religion is in that book." She answered, pointing to a worn book on the floor by the side of the bed. "I read Slim's Bible and that's all the church I need. And just because I was dipped in the river doesn't make me one of those dirty Mormons! "

"Oh, Hannah!"

"What do you know about it? Yes, I've heard about you, living in that fine house with a rich husband and no doubt, a Mormon girl to be your servant and do all the dirty work you wouldn't soil your lily-white hands to do. And look at the way you are dressed--gloves and all.

Margaret quickly removed her gloves and held up her hands, which were rough, callused, and painfully weather cracked. "Do these look like lily-white hands? I do my own housework and a lot more! We are trying to get ready to go to Zion and there is so much to do. I even made a pair of my own shoes."

"You think you know it all, with your happy, soft life." She replied sarcastically. "But you have never been left stranded."

Margaret fought hard to keep from answering Hannah with words that would put her in her place but asked instead, "Do you really want to know just how soft my life has been?"

"Yes." was the quick reply as she turned her head to look down her shoulder, squinting her eyes and sniffing her nose at her.

Margaret, ignoring her action began, "You think the Mormon Church has disrupted your life? How about mine? My first husband divorced me because I joined the Mormon Church as you call it. The divorce was terrible! James, my baby who was still nursing, was torn from my arms. I was even accused of putting a curse on my husband, of being a witch because of the growth over my eye. My husband, a lawyer, was eloquent in his accusations and the judge gave him a divorce, saying a Mormon was not a fit mother. I was forbidden to see my children again. My poor baby! And little Kathy, I can hear their cries now!

"I went to my parent's home, but news of my divorce had reached them and they wouldn't even let me in the door. My Father stood there and said, "Margaret? Margaret? Who's Margaret? I don't have a daughter by that name."

"I found the Elder who had baptized me. He took me to a member's home where I stayed until they left to join the Saints, but we ended up in California. I drove one of their wagons. Gold changed their minds about going to the Valley.

"Oh, how I miss my five children! But my life would have been in danger if I had tried to see them again." Tears were streaming down her cheeks as Margaret continued, "My oldest son found out where I was staying and on this very cold night, he walked more than a mile carrying a bundled-up baby. He said my baby was crying all the time since I left him and his Father wasn't home and he didn't know what else to do.

"After feeding him, we carried the baby home, but Mathew returned. He didn't touch the baby, but he beat both my son and me and said he would kill me if I ever came to the house again.

"You don't know how I've worried about that poor little one. How I hope he wasn't left to starve. Oh, my poor children! No one will answer my letters and let me know how they are." Margaret was sobbing, remembering that terrible day. "Oh no, you don't forget those you leave behind!"

Hannah was crying, too. She reached over and held Margaret's hand.

Just then the door opened and Slim came in. Seeing Hannah Marie crying, he assumed Margaret had caused the tears.

"What's this old biddy doing to you?" he bellowed and before Hannah could explain, he grabbed Margaret by the arm, walked her to the door and threw her down the step. He didn't look back after seeing her lying in the dirt as he closed the door behind him.

The dirt was soft and Margaret wasn't hurt. She got up, brushed herself off, climbed on her horse and returned home, feeling it had been a bad mistake finding and trying to help Hannah Marie. She would write to her parents and tell them she was all right, but not wanting to leave California.

# Chapter 7

"Here is a letter you'll be interested in." John said as he came through the door. "It's from your Father."

As Margaret grabbed for the letter, John teased her by pulling it away.

"Let me have it!" she cried and seeing it was truly from her father exclaimed, "This means he has forgiven me! He has finally forgiven me!"

"He forgave you a long time ago, else why did he ask me to find you when he heard I was leaving for California?"

But Margaret didn't listen to John and her excitement faded and her shoulders dropped. She was afraid to open the letter.

"Does he write to tell me about a death? Is it Mother?"

"No, read it." Having read the letter while walking home from the post office, John couldn't hold back the news any longer.

"Your family is moving to California!"

"California, here?"

"Yes, they are coming on the next steamer and your Father wants us to meet him in Sacramento. He will send us word when they arrive in San Francisco and tell us where and when to meet him."

Margaret's spirits soared as she eagerly read the letter. She began planning at once what she was going to wear and started making a new dress for Elizabeth and a new outfit for Johnny. Although she had been working hard getting ready to go to Utah, with this news her efforts were doubled and she soon had all their clothes ready for the trip.

Then the letter came!

When John read the letter informing them where and when, he exclaimed, "Oh, no! We can't go!"

Margaret looked at him in disbelief. "Why? This is the only chance I'll have to see my folks before we leave for the Valley."

"Margaret, I'm sorry, but this is the same and only time the judge will be in Nevada City and he has agreed to settle my two property disputes while here. I must get these cleared up now while I have the chance. I have to stay."

"Let's send word that we will meet him later."

"You know your father. When he says where and when, he means there and then."

"Could I go and take the children?"

"How could you manage with a baby and a very active little boy?"

"I could take the baby and leave Johnny with you."

"Take him to court? Hardly, Margaret!" he laughed.

"There must be a way. I just have to go!"

"I can't see how."

"Well," she sighed, "I can still hope and pray." And she did. She prayed night and day.

It was October; a few days before Margaret was to meet her family in Sacramento, when she heard a knock on her front door and when she opened it, there stood Hannah Marie. The first thing she said was, "Can I go to Great Salt Lake with you?"

Margaret saw Slim on horseback riding away and knew why she had come. As she invited her in she asked, "His wife came didn't she?"

"Yes." she answered softly, then much louder, "I'11 help you any way I can if you will only take me to Utah."

"Hannah Marie, are you sure that's what you want to do? You'll be among us Mormons."

"Yes, I've thought about it and I do want to see my folks again. I'm good at cleaning and I'm good with children. I'11 earn my way if you will just give me a chance."

"We won't be leaving until next year."

"Good! Until then I could work for you thereby pay my own way. Oh please take me," she pleaded.

Margaret hesitated a few minutes then said, "All right, Hannah." and agreeing led her to the spare bedroom, thinking, "She may be the answer to my prayers."

Hannah proved herself. She helped with the chores; followed instructions and little Johnny loved the attention she gave him. She made a big fuss over the baby and gave it loving care. Margaret felt comfortable leaving the children with her.

Very early in the morning on October 21st, Margaret started her journey to Sacramento. John took her to meet the stagecoach in Nevada City. When he lifted her heavy trap and valise to put them on the top of the stage, he complained, "What have you got in here? Lead? Or are you planning to stay for a month?"

Margaret laughed. She hadn't told John about the confections, books and gifts she was taking to give to her family. He would have thought her extravagant. As it was he had complained about how much this trip would cost her. He figured nearly $30 and gave her very little money for extras.

The ride was uncomfortable and tiring but at times she could see the beautiful autumn colors of reds, yellows and gold outlined by the background of dark green pines, which broke the monotony of the trip, and a fellow passenger sitting next to her, was interesting. He pointed out the spots where outlaws had robbed the stage in the past. He had personally been robbed two times. They took his gold watch and all his money the first time and the second time his ring and his money. And once he was on the stage when Indians attacked it. She felt he was a little disappointed when she didn't show more fear when they passed these spots. Also, disappointed that this trip was uneventful since no outlaws or Indians came to stop the stagecoach.

When they stopped for the night, her bed was considered deluxe only because it was private. It was very uncomfortable. A thin straw-filled tick lay over a board shelf. Margaret wouldn't have slept anyway. She was so excited about seeing her loved-ones again.

In the morning when the stage was moving again Margaret was entertained, as were the other passengers, by a vivid commentary of the events and happenings at different places as they passed through them, by the same man who had spoken to her before.

"My destination is Fort Sutter," He told Margaret, while waiting for another place of interest to turn up along the road.

"Isn't it the place gold was first discovered and that started the gold rush?"

"Yes, James Marshall found gold in 1849 in the American River at Sutter's Mill."

"Is there more gold there?"

"Well, it could be, but finding gold isn't the reason I'm going there. It is strictly for business. It has become a western terminal, a trade center with many wagons passing through. Sutter's Fort is real close to Sacramento, which is a lovely place and is getting to be quite a city. A beautiful grand hotel was recently built there. You should see it, or is that where you are planning to stay?"

"Oh, no! My Father would never have us stay there, even if he could afford it. He is bringing part of our family. There would be too many of us to stay in that kind of luxury."

"Well, try to visit it anyway. It's magnificent."

"Did you know Sacramento was founded by Captain Sutter on a land grant from the Mexican Government in 1839? At that time he called it New Helvetia. Then in 1848 when it was laid out as a town the name was changed to Sacramento. It was the first outpost in inland California. Now it is the center of the mining interests and has become a political center, too. How it has grown!"

As the stagecoach pulled into the Sacramento Station, Margaret saw her father waiting. She recognized him immediately – a tall man with a perfect posture. She was surprised he had aged so little since she last saw him. She ran and threw her arms around him, but he stood very stiff and rigid and didn't respond to her hug.

She stepped back from him and he greeted her with, "Where's John and the children?"

"John couldn't come. He had urgent business he had to attend to and wouldn't let me bring the children by myself."

He had hired a buggy to take them to the hotel and paid the driver to handle her luggage. As soon as they were seated he asked, "Do you still belong to that Devil's Church?"

"Oh, Father, it isn't the Devil's Church. It's Jesus Christ's own Church, restored in these latter days."

"Aye, and for sure it has brought you much happiness," he said sarcastically.

"Father, look at my eye. The growth is gone! Healed when an Elder in my Church blessed me. Aye, happy I am."

"Happy to leave your young'uns and be divorced?"

"That was Mathew's doing. Not mine."

"You must have given him good cause. Were you unfaithful to him?"

"No, Father, no! I never was." He shook his head and she knew he didn't believe her. During the rest of the ride neither of them spoke.

The driver stopped in front of this grand hotel, the one she had heard about.

"Oh, Father, are we staying here?" she exclaimed.

"Aye," he answered as he stepped out leaving the driver to help her down.

Her mother appeared and they fell into each other's arms, crying and laughing at the same time. Margaret asked her mother, "Does Father still hate me?"

"No, my child. It was him that wanted most to see you."

"But he didn't show it! He just glared. He didn't even smile or put his arms around me."

"Margaret, he has been very ill and this is why we are moving to California. To lift his arms or use his hands is very painful for him but he won't admit it. He just bears the pain and is too proud to give in. Yes, your divorce hurt him but I know he loves you as much as any of his other children and you know he never was one to show his true feelings or show much affection. I don't know how he lives with so much pain, so forgive and accept him."

They entered the hotel while her father was seeing that her belongings were brought in and taken to her room. In the lobby her brothers and sisters joined them and filled the room with greetings of love and laughter.

Her father had spared no expense to have the best accommodations for his family. Margaret's room was large and lavish and intended for more than one occupant and Margaret felt lost in it until her sister Helen shared the room with her.

Oh, how good it was to be with her family again, to be teased by her brothers and reminisce the good and bad times they had shared. She asked about the children she had left behind and was told since the children were forbidden by their father to see or visit their grandma or grandpa, they had not kept in touch with them but knew Mathew had married again and the family had moved from Pittston. Where? They did not know.

Robert Mitchell's family was treated like royalty. Everyone staying at the hotel seemed to enjoy and share in the fun and enthusiasm of this merry group. With all the unusual and favorite foods she was served, Margaret had never enjoyed eating as much as she did while dining with them or remembered laughing as much as during the three days she was with her father's family.

The love and respect they gave her healed many of her self-inflicted wounds and hurt feelings. This visit proved to be one of the happiest memories of her life.

When her brothers lifted her trap and valise on top of the stagecoach, they also complained of the weight. It was just as heavy as when she came since an exchange of gifts included pictures of the family, a hand crocheted lace tablecloth and other treasures, but most of them were for Johnny and Elizabeth.

When saying good-bye she promised her father to have John come and visit him in Georgetown, as her father was unable to go to Nevada City to see him. She felt quite a letdown as she left

Sacramento having said good-bye to these loved ones, knowing she may never see any of them again.

As the horses slowed to a stop reaching Nevada City, John was there to meet her. The first thing she asked was "How are the children? How did you get along without me?"

"Just fine. Just fine," John answered to both questions.

Margaret pretended to act hurt. "If I'm not needed at home, maybe I should have stayed with my folks."

"No, Margaret," John laughed, "I could never get along without you." And he gave her a kiss on the cheek after seeing no one was looking.

It was a joyous reunion when Margaret entered the house. Johnny ran to her giving her hugs and enjoying her hugs and kisses and little Elizabeth quickly crawled to her following her big brother to get her share of the loving. Even Hannah seemed happy to see her, saying, "I'm sure glad you're home. I didn't know there was so much to do."

On Wednesday, October 26th, John started to go to Georgetown to see his father-in-law. When he returned, he bragged to Margaret that his trip only cost him $4. 25. "I went by way of Buena Vista Ranch, thence to Illinioa Town, thence to Ioway Hill, thence to Wisconsin Hill, then to Todds Valley and then to Fords Bar on the middle fork of the American River, then to Bottle Hill. I put up the first night at Yankee Jims. I visited your father for a day, and started home the next day and spent the night at James Moors. I'm proud of my horse. He was obedient and fearless."

Now that her visit was over, Margaret put her effort towards getting ready to go to Zion. Hannah Marie was a godsend and between the two of them, they had every thing ready for the move by early spring.

But John wasn't ready. His property and mining claims were not sold. He had to divide his time working on each claim to keep it from being jumped and when he started planting the garden with peas, then carrots and turnips, Margaret told him, "Don't plant another thing. We won't need them. We are going before this year is over, even if we have to leave with nothing but the clothes on our backs."

Knowing Hannah Marie's past history, Margaret watched her actions toward her husband but could find no complaint and felt confident that she had changed. There was only one incident that made Margaret wonder about Hannah Marie's relationship with her husband.

Margaret came in from the yard where she was doing the final washing of clothes and linens prior to leaving for Utah. The family was in the kitchen and she saw Hannah's dress was soiled and said to her, "Give me your dress and petticoat and I'11 wash them."

Margaret stood with her mouth wide open when Hannah quickly undressed and tossed them to her.

"Hannah, not in front of John! Go to your room and dress." Margaret demanded.

"This isn't the first time you have seen ladies underclothes. Is it Mr. Blythe?" she said as she left the kitchen.

## Chapter 8

"Zion! Here we come!" Shouted Hannah Marie and William in unison from the second wagon, as the small convoy of five wagons began to roll.

Margaret gave a sigh of contentment. Finally they were on their way. She was tired. In fact, if she would admit it, she was exhausted. Looking back and seeing the other four wagons following theirs a thrill passed through her. Now nothing could stop them. They were on their way at last. They were really on their way!

John looked at Margaret and smiled when he saw the expression on her face. She was surely a trooper, determined to go although her baby was due in two months.

When she first saw Margaret, whose dress didn't hide her condition, Sister Gordon, who was traveling in one of the wagons, had exclaimed, "Eight months and you are still going?"

"No, only seven months. Yes, I am going." She answered. "Why? I'11 have this baby in Zion, an ideal place to raise my family. Where my children can be brought up in truth and righteousness."

"More power to you." she said, marveling at the determination Margaret had but wondering at her wisdom.

Thinking of her lovely home, her treasured piano, the beautiful furniture and the security she was leaving behind, there was a moment of regret. Then she reasoned living among the Saints would be well worth any sacrifice she had to make.

They couldn't have chosen a better group to travel with than the kind, humble Gordons, the enthusiastic Browns, the far-sighted and practical Holts and of course Elder Naylor driving their second wagon with Hannah Marie accompanying him.

Margaret questioned having Hannah riding with William Naylor. When she voiced her concern to John, he smiled and asked, "Would you rather she ride with me and you with William? No?" He chuckled. "Then don't worry. They will be all right."

The first day's travel was easy, as the road was well defined. The air was cool and refreshing. All of the party had time to relax and enjoy the scenery. When they stopped for the night they camped in a beautiful little canyon. Tired from the work of getting ready to leave, the women prepared a simple meal and after Brother Brown said the prayer, they all quickly made their beds and turned in early.

The second day was also pleasant and they moved right along. As they continued traveling they drove through lush meadows, barren land and heavy wooded forests and crossed cooling streams. Twice it rained, but the refreshing showers didn't dampen anyone's enthusiasm. Such a sharing, caring group made traveling a joy.

One night after dinner when the children were in bed, Brother Brown brought out his fiddle and started playing lively dance music. Margaret was ready to dance but knew it would not be proper and thought, "The spirit is willing, but the flesh is weak," and she sat down on a log by Sister Brown. The Gordons soon joined them. John was tending the fire.

William and Hannah made the most of the music, swinging their legs high and twirling and stomping, as were the Holts. Watching the dancers, Margaret wondered why they had waited so long to go to the Valley. Traveling had been so pleasant and fun and she felt this was a little preview of what life among the Saints would be like.

"Yes, this is Paradise," she thought when John prayed that night as they were standing in a circle around the campfire with hands joined. She was filled with peace and contentment and felt she couldn't wait until they reached Great Salt Lake.

The canyon road led higher on the side of the mountain and twice the small train had to stop where small rockslides claimed the trail. Everyone pitched in and picked up the rocks to clear the way. Even little Johnny had fun taking small rocks and letting them roll down the mountainside.

They found a lovely place to camp and after the mules and horses were hobbled, four men went down to the creek to fish. William stayed in camp to help the ladies prepare the evening meal. John's line was a piece of twine tied to a-sturdy willow with a bent wire fashioned into a hook. He used a worm for bait.

Brother Brown was the only real fisherman. He caught four large trout, almost enough to feed the whole company. His were the only fish caught. He teased the other men.

"Well, sure you caught fish. You had a real pole. Look what we were using."

"Naa," Brother Brown laughed, "It was your loud talking and moving around so much. You scared the fish away."

Back in camp when the three men were telling each other of their near catches and of the large fish that got away. William entered the conversation.

"I like to fish, and I've caught many of them." He bragged. "Bet I could have brought some in."

"You think you could do better than us?" Brother Holt asked. "All right; let's see what you can do!"

"Here take my pole," Brother Brown offered handing the pole and bait to William. He left for the creek eager to show his expertise.

As William left to go down to the stream, Margaret wondered if he took this challenge just to impress Hannah Marie. She had seen the looks they had given each other when William offered to stay and help the ladies. He and Hannah had gathered firewood and although he had helped all of the ladies, he was with Hannah most of the time.

The fried trout was eaten and all signs of the meal had been cleared away before William returned with only one small fish still hanging on the end of the pole. It was growing dark and the men were sitting together telling fish stories. When they saw the tiny fish they laughed at him and Brother Holt teased, "The mighty fisherman returns with his big catch."

"Well, he did catch one fish. That's better than we did," Brother Gordon reminded.

Brother Brown took the pole from William and stood it against the side of his wagon that had been pulled in next to John's wagon.

During the night John and Margaret were awakened by something repeatedly hitting the side of their wagon. John looked out to see what it was and told Margaret who was sitting up in bed, "It's a bear – a huge bear. Strange, it seems to be fighting itself." Then Margaret could hear the growling.

Margaret started going towards John when he cautioned, "Stay there!"

"But I want to see." Margaret answered.

What began as a soft growl became almost a loud roar, waking the other men in camp. Most of them sleeping under the wagons as was little John. Margaret had given him permission to sleep with William whose wagon was across from their wagon.

The growling and confusion woke the whole camp. Ordering the women to stay in the wagons, the men gathered a safe distance from the big brown bear, which they could see in the moonlight as the bear continued growling and thrashing about.

"Oh," Mr. Brown exclaimed, "He tried to eat William's fish and has the hook caught in his mouth."

"The poor thing. I wish I could help him," Brother Gordon sympathized.

"I'11 get my gun and kill him."

"No, Brother Holt! That big thing! He would get you before your bullet could kill him. And he is mad enough to come after you, and then none of us would be safe."

"Yes, I think we should return to our wagons, calm our women and hope the bear will leave of its own accord." Suggested Brother Brown.

"You're afraid." Brother Holt accused.

"Yes, I am. That big angry bear is so mad he could tear all of us apart before we could do anything."

The bear continued fighting and flinging the pole in the air.

When William was awakened by the bear, he joined the other men thinking Johnny was sleeping but he was awake and seeing William leave he was afraid and crying loudly, he started running towards his father's wagon and headed straight for the bear.

"Oh, look!" Brother Gordon, who was the first to see him, shouted, "That's little Johnny!" and he started running towards him, but his father reached him first. John caught him just in time, picked him up and skirting around the bear brought him back and put him in the wagon with his mother.

The men continued watching fascinated by his actions. Then his paw got tangled in the fish line. They were unable to think of a safe way to help him.

As they were watching, another smaller bear showed up. "Could this one be his mate?" John asked.

Recognizing the other bear's predicament, she nuzzled him and as he calmed down she licked his mouth and the growling stopped. After helping untangle the line around his paw, she walked over to the pole, picked it up in her mouth and still holding on to it, she backed up to straighten the fish line then she sat down on the pole.

The suffering bear backed up stretched the line and with an accompanying sound of pain the hook was torn from his mouth. Then the two bears loped up the mountainside together.

The men couldn't believe what they had just seen.

Brother Brown retrieved his pole and carefully put it away. The men had little sleep that night realizing they were in bear country and wondering about the safety of their horses and mules.

In the morning while the men were hitching up the mules and horses and preparing to leave camp, Margaret hiked up the mountain to see the autumn beauty of the valley below. Standing on a rocky point she gloried in the display of colors that painted the beautiful view before her.

"Where have you been?" John asked when she returned.

"See that rock jutting out on the side of the mountain? I stood there and could see all around and all of you here in camp preparing to leave."

"But Margaret, you know this is bear country. What if you met the bears?"

"They went the other way."

"Sure glad I didn't know where you were. You worry me, Margaret. I don't know what I would do if something happened to you."

She gave him a hug before she got into the wagon.

# Chapter 9

Soon the landscape changed and the company found themselves traveling mile upon mile through heavy sand, sparse vegetation, small clumps of sick looking sagebrush and salt grass. The wind whipped the sand and dirt in their faces and clothing and those traveling behind the lead wagon received an extra dose of dust from the turning wagon wheels.

Little John took turns riding in William's wagon and with the Blythes. While in their wagon, Hannah carefully wiped off his face and tried to keep the sand from his eyes and mouth. Margaret was so grateful for Hannah's help and wondered at all the energy the young folks had as they were singing and shouting while Margaret was hot, exhausted and depressed.

Hannah and William were laughing and teasing each other. "You are a dirt ghost!" William told Hannah, "All I can see are your eyes."

Hannah retorted, "You look like a scarecrow caught in a dust-devil!"

"How do I look?" asked little John who was sitting between the two.

"Like a little mud pie." Hannah suggested, seeing the mud caked around his mouth, but William's description pleased him more, "A pepper covered Johnny-cake."

He learned and sang songs with them. After singing a song at the top of their voices, they would end it with the same chorus, 1-2-3 cough, 1-2-3 spit, with the accompanying actions, which delighted Johnny.

This part of their journey was without water or forage for their animals. Some of the extra feed they carried was hay and grass they had stuffed in their bedding ticks, making the ladies beds more comfortable until it was used. Here they passed old bleached animal bones scattered on both sides of the road. A rusty plow had been discarded and other rusty gardening tools lay near by. They saw more than one pile of sun bleached and broken furniture that told the story of misfortunes suffered by former travelers.

Then they came upon a more recent bit of bad luck. A dead cow lay by the side of the road. The air was filled with the stink of the rotting animal. Little Elizabeth had been fussing, crying and crawling all over Margaret trying to get comfortable. Exhausted she finally went to sleep and Margaret laid her in her bed behind the wagon seat.

Then she reached for the water bottle to get a drink but found it empty.

"Oh, John, please stop and get me some water," she pleaded holding up the empty bottle.

"Stop here in this stinky place! Wait just a little longer and we will stop for the night."

"I've got to have a drink right now or I'll die! I can't stand it any longer!"

"All right, Margaret, all right," John soothed, but kept his wagon moving so none of the other wagons would have to stop near the dead cow.

After explaining to William, who came to see why they had stopped, John showed him on the map a good place that was just beyond this desert stretch of road and asked him to lead the other wagons out of this smelly place. He would follow as soon as he got Margaret a drink.

"That was a dead cow we passed. Can you believe anyone would try to bring a cow with them?"

"Surely foolish, wasn't it?" John commented remembering he had had the same idea. He wanted to bring his prize cows rather than sell them but Margaret convinced him otherwise.

As William pulled around the Blythes' wagon, John spoke to each of the other drivers asking them to follow William.

John had to tip the water barrel to fill the dipper. "It's warm," he cautioned. "Almost hot." "Then we'll make tea," Margaret answered grabbing the dipper and gulping down the water.

"Feel Better?" John asked climbing back into the wagon. She nodded and they were soon on their way.

Margaret gave a sigh of relief as she stepped down from the wagon. This green oasis seemed like heaven compared to the thick, hot dust they had traveled in throughout the day. She wondered which to do first, lay down under the shade of the trees or to go to the little stream which ran to meet the Humboldt River and drink of its crystal water. The crying of little Elizabeth who had awakened interrupted her plans. Bringing the child from the hot wagon and putting her down in the shade, she started looking around for her son, Johnny. Finding Hannah Marie and William sprawled out on the ground half asleep, she asked about her son.

"I don't see Johnny. Where is he?"

"He was riding with you." Hannah Marie responded without changing her position or opening her eyes, but William sat up and explained, "At our last stop, he wanted to ride with you so I lifted him down and Hannah saw him running towards your wagon."

"He never came with us!"

Margaret and William went around and asked if anyone brought Johnny with them. No one had. John was unbridling the horses when Margaret ran up to him and cried, "Johnny's not here! He has been left behind!"

William, who had followed her, started re-bridling the horses. Margaret and John climbed into the wagon and soon all three were on the road going back towards the place where they made the last stop. The weary horses were hurried and pushed almost to exhaustion before they came to a place in the road where Margaret was sure they had stopped pointing to the wagon wheel marks made in the dust by the four wagons which had gone around their wagon.

The land was barren except for a few scattered scrubby bushes of Oak brush and they could see all around the area, but no Johnny.

Fear gripped Margaret's heart. Where could he be?

John and William jumped off the wagon. They spotted a pile of dirt with a piece of cloth sticking out of it over which the four wagons had passed.

"Please, Dear God," John prayed, "Don't let it be him."

John pulled a woman's sunbonnet out of this pile of dirt. How thankful he was that this wasn't his son's grave! But where could he be?

William's extended search took him up the road towards their camp and John and Margaret started in the other direction. Margaret was exhausted but would not give up. They explored every dip and shadow in the area without results. They came across dry bones of animals, some whole and some scattered about, discarded furniture bleached and weatherworn. Margaret could see some of them had been beautiful, expensive pieces, now they were cracked and split. There was even a small organ corroded by the sun.

"Why?" Margaret asked.

"To lighten their load, having one less animal to pull their wagon."

Then they came near the stinking place. There were boxes and a small pile of furniture here, too, apparently left more recently.

"Look!" John exclaimed pointing to small footprints in the dirt by the furniture.

The hunt was on. They looked in, around and over the pile of wooden boxes, table and chairs and other discards, but still no Johnny.

Margaret sank to the ground and started to cry.

"Oh don't give up, Margaret. We'll find him." He knelt down beside her and prayed they would find their son.

Then he went down the road where the old stinky cow lay and there he was sound asleep, cradled in the crease between the bloated stomach and the dead animal's leg.

As John picked him up, he opened his eyes, hugged his father around the neck and shouted, "I knew you'd come! I knew you'd come!"

Hearing his voice, Margaret forgot her weariness, ran over to them, and grabbed Johnny from his father's arms and held him tight thanking her Heavenly Father for this answer to their prayer.

During the night Sister Gordon was summoned to help Margaret when she gave birth to a little daughter. She was a healthy, beautiful baby with a head of dark hair. Only her mouth marred her beauty. She had a harelip.

The last few days journey had been rough on Margaret. Hot and painful each time the wheels ran over a rock or rut and she was so uncomfortable riding on the hard seat next to her husband. But now the baby was born. That part was over and she was holding this little girl in her arms. Seeing the harelip that ran almost to her nose, Margaret wondered if she would have trouble nursing.

"Little Jeannie," she said, calling the baby by the name that was chosen before she was born, "We'll work it out." She put Jeannie down next to her and soon she and the baby were sound asleep.

Margaret woke up when Sister Gordon came to check on how she was doing. Gathering up the soiled bedding she said the ladies were going to do their washing. All had agreed to camp here for a day or two while she regained her strength, "Your husband suggested it and we are happy for the chance to rest a bit."

"Your husband has taken the horses and mules up the canyon to find good grazing for them."

Looking down at the baby she said, "Such a pity, this crouch-lip." Margaret started to cry and turned her head so Sister Gordon couldn't see her. She didn't notice as she picked up the bundle and went off towards the stream.

"This is silly," Margaret told herself, " just self pity." She was surprised how quickly her tears stopped as she started to plan on how she would take care of little Jeannie.

She was about to doze off when flies started bothering her. They would land on her face and on the baby, too. So intent on shooing the flies away, Margaret hadn't been aware of the bee that had found the baby's head. She brushed it away, but it was persistent and kept returning, exploring the baby's eyes and nose. When it landed on her mouth, Margaret wouldn't stand for that She tried to pick it up intending to kill it. Before she had a chance, the bee used its defense weapon and stung her hand a number of times.

"Covering the stings with mud will keep the swelling down and ease the pain." Margaret thought. She called Sister Gordon but she was too far away and didn't hear her.

Margaret got out of bed and peering around the wagon cover saw a place where she could get a handful of mud without anyone seeing her. This was behind the willows where the sisters were hanging their clothes after washing them. The men were resting in the shade over by the women. Brother Holt was snoring and Brother Gordon was entertaining the children. Since she wasn't properly dressed, she saw she would be hidden from the men's view, too.

She climbed over the seat in front of the wagon. She hadn't realized how weak she was when she started and felt proud of herself when she reached the ground without losing her balance.

When she reached the mud she heard Sister Gordon say loud enough for all to hear, "What a shame the baby has a crotch- lip. I wonder what causes that?"

Quickly Hannah answered, "I know why. God is punishing the Blythes for their sins."

"Oh, no," Sister Gordon answered, "Those things just happen."

"It's this travelin' that's caused it," Sister Brown suggested. "God has nothing to do with that."

"Oh, yes he does. If they have committed adultery!" Hannah argued.

Margaret couldn't believe what she was hearing.

"Well, that lets them out. They are a good religious husband and wife."

"Oh you didn't know Mrs.Blythe was divorced by her first husband?"

The men became interested in the conversation when they heard the word "divorced". None of them had ever known anyone personally who had been divorced.

"She was?" gasped Sister Holt.

"And you know," Hannah continued, "there has to be a definite reason for a man to legally divorce his wife."

Margaret wanted to shout, "And you know the reason. It was because I was a Mormon!" but the hurt and the anger had filled her until she couldn't make a sound.

"And by marrying her, that makes Brother Blythe commit adultery, too."

"Ah, no," Sister Gordon answered, shaking her head. "No, No."

"Oh, yes, the Bible says so," insisted Hannah Marie, taking the bible from her pocket and flipping over the pages until she reached Matthew chapter 5 verse 32 and started reading, "But I say unto you, that whosoever shall put away his wife, saving for the cause of fornication, causes her to commit adultery and whosoever shall marry that is divorced committeth adultery."

Margaret had heard enough. Forgetting the mud she started running toward the wagon. Because of her tears she was clumsy and fell twice and then she didn't have strength enough to climb into the wagon, so she plopped down by the wagon wheel and began crying in earnest.

On returning, John found her there. He picked her up and gently returned her to her bed. John had seen this uncontrollable sobbing before and tried to comfort her. Being unsuccessful, he decided it accompanied the birth of each of her children and gave up.

Seeing John was about to leave her, she stopped crying and held up her arm and said, "John, I need some mud to put on my hand."

John looked at her swollen hand and asked, "A bee sting? Is that why you were crying?"

"No." Margaret told him what she had heard.

"How could she talk like that when she is guilty of the very sin she is accusing you! I'll tell her a thing or two!"

"No, no. It will just make matters worse. You and I know we haven't sinned to cause this crotch lip."

"She can't get away with that!"

"Please, no! Let's not stir anything up. I'd hate to have her for an enemy. Even with all our problems and trials, so far this has been a pleasant journey, with everyone so willing to do all they can to help each other. We can't afford any contention among us. I'11 pretend I never heard what she said, but she has lost all the love and respect I had for her. I hope I can forgive her and treat her nice."

## Chapter 10

The rest of the trip held many perils and would have been pure misery for this small company if it hadn't been for the optimism and great desire each had to reach Zion. Prayers, aching muscles and hard work mixed with the entertainment of Brother Brown's fiddle and the frequent singing of the "Laughing Song" by Brother Gordon kept this faithful group in high spirits.

They reached the valley in early October and were led to a gathering square. A place where new arrivals to Salt Lake City could put their wagons and feed their animals and rest after their long journeys. Here was a bowery to shelter them and a few conveniences. A number of wagons were already parked in the square.

Brother Holt was the first to jump from his wagon and as the others climbed out of their wagons, he shouted, "We made it! We are here in Zion!"

The Blythe party automatically grouped together. "Yes," Brother Brown replied," Aren't we blessed. All of us came through alive and surprisingly we didn't even lose an animal."

Sister Holt laughed and glancing around the gathering said, "Remembering how we looked when we left California? Clean and all spruced up. Look at us now. We and our animals are a sad-looking bunch."

"Nothing that a little soap and water won't cure." Sister Gordon replied.

"And a little rest." added Margaret who was holding tiny Jeannie.

Brother Gordon suggested they offer a prayer of thanksgiving. For the last time they linked their hands together and John offered the prayer.

"What are you going to do now?" John asked the Brethren.

"I sent money ahead to have a cabinet shop built for me. I'm anxious to see it." Brother Holt answered.

"My son has been in the valley for a couple of years. He wants us to live with them." Was Brother Gordon's answer.

"I don't know what I'll do." Brother Brown said.

William asked John if he could borrow a horse and as soon as he could saddle up, he took his few belongings and went to find his folks.

As soon as John and Brother Holt washed and cleaned-up and had a bite to eat they went to town. Brother Holt to find his property and

John to find the whereabouts of Gordon's son and Hannah's family. When John returned, he brought the Gordon's son with him and told Hannah Marie, "Your folks were sent by Brigham Young with other families to colonize and start a city north of here. We will try to get word to them and let them know you are here in the city with us."

Hannah was so disappointed. She hadn't realized until now how much she had been looking forward to seeing her mother and father and her brothers and sisters. To add to her disappointment, William returned the horse and brought a lovely girl with him and introduced her as his future bride, telling them "We were about to get married when I was called to go on a mission to the Sandwich Islands. I didn't dare hope she would wait for me, but she did. How blessed I am! You are all invited to the wedding and I'm sure it will be soon."

After everyone congratulated him, he went to find Johnny to tell him good-bye.

Brother Holt came back, excited about his shop. It was built just as he had planned and the workmanship was superior. He had also found a place for him and his wife to live.

William and Sarah were the first to leave. Then the Gordon's wagon left with the Holt's wagon following close behind. As they said their farewells, it was hard for Margaret to see this intimate group break up. Although there had been promises to keep in touch she knew it would never be the same.

"Doesn't it seem strange without the others?" Hannah Marie asked Margaret as they were preparing the evening meal.

"Especially without William," Margaret teased.

Hannah ducked her head and smiled but her smile soon turned to tears.

"I'm sorry," Margaret sympathized realizing how disappointed Hannah felt. We are both tired. We've had a long eventful day."

In the morning John and Brother Brown called on Brigham Young who received John with a firm handshake. "I've wanted to meet you. The $4,000 dollars you sent with Brother Cannon was an answer to prayers. It helped us move south during the Johnston's Army threat."

"I wondered what was happening in Salt Lake when I received the Deseret News printed in Fillmore. I don't understand. Why did the President of the United States send an army out here? I heard General Scott was going to lead an army from California to fight the Mormons, too. Why?"

"Oh, unscrupulous men going back to Washington with their lies and the ambitious politicians not wanting us to become a free state, claimed we were rebelling against the Government. This make it desirable and an excuse for President Buchanan to send an army to bring the Mormons under their subjection."

"You said my money helped you to move south. Is Fillmore where the Saints went?"

"Some of them and some scattered out along the way and are building their homes there, not wanting to return to the City. I went south to Provo."

"Yes, the printing press was moved to Fillmore. You see, Fillmore is the center of Deseret, the territory we wanted included when we applied for statehood. Because of its location, we planned Fillmore to be our State Capitol, but our petition to become a State was refused."

"Receiving the information that the U. S. troops were sent out by President Buchanan to get rid of us Mormons, we prepared for war. Determined not to be driven from our homes again. We covered the foundation of the temple we had started to build, and had all of the Saints leave their homes. Most of us moved south and the printing press was taken to Fillmore. We left a few men to torch all of our homes and buildings if the Army reached our city, so they would find nothing but ashes." The President explained.

" We had no idea an army was coming until two of our men, Porter Rockwell and Judson Stoddard, Pony Express riders bringing the mail from Independence Missouri saw them and found they were bound for Salt Lake. Then scouts disguised as California emigrants mingled with the camp. The soldiers and officers boasted they were coming to drive out the Mormons and plunder the City. He chuckled as he added, " They also said they were going to scalp old Brigham."

"This was a bloodless war. The only shots fired were at Lott Smith, but they only hit the horse he was riding."

"That Major Lot Smith and a few other men kept the army from ever reaching Salt Lake City. They burned the supply wagons and ran off the cattle from the army encampments and burned the grass so their animals wouldn't have any feed. They burned Fort Bridger and Fort Supply so when the army reached these Forts they found nothing but ashes. Then the army had to return and winter up on Black Fork."

"Well, it all ended. We accepted Alfred Cummings as the Governor of Utah and gave permission for the Army to pass through the City on condition they didn't stop but set up their camp at least 40 miles from the City. This they did and the army is now stationed southwest of us at Camp Floyd."

"Then you are not the Governor of Utah any more?"

"No, and we are not a group of secluded Mormons any more. We are getting a rough element in our city and many anti-Mormons. But I am still the President of the Church of Jesus Christ of Latter-Day-Saints and with God's help, I shall take care of my people."

John felt a keen disappointment realizing Utah wasn't the Zion, as he had believed it was.

"Where can I find Brother Cannon?" John asked. "You know George Q. Cannon baptized me in the San Francisco Bay and I would surely like to see him again."

"Well, you would have to travel quite a distance to see him. He is in Great Britain on a mission. Now, Brother Blythe, what can I do for you?"

When John said he was looking for a place to live and build a home, President Young called in his brother-in-law and told him to take John and help him find a place.

John had Margaret go with them and they were shone a number of places they could buy. The one they decided on was the warm springs just north of the city.

When Brigham Young heard of their choice, he shook his head and took them to a city plot on the southeast corner of State Street and Second South and suggested he buy this place. There was a large "L" shaped building already on the land. Margaret hesitated giving her approval, thinking how wonderful it would be to have all of the warm water they could use right at their doorstep and her dream of a new house wasn't anything like the building she saw in front of her.

"This is it." John said to Margaret.

Seeing Margaret's face, President Young laughed then prophesied, "You will live to see this place grow one hundred times its present value." John knew he had made the right choice.

Margaret and John, with the help of other hired workers, divided, cleaned, painted, heated, furnished and decorated this building and when they were finished, all were proud of their work. During the remodeling Hannah helped take care of the children. Little Jeannie was growing and gaining weight, John also found time to attend the Academy and studied math and grammar.

As members of the 13th Ward they enjoyed the friendship of Bishop Wooley and his family and quickly made other friends.

"Let's have a dinner and invite President Young and his counselors. Heber C. Kimball said we should tear the place down. I want him to see how nice the place looks now. And we'll invite Bishop Wooley and his family and they shall be our first guests." Margaret suggested.

John did the inviting and hunted and bargained to get the fixings for this special dinner. Margaret and Hannah outdid themselves cooking a delicious meal. Checking on the table setting and the prepared food, Margaret felt everything was just right. "Almost perfect," she said to herself as the guests started to arrive.

Brigham brought one of his wives, Heber two wives and the Bishop one. Then the other guests arrived and all were made welcome.

"My!" Hannah exclaimed when she and Margaret were in the kitchen, "Every one of those women are pregnant."

"In a family way," Margaret corrected.

Their guests were seated. Jeannie and Elizabeth were sleeping but little John had a chair at the table propped up with books and pillows. President Young was asked to bless the food. The food was served and the guests were starting to eat when Johnny shouted, "A hair! A hair! A horse hair!" Lifting one of his mother's hairs off his plate.

Brother Kimball and Sister Wooley jumped up and dashed for the door. The Bishop's wife didn't make it to the outside but Heber Kimball did. Bishop Wooley seeing his wife's humiliation, gathered up his family and apologizing for his wife, left.

Heber Kimball came back in. His face was white. He sat down on his chair, smiled at his wives, placed the napkin on his lap and started eating.

Margaret was upset as she cleaned up the mess by the door but John and President Young couldn't control their laughter and soon all were laughing, relieving the tension, and the remaining guests enjoyed their dinner.

After the guests had left, Margaret said to John, "And I wanted everything to be just perfect. I was so proud of my home and our big dinner, but no one seemed to notice."

John smiled and said "Pride goeth before the fall." and they both had a good laugh.

One morning returning from the Academy, John asked Margaret, "The Brethren tell me I should get a second wife. How would you feel about it?"

"Not good. Oh, John, we've talked about polygamy before. Why do you ask?"

"They explain I have the means to support another family. I have good morals and this is one way I can further the work of the Lord."

"How?"

"You see, there are many more women here in Zion than men, especially worthy men."

"But polygamy, John! Didn't you say the idea was revolting? Is every man asked to have more than one wife?"

"Only a few of us worthy members are asked. We have to qualify for this privilege."

"Well, did you have someone in mind?"

"They suggested Hannah Marie."

"No! No! No, she shall not take my place! She has already won the hearts of my children and now you want her for a wife! If that's how it is, I won't wait for her father to pick her up. You will have to get her out of my house. Find her a way or take her yourself."

By a happy coincidence a Brother who came for winter supplies was asked by her father to get Hannah Marie and bring her back to their settlement. He called on the Blythes that very day.

They were surprised to see how anxious Hannah was to leave and go to her family. She left the next morning.

The weather was cold but the sun was shining. Margaret heated rocks in the oven and was sure Hannah had warm clothing, quilts and even a bearskin to cover her while making the trip. She had John put the heated rocks at their feet. They sent molasses, rice and beans, soap and dried fruit to her parents.

One of Margaret's best dresses was placed in Hannah's bag and she gave her clothes enough to serve her for a year.

Then little Jeannie became ill. She had a fever, was fussy and refused her milk. Margaret held her and rocked her but couldn't pacify her. A lady doctor came and gave her some medicine.

It did not help. Even with all the care and prayers said in her behalf, she died.

Her grieving mother dressed her in the beautiful white dress and bonnet she had made for her to wear the day she was blessed. Earlier in the month during a Sunday meeting in the 13th Ward, her father gave her a name and a blessing. A blessing she would never fulfill in this mortal life.

As she was laid down to rest in a tiny grave in the City Cemetery, John said, "This is where I want to be buried. Up on this hill overlooking the City. It is such a lovely spot."

Hearing this, Margaret could hold back her tears no longer and broke down crying. John put his arm around her and tried to comfort her saying, "Our Jeannie's little body is here, but her spirit is with her Father in Heaven. I'll bet my mother met her and held her in her arms as she passed through the veil. Margaret, don't cry. You will see her again. She is so much better off now. No hurting. No crying. No pain."

As the days passed Margaret felt the loss of Jeannie almost too hard to bear. "If I'd only taken better care of her. Why did I leave her when we were remodeling? I should have found a better way to feed her. I loved her so, why did God take her away from me?" she lamented.

John remembering how Margaret was finally comforted after little Daniel died, believing he would always be one of her eternal family, he wondered why she couldn't feel the same way about Jeannie's death. "Don't blame yourself or God. You did everything you could for her. She is in Paradise, a beautiful place and has a perfect body. She won't have a hare-lip."

"I won't know her without a hare-lip." Margaret wailed.

"Yes you will. You are her mother and she will be your daughter forever!"

Margaret was just getting over the loss of Jeannie when she heard about a grave robber. He had been caught and found among the things he had removed from the bodies of the dead were little Jeannie's dress and bonnet.

"I could kill that man!" Margaret said fondling the little dress.

"You aren't the first one to say that. A number of the victims loved ones have said the same. That is all I've heard the last three days. He has caused quite a stir."

John was a member of the High Council having been ordained under the hands of Brigham Young, Heber C. Kimball, John Taylor and Wilford Woodruff. Brother Kimball was the mouthpiece and as such John was one of those asked to pass judgment on the grave robber. He refused saying he was too close to the case to give an impartial judgment.

"When did he have access to the coffins?" asked John.

"As Under Sexton, his job was to cover the coffins and fill the graves. After the mourners left he apparently opened them up and stripped the corpse. When he was caught, they found in his home on Third Avenue, boxes of clothing, jewelry and other effects that had been buried with the dead."

The feelings of many of the people were aroused and because he had received death threats the City council decided to quietly and quickly banish him to Fremont Island where he was taken and left with a ball and chain around his leg.

Years later a skeleton was found on that island and around the ankle was a ball and chain.

# Chapter 11

John's life was a busy one. He took classes at the academy and went to singing school with Margaret. He did his block (home) teaching faithfully, attended all church meetings and his prayer circle and still had time to attend the parties, dinners and other social events given by friends and the Church.

He worked on the state road and on the ditch that ran along the side of the road. Part of the time, John was put in charge of making the ditch and had from ten to twenty men working with him until it was completed. The men were instructed to make this ditch 12 feet wide and 6 feet deep. This ditch drained the water from the road so the heavily loaded wagons bringing granite for the temple from Cottonwood Canyon wouldn't get bogged down in the mud.

On New Years Day, 1861, Margaret and John went to the dedication of the 13th Ward. Members of that ward now met in that chapel instead of the Assembly Hall on Temple Square. Brother Woodruff offered the dedication prayer.

One of the speakers was President Brigham Young and what he said impressed John. 'The key to his power and capacity to transact the duties incumbent upon him was in training his mind to concentrate entirely on the present business and as each succeeding piece of business was attended to in its turn, it was immediately discharged from his mind. Striving at all times and under all circumstances to be guided by the Spirit of God and by so doing, at night when he lay down to rest, his mind felt as clear and blank as a sheet of white paper.' John determined to so train his mind.

At the next meeting, Bishop Wooley plead with the members to give every thing they possibly could for the Perpetual Emigration Fund, as many poor and worthy members needed this help so they could join the Saints in Zion, but lacked the means to cross the plains. John gave money, Margaret gave the little jewelry she had - a pair of earrings, a finger ring and a broach and sold two of her best bonnets, giving her money and her jewelry to Brother Calder to aid in bringing the poor members to the Valley. She also took two more fine bonnets and a silk mantilla to Bishop Wooley and asked him to dispose of them for what he could get and use the means to assist in gathering the poor.

As a member of the High Council, John met with the brethren to settle disagreements between members. One of the disputes he helped settle was between Brother Roper, plaintiff, and John Stacks, defendant. It concerned a speculation entered into by Stacks. He bought a small vessel at Port Elizabeth near the Cape of Good Hope in South Africa. Brother Roper helped him buy the ship, which cost twenty-five hundred pounds sterling, by advancing him fifteen hundred pounds. One thousand pounds as a loan, the other five hundred pounds paid for one-fifth share in the vessel. He was also to receive half of the profit from the first trip, which he had not received.

The ship was freighted to London and brought 17 Saints from London who paid one thousand pounds sterling for their combined fares.

During the hearing Brother Roper said he wanted no further connection with the vessel and asked the elders to sell his one-fifth interest in the ship. He said if they could get the 500 pounds, the amount he paid for his interest, to give 100 pounds towards the building of the temple and to put the remaining 400 pounds in the Perpetual Emigration Fund.

Both Brother Roper and Brother Stacks had been disappointed with the results of their venture. Their original plan was to help the Saints come to Zion, but found very few members of the Church who could afford to pay the fare.

The two men agreed on a plan for Brother Stacks to pay Brother Roper the profit money now and a way for Brother Stacks to pay the loan, which meant selling his ship. After talking the matter over, Brother Roper changed his mind, by buying more interest in the ship with the 1000 pounds he had loaned Brother Stacks. Before they left they began sharing ideas for the future use of their ship, which did not include bringing members from England.

When the men first came to court there was contention between them, but when they left they were very amiable and willing to do everything they could to solve their problems.

"Well, we lost a hundred pounds for the temple and 400 pounds for our Emigration fund." One Council member remarked.

"More than that, I think the Church just lost two wealthy members as they both plan to return to their homes in London."

At another time, John met with the High Council to judge the difficulty between Brother Charles Christman and Dr. Whitmore. Christman claimed Dr. Whitmore defrauded him of $3,040. While they were investigating the matter, President Young came in and suggested a settlement which was that Brother Whitmore pay Brother

91

Christman $1500 now and the balance at ten percent interest from the time it fell due until it was paid in full.

Dr. Whitmore agreeable to everything except the interest he was asked to pay.

"You didn't pay any interest on the money I loaned you." Whitmore accused. "Why should I pay interest on this money?"

"That was money loaned to the Elders to gather the poor in the President's name and you are as able to lose the interest for gathering the poor as I am to pay it as I never handled a dollar of that money. The Church pays hundreds of dollars out annually in such cases. We owe Blythe, who sits there, money now, but he has never seen a dollar of it, and I reckon I will not pay interest on that or any money used for the gathering of the Saints and for building up the Kingdom."

A few days later when John was in need of another team of mules and after hunting and unable to find one, he went to the President and asked him if he knew where he could get a team. Two days later John received a large span of mules from President Young valued at five hundred dollars, which was deducted from the amount due him from the Church.

Hearing of the discovery of silver and gold and other precious metals found in the mountains near and around Great Salt Lake City John had the urge to find a claim for himself.

"Then I could build you a grand home. I could give the money I didn't need to the Church. I'm a miner, Margaret, and that is what I should be doing."

"I don't know, John. If we were to become rich, how would we use our money? Buy costly things; forget God and our Church in our pride? Think we are better than others? Like some I know? I don't know if I want to be rich."

"No, we could help the Church. In fact I could put my claim in the name of the Church and just use what we needed."

"Then go see President Young and ask him if that is what you should do."

When John told Brigham Young of his desire and that mining was the only way he knew to make money, saying, "I started working in the coal mines in Scotland when I was a small lad and that has been my occupation ever since. I know I can find gold and silver and use my time mining for the benefit of the Church."

"And for your own benefit?" asked the President.

"Only for my family's needs."

"No, John. What the Church needs now is food. Do you know how many hungry people are in our midst? We need to fill the Bishop's Storehouses so our members will not go hungry. You can't eat gold. When there is no food to be had, no amount of gold can ease hunger. If you want to mine, I suggest you mine the earth. There you will find rich rewards. You have had some experience with gardening and tilling the soil shown when you brought alfalfa seed and other seeds from your ranch in California. Buy land next to the Jordan River where you can get irrigation water. Mine the earth, John. Mine the earth."

When he left the President, John went right out and bought some land near the river. Then he bought a second field and he didn't stop until he bought three plots of land, which he cleared, cultivated and planted.

The little house that was on his Second South property, originally the one the family lived in while they were remodeling the big building, was rented as soon as the Blythes moved out. When the tenants moved to Bountiful, John let Wm. Jamison live there and he hired him at $35 a month for six months. He agreed to receive his wages for the six months in supplies instead of money. He was paid 1 suit of clothes, 2 undershirts, 1 pair of boots and 1 pair of shoes and the rest in wheat and flour. (Wheat at $2 a bushel and $6 a hundred pounds for flour} Brother Baxter and Ide Blyth, who was not related, also worked for John.

The big house was full, too. When Bishop Wooley asked John to let two single ladies live with them, their board and room furnished in return for their help around the house, John consented after getting Margaret's approval. Already living with them was Sister Albertena Hansen, a dear old Danish woman who was always optimistic and pleasant. She was loved by Johnny and Elizabeth and became their 'Grandma'.

Sister Taylor brought a wagon loaded with her belongings and as soon as she was settled let John know she would like to become his second wife. John hurt her feelings when he told her he was not interested.

Anney was rather pretty and a hard worker but very domineering and set in her ways. She had been raised on a farm and loved working with the animals and out-of-doors.

A married Sister, Mrs. Bushby moved into part of the building, too, agreeing to pay $6 a month for two rooms. This made quite a full house, but Margaret didn't mind. She loved their company and their help and thought nothing of sharing her home as her mother once did, when she ran a boarding house for the miners in Pittston, Pennsylvania.

Now Margaret had time to take music lessons. She sewed for the children and made a best dress for herself. Along with Anney, she worked out in the fields planting and weeding and helped John cultivate and irrigate. She organized the household chores and planned the menus and the girls cooked an abundance of food every day, never knowing if there was to be eight or twenty come in at noon for dinner.

They planted orchards of plum, pear, apricot, peach trees, berry bushes, and grapevines. They planted vegetables, every thing from peas to corn. Ten acres were put in wheat and even sugarcane was planted.

John had much help from Church members since he had deeded all his fields to the Church except another field he bought. This one he kept for his family as well as the garden he made behind his home. Brigham gave him stewardship of these fields, which added to his responsibilities.

Many times returning from a hard day's work he felt he would rather go to bed than go to a party or a social but he went for Margaret's sake and found after eating and a short rest, he was as eager as Margaret was to attend these affairs.

President Young handed John tickets for the opening of the Salt Lake Theater, and in the evening of Thursday March 6th, 1862 he took his family to the dedication.

"Oh, not little Elizabeth," Margaret protested. "She's too young to go."

"But I want my children to be able to say, 'I was there at the grand opening of the Salt Lake Theater.' It's something they can tell their children about."

President Brigham Young was at the entrance receiving the people. The family had good seats, close to the stage. Daniel Wells read the dedication prayer and afterwards Brother Brigham addressed the people and stated the reasons and purpose he built this theater. He wanted the audience when they came to the theater to come with pure motives and to exercise faith in behalf of those who perform, that no impure thought or desire might have place in their midst and that the actors might each be able to act their part. He hoped and desired that the building might long stand to be a place of amusement for the Saints and rather than see it polluted by the wicked, he prayed God would let the building return to its native elements again.

Then he left the stage and a play, <u>The Pride of the Market</u>, was enacted. John felt it was performed in good style, the scenery and wardrobe in good taste and he felt very pleasantly entertained.

Little Elizabeth fell asleep in Margaret's arms while President Young was speaking. She woke up when she heard a loud noise on the stage and sat up staring at the actors. Then she squirmed from Margaret's lap and ran down the aisle shouting "Hannah! Hannah!"

Margaret ran after her, caught her in her arms and carried her back to their seat. She was fighting to be released all the way back calling "Hannah."

"No, No, that's another lady." Margaret tried to sooth, but when they sat down, Margaret embarrassed by the people trying to shush them was more upset when Johnny added, "Yes it is. That's Hannah Marie!" and when Margaret looked at her closer, she saw the lady was indeed Hannah Marie.

"What's she doing up there?" John asked and he received more orders to quit talking from the seats behind him.

"Let's be quiet and watch the play." Margaret answered.

The Blythes would have liked to go back stage and talk to Hannah but that was not allowed.

The next day Hannah honored the Blythe's with a visit, telling them she had been too busy learning her part to come and see them. She had left her family more than a month ago because she had to get away. There was no one there her own age and the only future she saw was to become a plural wife to some old man.

"I couldn't stand that. I have a life to live! And now I've found my place."

She had an audience right in the Blythes front room as all of the ladies and John and the children hung on her every word. Then she came to the real reason of her visit. "It looks like, you have a house full. It's so crowded living with the girls and there is no place to learn my lines. You live so close to the theater I was in hopes you would let me stay with you, but I guess you have all of your rooms filled.

"You can have my room." Anney said, awe struck by the idea of having an actress living in the same house she lived in.

"And where would you sleep?" asked Margaret.

"She could sleep with me." Sister Taylor offered.

Margaret could see she was also under Hannah's spell, and she couldn't believe it when John said, "There is always room for one more." He went on to say perhaps Sister Bushby wouldn't mind letting her live in one of her rooms, and Sister Bushby agreed.

John could see how annoyed Margaret was over the idea of having Hannah live with them and when they went to bed that night he couldn't resist teasing her.

"See if you had let me marry her, she wouldn't be looking for a place to live and I'd be married to a charming actress." He knew he hit the mark, as she didn't speak to him the rest of the night.

Hannah was accepted as someone special and she took advantage of this. She was never asked to do anything around the house. "Nothing to dirty her lily-white hands." Margaret was heard to remark. She was gone most of the day but on the mornings she didn't have to go to the theater she slept until nine. Then the ladies in the kitchen felt it a privilege to take breakfast to her so she could eat it in bed. This irritated Margaret.

This arrangement didn't last. Within a year everything changed. Sister Bushby joined her husband, and Sister Taylor met a man in the 13th Ward who proposed to her and she became his third wife. John bought a ranch in Rhoades Valley and Anney went to help his partner run it. Margaret gave birth to a son, again named Daniel. When Hannah had to fend for herself she moved. Ide Blyth and his daughter moved to Greeley, Colorado. William Jamison went to Alta to try his hand at mining, but Baxter who never did live on the premises continued to work for John.

Sisters Mary Benson and Martha Dedman joined the family and Brother Thomas, who worked for his room and board, appreciated the comfort and acceptance he felt living with the Blythes. Everything was running smoothly except for the complaints coming from Rhoades Valley. Anney and Lewis Smith, John's partner, couldn't get along. They were constantly arguing and disagreeing.

In the dead of winter when John couldn't get away, Margaret went to Rhoades Valley by sled to see if she could help them solve their problems and to keep Lewis from moving out leaving Anney alone on the farm as he had threatened to do. He had asked John if he would buy his half of the ranch because he just couldn't live with that woman.

After Margaret's visit, peace reigned for about a month. Then John went frequently the forty miles to Kamas and would stay a week at a time to arbitrate their disputes.

When he came home after one of his trips early in June, he found Albertena Hansen very ill, near unto death. She called John to her bedside and requested to be sealed to him as a wife. Which he agreed to and Margaret covenanted with her to attend to the ordinance acting as her proxy as she was too far-gone to act in her own behalf. She died and was buried in John's grave plot. He arranged her funeral, paid for her coffin and the other costs of her burial. Margaret kept her promise.

Lydia Ann, called Anney, had also married John before she left to live in Rhoades Valley. She let John know he was not to touch her, a platonic marriage only, not sexual but purely spiritual. She felt she had to be married in mortality to be a queen in her life after death. She was so insistent that she convinced Margaret as well as John.

The New Year, 1863, found Margaret very ill. She couldn't get out of bed and had much pain in her stomach. Martha was also very ill, suffering with pain all over her body but mostly in her back and bones. Little Daniel was sick too. In the evening John called in Brother Atwood and he brought another Brother and by the Priesthood they held, they administered to each of the sick in turn and they all had a better night.

In the morning Margaret was a little better yet still very ill and Martha was still in pain. Little Daniel had fully recovered. A week passed, still Margaret and Martha had not improved. John felt the evil power of darkness had crept into his home to rob his family of the health, peace and comfort that belonged to the faithful Saints. He intended to combat every evil influence that came in contact with his family with the help of God and the Priesthood.

John called in a doctor who said he could see no permanent cure for Martha but thought she might be relieved a little by blistering and medication. He didn't know what to do for Margaret. Ruling out appendicitis he gave her a liquid that proved to be a laxative.

Margaret started improving after she had a miscarriage. At the time this happened, the doctor told John if this happened again she would die. This meant she would have no more children.

Margaret consoled John with, "Well, we did have the five children we said we wanted, three living and two to raise in the hereafter. All five of them will be ours forever!"

Complications from measles were the cause of little Daniel's death. Almost two years old, he died in spite of all the tender care given by his mother and others, and the faith of the members and the prayers said in his behalf.

Margaret became ill and couldn't get over his death.

John decided she wouldn't improve until he took her out from her familiar surroundings. For her health he moved the family from Salt Lake to Rhoades Valley. It was the right decision.

Anney insisted, since Margaret was John's first wife, she should take charge of the household. It would free Anney to do the outside work. This responsibility brought Margaret out of her depression but she had to remind Anney, more than once, when she was ordering persons and insisting they do things her way that she was in charge of the house and the kitchen and not to be concerned if everything wasn't done perfectly. But Margaret would appreciate any suggestion Anney had to help her do a better job.

Margaret tried to give Anney the indoor work she liked to do. One was to bake an apple pie, her specialty. It always brought praise from the men folk. She was good with the children but showed partiality to Johnny. He would follow her around and willingly do any job she would ask him to do. She taught him to love the animals and how to take care of them. She let him ride on her horse with her and taught him to love the earth and the fields.

Margaret felt she was a special person and they enjoyed working together whether it was in the house or in the yard and fields where Anney had her say.

Lewis and Anney argued constantly. Finally Margaret insisted they not argue in the house and many times a going argument would stop just as they opened the door to step inside. Once, they came in the house, turned around, went out closing the door behind them and came back in after they finished their argument. John and Margaret couldn't help laughing at them although they couldn't see anything funny about it.

It took over a year before Margaret was her old self again and for her optimism and sense of humor to return. During this time John made frequent visits to Salt Lake to take care of business and his Church responsibilities leaving Lewis to take care of the ranch, which he did very well. Margaret couldn't understand why Anney couldn't get along with him.

"It's time we went back home." John told Margaret returning from one of his trips to Salt Lake after making sure Lewis could get help to finish harvesting the crops. Although they only took one wagonload when they went to Rhoades Valley it took two wagons to bring their things back because they had acquired so much while living at the farm.

When John complained for now they would need another driver and Lewis could not leave everything right now. Margaret said, "It's all your fault, John. If you hadn't brought all these extras from Salt Lake just because I asked for them, we wouldn't need a second wagon. But, I'm glad you did."

Margaret insisted on driving one of the wagons. Traveling the 40 miles was slow. The weather was good and they camped out at night. While they were traveling Margaret became restless and for the first time in a year wanted to go back to her home in Salt Lake.

"I've got a little surprise for you." John said at their last stop before they reached the city.

"Tell me. What is it?" Margaret begged but all she could get out of him was, "You'll see. You'll see." and she went back to her wagon very curious.

When they were in the City, going down State Street, Margaret pulled her wagon along side of John's and shouted, "What is it? What is the surprise?"

And he answered her, "If told you it wouldn't be a surprise."

As they drew near her home Margaret could see something was different but couldn't make it out until they stopped in the yard.

A little surprise! Margaret could not believe her eyes when she saw a beautiful new home standing where the little old house had once been. She jumped from the wagon and ran to the house with John following close behind.

He unlocked the door then picked her up and carried her over the threshold.

They were laughing when he put her down. "Where did you learn that?" she asked but didn't wait for an answer as she ran from room to room and was standing admiring the kitchen when John caught up with her.

"Do you like it?"

"Oh, John! It's wonderful! It's beautiful! Pinch me. See if I'm dreaming!"

He brought the children in and those persons who were in the yard that knew of the secret and wanted to see her reaction. John had them all kneel down and he dedicated their new home to the Lord asking for His spirit to always be in this home filling it with love and peace.

A few weeks later Lydia Ann and Lewis came to see them.

"Oh-oh," Margaret said when she saw them approaching the house. "It looks like their separation is about to become permanent."

"We've been so busy; I've never given them a thought. Margaret, maybe we shouldn't have left them. I wondered what would happen. Sure hope it isn't too serious."

After they were greeted and brought to sit in the parlor John asked, "What are you doing here? Is something wrong at the ranch?"

"It's the ranch I want to talk to you about," Lewis replied. "Is there any way I can buy your half of the ranch? I'd still feed and take care of your mules in winter." That was how John came to buy this property in Rhoades Valley in the first place. He had wintered his mules there a few years earlier.

"I think that can be arranged," John answered. "It's quite a distance for me to travel back and forth as I found out. Yes, I think that can be arranged."

And seeing Anney almost exploding with what she wanted to say, John asked "And you wanted something, Anney?"

"Yes, a divorce!"

John and Margaret's mouths dropped wide open in shocked surprise.

Anney went on, "You see, Lewis and I want to get married."
"But--but."

"She's right!" Lewis exclaimed, "We want to get married."

"But--but," John still stammered.

"We want to get married, have our own home at the ranch and have children," Anney explained.

"You really know what you are doing?" John asked.

"Oh yes, we love each other," they said in unison sounding like it had been rehearsed. Then Lewis walked over to Lydia Ann and put his arm around her shoulders.

Because it was a platonic marriage, John was able to get the marriage annulled and before they left to go back to Rhoades Valley, they were married and Margaret gave them a party, the first in her new home, to celebrate their wedding.

Chapter 12

John was made a private in the Nauvoo Legion, the Valley's militia. It was called by President Young to go to Gunnison. There had been men and families killed, livestock stolen, and houses burned by the Indians in many of the small settlements in the Sanpete and Paiute Counties. Houses and towns had been abandoned and a good number of families went to Gunnison where they formed a military unit of their own. Here the settlers had built their homes close together surrounding a number of acres, which had been their Town Square but was now used at night for keeping cattle and livestock safe from the Indians.

Sixty-five men, members of the 5th Infantry Regiment of Utah, Co. B and their officers responded to the call. These men left their homes, fields that needed to be planted, and the little comforts they had. Some made sacrifices in order to bring food and supplies needed for this expedition, which was a part of the Black Hawk War.

This war started when a small delegation of Ute Indians came to Manti to settle a dispute over a few beef the hungry Indians had killed and eaten. During the talk, one of the settlers became irritated and losing his temper brutally knocked the Indian Chief off his horse. This act infuriated the Indians and after swearing to get even, they swiftly rode away. Their threats were not idle.

Within the next few days they chose Black Hawk to be their War Chief, and they went about killing and raiding the Mormon settlements and homesteads. Other Indians having eaten beef from Black Hawk's spoils joined him in further raiding and killings.

Pleas to the U. S. Government to send troops to protect these settlers fell on deaf ears. One Federal Official was heard to say, "Why send troops? Wasn't our plan to exterminate the Mormons? The Indians will do our work for us, so let's not interfere."

In the meantime, Brigham Young had his people build many forts and the members living in the most dangerous areas move to these forts for protection. Many farms and towns were abandoned. He also had a military organization formed in each of these places.

A call reached Church headquarters for help. The people at Fort Gunnison were losing too many of their stock to the Indians, so this expedition was sent to strengthen the fortification and help protect the cattle and settlers who had gathered at Gunnison.

John left his home about four in the afternoon on April 22nd, 1867 taking a light spring wagon furnished by Captain Brockbank and a span of mules furnished by Charles Bagley. He met the Company near Christman's gristmill. They camped in Bishop Wooley's pasture.

Since Captain Orson Miles had not yet arrived, Major Winder placed the camp in John's charge. At eight o'clock John called the Company to order and prayer was said. Then he arranged a horse and camp guard. He went to bed about nine and had a restful and peaceful night.

At five in the morning, camp was called up to get ready to travel. Captain Miles arrived and they started about eight o'clock. They stopped at Willow Creek at noon and reached American Fork about sundown, camping near the Tithing Office. Bishop Carrington gave them hay and grain for their animals that were from the tithes given by members of the church living in American Fork.

In the morning they reached Provo City about noon. They waited two hours for General Pace who was in charge of this expedition, and the men called from Utah County and Provo. The Company spent the night at Spanish Fork. Here John, Captain Miles, and Doctor Ormsby, the ones riding in John's wagon, were invited by one of the members to have supper and breakfast at the member's home. They gladly accepted. They all had hardy appetites and made quick work of their meals.

They reached Payson, a distance of six miles, and halted for about an hour to load a supply of grain from the Tithing office for their animals.

When they started again, they passed President Young and his party at Summit Creek settlement. The President's party over-took them a few miles down the road. He rode slowly along as he passed, saluting them as he went saying, "Brethren, be of good cheer. You are on Zion's side." And he blessed them as he went by. When the men reached Salt Creek that night, the President and his group were holding a meeting with the members living in Salt Creek.

The next morning at eight o'clock the bugler sounded prayer call and when they were assembled, General Pace addressed the boys.

"Brethren, we have been called to protect our brethren and their families on the frontier settlements and wherever our services might be most required for the good of Israel." He said that he viewed this mission as honorable as if they had been called on a mission to preach the gospel among the nations of the earth. He impressed on the minds of the men the necessity of cultivating the spirit of obedience, of peace, of love and unity. "Ever be ready to perform any duty required of us united, as a band of Brothers."

Saturday morning they traveled near the banks of the Sevier River. The stream was riley and not good drinking water but the best they could find. The road was sandy, which made traveling slow but about one o'clock they came in sight of Fort Gunnison. It was quite a settlement. The houses were built of stone, adobe and logs. Most of them had dirt roofs.

The men were complaining as they made camp. The ground was bare and sandy and the wind was blowing. The cook, William Goforth, said to John as they were unloading the food supplies from the wagon, "It looks like all the food I cook and we eat will be well seasoned with sand." John readily agreed.

After the tents were pitched and the men and animals fed, the military organization belonging to Gunnison, marched to the beat of a drum in front of the new encampment. Their Officers commanded them to have an inspection of arms by Lieutenant General Wells, and Major General Burton and Brigadier General Pace. A few of them had pretty good guns and some of them no better than a good club. There were about ninety in number.

When Lieutenant General Wells addressed the men he told them to build a stone and lime fort -- one that was good and substantial and would afford ample protection from the Indians. Yet he counseled every man to never allow any feeling or desire to slay the poor Indians but when they found them in the act of stealing and plundering, "Then was the time to lay them low, only slaying them through a sense of duty. To teach them we will not be trifled with."

He told of an incident that happened to him and General Pace. He was instructed to go and wipe out some Indians. He wept tears at the very time they were slaying them, as he had no malice towards them but stern necessity required it and it was done to the letter. When he returned, he mentioned how he had felt to President Young and his reply was that as long as Israel could go to battle with those feelings they would gain victory over their enemies.

He told the Brethren of the Indian's subtlety and, their mode of warfare and to compete with the Indians where to put their cattle guards.

Then he prayed that they all might be preserved from sickness and death and that they would return to their homes, families and friends having faithfully accomplished all that was required of them. After this talk, the men had a clearer understanding of why they were sent here and there was much less complaining.

"Whether we see any Indians or not, we'll build the best and highest damn wall ever seen in Zion!" Exclaimed the company stonecutter, expressing the enthusiasm felt by the men.

Monday the assigned men went to the quarry and were back before noon. The rock was so hard they had worn out their tools and broken the wedge. They had to wait two days before the blacksmith returned from planting his fields to sharpen their tools and make a new wedge for them. This dampened their enthusiasm. On other occasions the building of the wall had to wait as the men were called on to do more important duties, as thought by the Officers, but the stone-mason had a difference of opinion. The wall was finally completed. Maybe not the best in Zion, but it still was one that afforded good protection for the people in Gunnison.

The meetinghouse built of logs with a willow and dirt roof was already filled to overflowing and as many people outside when John went for Sunday Services but he was fortunate to get a seat next to an open window where he could hear and see the speakers, who were Legion Officers, Wells, Burton and Pace.

In the afternoon he wrote a letter to Margaret and caught the mail carrier before he left at 3pm.

"Aren't you afraid of the Indians?" John asked. "Traveling alone on horseback?"

"They haven't bothered me yet." He answered spurring his horse and leaving Gunnison.

Most of the men, members of the 5th Infantry Regiment of Utah, never saw nor had any contact with Indians during the time they were at Fort Gunnison. However, a number of times the Indians presence in the vicinity was evident. The men lost one of their horses while they were on guard during the day. At different times two beef were stolen at night when they were right inside the protection of the fort.

The two Scottish ladies from Glenwood, who John hired to wash his and the officers' clothes, told him why they had come to Gunnison for protection. The mother's husband had died and she was living with her daughter whose husband was shot.

The daughter said, "We saw four Indians riding through our farm and coming towards our house. My husband went out to meet them carrying his gun. When he found they were hungry and asking for food he went to the corral to find a beef for them. At the gate he laid his gun against a gatepost. One of the Indians picked it up and shot him in the back, killing him. I was watching and afraid to go to him for fear of being shot, too. When they left, they took his gun and drove off all of our cattle."

"That's when we came to the fort," the mother said.

After they had been living under military rule for about a month, Lt. Adam Paul accidentally shot himself in the ankle. Dr. Ormsby was brought from Manti to look after him. He extracted the ball and cleaned out the wound and remained all night looking after Lt. Paul.

In the morning John was ready to go to the quarry as assigned, when his orders were changed. He was to take Adam to Manti so he could be under Dr. Ormsby's care. John quickly agreed for he wasn't too eager to return to the quarry.

Two days earlier John was one of the eight men called to work at the quarry. Some of the men were hard at work while some were fooling around. John became disgusted with them when they were trying to keep the others from working. They were acting wild and reckless. When they became vulgar in their expressions and used profane language, he took the liberty to reprove them in a kindly manner. The men returned to work and after that often hushed each other up when they saw him near by.

William McCallister was asked to go with him. It took them five hours to reach Manti a distance of fifteen miles. Taken to Dr. Ormsby's Office Lt. Paul received every care and attention that could be had for his comfort. The next few days John had very little sleep spending so much time sitting at his bedside changing cold water packs and taking care of him.

Sunday John was relieved for a few hours and attended the Elder's meeting and Sacrament meeting and had a chance to see the incorporated city of Manti and told Adam Paul about it.

"It is beautifully situated on a gradual sloping hill with many fine buildings of all descriptions which are principally built of stone as they have stone quarries near the city. A large two-story building is used for meetings and school. This is the finest settlement I have seen in Sanpete County. The public square is enclosed with a strong stonewall, some ten feet high. It is used at present as a public corral to protect the stock belonging to the settlers from the Indians. Here is a herd of some nine hundred horses and mules and horned stock taken out every morning to feed and brought in at night. The milk cows are taken home and the rest kept in corrals in the square."

"Fourteen mounted men accompany the stock to herd and guard them. Each man receives one and a half bushels of wheat per day, which is paid by the owners in proportion to the number of stock they send out."

"That makes twenty-one bushels a day the people have to pay for guarding them." Adam calculated. "I wonder where they grew all that wheat?" Adam asked, and then added, "They should get our men over here and get them guarded for nothing. Say, where did you get all of that information?"

"I met the city clerk and he told me."

John sent a letter to Margaret. He wrote a few lines telling her about Adam Paul, how he was wounded and asked her to call on his wife and let her know how he was getting along and that he was receiving every comfort. He mentioned the people here were very kind and obliging and he would start home with him as soon as the doctor pronounced him fit for the journey.

But his foot was not healing very fast. John went about a mile down the creek and dug some flag root and prepared it with some slippery elm bark for a poultice and put it on his wound.

At Adams request, the doctor invited a few of his lady friends to come and spend the evening in the office with them. Five ladies from the most respected families and three young men accompanied them. One brought an accordion.

They all had a good time singing and dancing, except Adam who couldn't put any weight on his foot, but he joined in the fun and frolic and sang along with the rest of them. As the evening wore on, John could see Adam was suffering a great deal of pain but Adam kept asking the group to stay. It was ten-thirty before they parted.

When they left, John could see Adam was more restless than usual. John removed the poultice, washed off his foot with a sponge and then anointed it with consecrated oil that he brought from home. Adam rested a little better but kept John up all night. He made a poultice of bread and milk and this seemed to ease the pain.

Adam continued to get weaker as the days passed and his foot and leg more sensitive and the anxiety to go home increased. Dr. Ormsby was opposed to his going until his foot was out of danger. Not having his own way he became a complaining and demanding person. He also became quite a mimic. He often made fun of the way some of the members bore their testimonies. Today it was old Father Miller who baptized President Brigham Young.

Adam pretended he was Old Father Miller. John told him he did not like to hear him do so. "Many who thought themselves so smart might fall far short of those men they make jest of. The Lord has chosen weak things of this world to confound the mighty and I consider Father Miller's case as one striking illustration of the fact. For as unlearned and uncouth as he was, when he received a portion of the priesthood of the Son of God, he was called to go forth and testify before the world to the truth of the Gospel." John continued, "He did so in humility and in his weakness, but the power of God accompanied his testimony to the convincing of many, even Brigham Young who I believe to be one of the best men who lives on the earth today."

Adam apologized and stopped making fun of other members.

Saturday, the first of June, Captain Miles, Major Vance, Sergeant Houtze and Private Nathan Tanner came from Gunnison to drill the militia belonging to Manti. After the drill the Captain and the Major visited with the men in the Doctor's office.

After hearing Doctor Ormsby say Adam's foot was doing well and he thought he could leave for home next Saturday, Major Vance asked John, "If you got home next Saturday evening, would you start back Monday?"

"I think not!" John answered decisively, feeling ill from lack of sleep. Then he realized his position. He was still under the command of his officer, Major Vance. He apologized then said, "It is my desire to show all due courtesy to those placed over me. What time do you want me to start back?"

"I have full confidence in you. Come back whenever you feel rested and are ready to come back."

Waiting to hear from General Pace, who had gone to Provo when he heard one of his wives was sick, the two officers and Houtze and Nathan Tanner didn't leave to return to Gunnison until five that evening. Then they received little news from General Pace only to double the guard at Manti and Gunnison. After shaking hands with John and wishing him and Adam a safe and a pleasant trip to the city, they left.

Three hours later, Orson Miles and Tanner came galloping back to the fort. At Sundown, Indians who were secluded near the road had fired upon them and at first shot Major Vance fell from his horse mortally wounded. As the other three wheeled their horses Sergeant Houtze's horse was shot out from under him and he was left on foot. Not knowing whether he was dead or alive and seeing Indians ready to fire on them, Miles and Tanner put spurs to their horses and swiftly retreated with five Indians following close behind. This happened at Twelve-Mile Creek, twelve miles from Manti and three miles from Gunnison. They left their two comrades without firing a shot at the Indians, although both had revolvers and Tanner also had his rifle.

Major Vance's horse followed Miles and Tanner. The Indians chased them at least five miles but it was growing dark and the men couldn't tell whether the Indians were still chasing them or not. When Vance's horse stopped they drove it in front of them. At Six Mile Creek Orson's horse began to lag and Vance's horse stopped so Miles jumped off his horse and made a trade, driving his horse in front of him. Tanner had to use his gun barrel on it to keep it moving.

The town was alerted by the sound of a big base drum as soon as the Indian attack was reported. When the quiet of the night was broken, John could immediately hear the sound of treading feet responding to the call. It was considered wisdom to send twenty mounted and well armed men who were acquainted with the lay of the country to check on their brethren in Gunnison and go after the Indians.

The night was pitch black and the men had to swim their horses across the stream and make their way along the mountains on the north side of the creek. They reached Gunnison at daybreak and informed the men at the fort of the supposed fate of Vance and Houtze. It was discovered a few hours later that the Indians had been prowling around Gunnison during the night and again had stolen some cattle and horses.

As soon as the men from Manti had breakfast and their horses fed, Lt. Afton Davis and twenty men from Gunnison accompanied them back by way of the road. When they reached 12 Mile Creek, they found Major Vance lying where he had fallen. He had been shot twice, but his body had not been mutilated. They also found Houtze. He had run over a quarter of a mile from where his horse fell. His body was very much mutilated. He had been shot three times with a rifle or pistol and by seven arrows. His nose and face was badly bruised and cut up, showing there had been a desperate struggle.

They arrived in Manti with the bodies that morning. They were wrapped in blankets as they had been stripped of everything except their shirts. Houtze was still wearing one glove. As the company passed in front of the doctor's office with the corps in a wagon, Adam Paul wanted to see the bodies so John got them to stop until two men carried him out in their arms to the wagon.

The blankets were removed revealing a sad sight. Even with the aid of the gospel, onlookers would have feelings of revenge, John thought. Seeing them made John sick. Adam asked for one of the arrow that was buried in Houtze's back and it was given to him.

The bodies were taken to the school. Here they were washed and their wounds were sewed up and they were wrapped in sheets, and with a good escort they were taken to their homes - Vance to Mountainville, near Lehi and Houtze to Great Salt Lake City. The party traveled night and day and reached the city the following night, a distance of one hundred and sixty miles.

A number of men were calling Captain Miles a coward and seemed to lose respect for him for leaving the two men to the mercy of the Indians without even firing a shot. John knew Orson Miles was a good, quiet, unassuming man and how devastated he felt over this sad and unexpected affair. John wondered how anyone could blame him for his action. John asked those men around him what they would have done if they had been in Miles or Tanner's shoes?

"Of course you would try to save your own skin. Miles did the right thing. Retreating would be the only thing he could do."

On Saturday morning Adam, McCallister and John had a mounted escort of three men as they traveled back to Adam's family in Salt Lake City. Arriving at Fountain Green six men escorted them. John felt fortunate to have them since they would have to travel through Salt Creek Canyon before reaching Nephi. This canyon was a rough place, well adapted for Indian attacks. Having no problem they reached Nephi at seven in the evening and put up at the Nephi House. Here some of the boys entertained Adam with music.

They left Nephi in the morning without escorts. They considered the going safe now. But they were forced to drive carefully because of Adam's sore foot, which was painful. The pain wasn't helped when McCallister accidentally hit it with his elbow in his anxiety to see the infantry drilling on the public square at Spanish Fork.

The horses were tired when they came to Springville but Adam was anxious to go on to Provo. John stopped and changed one of the horses that had given out and drove on to Prove but it was hard on the team and difficult traveling. McCallister had to get out and coax one of the horses along.

They spent the night at Kimball Bullocks. He had two wives. One was a good housekeeper and good looking but very high strung. The second one free and easy and good with the children and there was a number of them. Again there seemed to be peace and harmony in this home. John started wondering about having a second wife.

Leaving at seven, they reached the city about one, where they left Adam at his father-in-laws. John drove home exhausted. As soon as he greeted Margaret and the children, he went to report to Major Winder who was anxious to know about the death of Major Vance and Sergeant Houtze. John told him what he knew and how Captain Miles and Tanner had been blamed for their deaths because they didn't stay and fight the Indians.

John completed his report with "How could anyone talk that way if they weren't there in their place? No man would stop to be killed. Of course he would ride away panic-stricken."

"The facts are far from what we were told. Let me show you what The Daily Telegram published. And here's a cartoon-drawing of the incident." The Major handed John the newspaper.

After seeing the article and drawing John exclaimed, "How could they censor and make fun of that humble man! The newspaper editor must be anti-Mormon or why would he ever write something like that?"

"Well, it sure sold a lot of papers."

It was two days later when John had an interview with the editor, Stenhouse. He asked him why he heaped the blame and censored Captain Miles and Tanner without knowing the facts. Why did he publish false rumors and give these vicious lies publicity by backing them up?

Stenhouse had John follow him and took him into his office. He picked up a copy of The Daily Telegram published that morning and showed John how he had corrected those statements. He said he was sorry that anything had been published that wasn't correct. Then he changed the subject by wanting to know all about Adam Paul and how he got injured and about John's trip coming home. He published this information the next day.

# Chapter 13

Margaret McKie will always remember the day she came to live with the Blythes. The city was celebrating the 24th of July 1869. She came with the intention of marriage.

Margaret McKie was a young, pretty little Scottish girl, who came full of romantic ideas anticipating being married to a prominent, good, Latter-day-Saint. Although he wasn't wealthy she heard he was well off and could well afford a second wife. She dreamed of a beautiful home, of being adored because of her beauty and she would return his love and bear him many children.

Shortly after the holiday, John took her into the parlor to talk to her and ask her if she was ready for marriage. He called her Maggie. "I don't want to be disturbed," he told Margaret, his first wife. "Would you sit by the door and keep the children out?"

Margaret agreed as John closed the door imagining the romantic way he would ask her to be his wife. She was embroidering on the beautiful white dress John's new wife would be wearing on her wedding day. Yes, it would be different, she thought, having another wife around. John needed Maggie. She would accept her and love her.

She had to stop both Elizabeth and John Jr. from entering the room. Elizabeth wanted to know why she couldn't go into the parlor. It had never been off-limits before. Margaret knew they were as curious as she was about how John was proposing to her. All three would have been disappointed.

He didn't get on bended knee. He didn't kiss her or hug her. He didn't even touch her but asked unromantic questions like: "Are you ready to live the law of celestial marriage? Do you want children?"

"Yes," she answered.

"Could you live in the same house with my first wife and her children?"

Maggie's first bubble broke. No home of her own.

"Since both of you have the same name, we will call you Maggie or Mag. Didn't I hear the children call you Mag?" The second bubble broke. She always hated anyone calling her Maggie. Her name was Margaret and she told them so. And –Mag- a name for a bird, reminding her of a screeching magpie! She thought in disgust, "I'11 not only lose my last name, my first name too."

"Will you as my second wife show Margaret the respect she deserves? And keep peace and harmony in our home?"

Margaret agreed to everything John asked.

Then he said, "Margaret can't have any more children so I'll come to your bed quite often." He didn't hold her hand as they stood facing each other while John prayed that they would live the law of celestial marriage in its purity and honor it to the best of their ability, and the interview ended.

It wasn't until August 16th when they were married in the Endowment House by Squire Wells. Only two witnesses and Margaret attended the wedding.

"No party," John instructed Margaret. "I have work to do in the hay field that can't wait." Coming home very tired he slept alone in a single bed.

He never entered Maggie's room until they had been married for over two weeks, which proved a disaster. After that night, Maggie stayed in her room locking her bedroom door and refused to come out all day, even to eat. Listening by the door, Margaret could hear her sobbing.

John went to Squire Wells and asked for his marriage to be annulled. She had deceived him and had refused to consummate the marriage. Brother Wells laughed at John's insistence and after asking John some intimate questions gave him some suggestions and a few pointers on the art of lovemaking.

After much coaxing, Margaret was finally allowed in Maggie's room. She held her like a child comforting and soothing her injured pride.

"He didn't even say he loved me. He never has," she sobbed. "He frightened me with his demand of carnal-connect without even holding me or kissing me. I don't think he loves me. He has never told me so. I'm a virgin and heard the first time might be painful and I was prepared for that, but planned on a little tenderness and romance and understanding on his part, but he gave me nothing. So I refused him. Did he treat you like that?"

"When I married John it was different. I had been married before and knew what to expect. He seems embarrassed to show his love, even vocally, but never in public. He hugs the children and me sometimes. I know he loves me dearly by the way he treats me. The way he smiles at me. The many little things he does for me.

"Perhaps he felt if he showed you he loved you he would hurt my feelings. Or maybe he felt he was being untrue to me. Or that I would be jealous and I would have been at one time, but I got over it and I have accepted you as an equal and hope I'll never hurt you or take advantage of you. Be patient, my dear. I love you and so does John. You are a sweet addition to our home."

What Margaret said to John that night was almost a lecture. It worked. A few days after this Elizabeth tattled on them, confiding, "Mama, I saw Father hugging and kissing Maggie!"

Margaret answered, "That's all right. They are married and when you are married, I hope your husband holds you and kisses you."

With the birth of her first child, Maggie wanted a home of her own. John had one built for her. Here she gave birth to one more girl and a boy.

Now that Elizabeth and Johnny were getting older, Margaret hungered to have little ones around. Ten-year-old Elizabeth brought babies and small children into her home, tending the children of the players who were currently performing in the Salt Lake Theater. That was different. She yearned for one of her own. One she could hold and love and watch it grow.

Before Maggie had her first baby girl, Margaret's desire was realized, three children were added to the family in the same year. She was asked if she would raise two orphan boys, William Wright, Edward Jones and a tiny baby, Charles Alphonzo Underwood.

"When I ask God for a blessing, He showers me with three." she told John.

When Margaret and John went to the jail to find the baby's guardian to see if they could adopt the baby, they found the baby with an old prisoner who was trying to take care of it since his mother was insane. It was believed that insanity ran in families and that the baby might turn out to be as crazy as his mother.

"The poor little thing." Margaret took the baby from the old man's arms. "Of course we'll take him! Won't we John?"

John nodded. He knew it had been decided before they came.

They named the baby Robert Blythe. "Robert?" John questioned, "After your father?"

"Yes," Margaret answered. "That's my grandfather's name too."

Many times she was proud of his accomplishments and he grew up to be a fine, outstanding man. However, when he found his birth name was Charles A. Underwood and learned the sad history of his father and mother, he had his original name restored, but Margaret always considered him as one of her own.

John was shocked when he was arrested a few days before Christmas on suspicion of murdering Dr. J. King Robinson. Why would they ever suspect him? He could never understand, as he hardly knew the man. Yes, he knew he ran a billiard saloon and he was connected with a very anti-Mormon Church but he had no dealings with the man. This murder happened five years ago. Why was he arrested now? The only answer he was given to his questions was, "New witnesses were found with new evidence." Four other men were arrested at the same time for this murder. These men were Alexander Burt and Brigham Y. Hampton, who were police officers; James Toms, a gunsmith and one of the special police, and the fourth John Brazier.

The murder occurred Oct. 22,1866. Dr. King left his home just before midnight on pretence that his professional services were needed. He had been an Army surgeon. Going a short distance from his home he was severely beaten by a band of ruffians and then killed. The reason remains a mystery. Some believe his assailants only meant to give him a good thrashing but being recognized he was killed to protect them from exposure.

At the time prominent attorneys openly accused the authorities of the Church responsible for his murder. Indignant President Young asked these men to produce their proof. Saying he was willing to go to court and be examined and to have them make the most thorough investigation the country could furnish. He denounced the crime and offered $500 to anyone who brought the real criminals to justice. This fund grew by private subscriptions to the sum of nine thousand dollars. It was never collected.

The first investigation at the time of the murder found neither witnesses nor evidence to involve the Church or any other persons.

Ever since the armies were sent to Utah to put down the 'Mormon rebellion', very fanatical persons had invaded the Mormon sanctuary. When Brigham Young was relieved of his Governorship, the Mormons had no direct control over the evil and vices that crept into Great Salt Lake City except through the faithful members of the Church and its teachings. The worst administrator by far was Governor J. Wilson Shaffer, who appointed an adversary, Chief Justice James B. McKean. He came to destroy Mormonism and its leader, Brigham Young. He was helped by an organization of "crusaders" which he condoned and encouraged.

After the lapse of five years these crusaders brought up this matter of Dr. Robinson's murder. Feeling assured that under the changed conditions now prevailing, they had the power to secure convictions. Of course they preferred getting men "high in authority" but since the first trial proved unsuccessful they targeted prominent Mormons. With Judge McKean upon the bench and the grand jury made up of like men, one a confessed murderer, Bill Hickman, convictions would be assured. So several well-known Mormons were arrested on bench warrants and they were confined in the City jail.

The day after the arrests the trial began. Numerous witnesses were examined, some whom testified at the former inquest but they were now not able to add anything further. They had heard a shot and heard a scream and had seen men running away from the spot where the deed was done, had recognized some of them, but those men they were still unable to identify.

Now they had two new witnesses saying they knew considerable about the murder, claiming they had left town before the first trial began. They were Charles W. Baker and Thomas Butterwood.

Baker's testimony was he and his partner stopped in Salt Lake on their way to Arizona and the night of the murder they attended the Salt Lake Theater.

The name of the play he couldn't remember, but it was one in which Julia Dean Haynes took part and after the performance they walked down State Street as far as Tuft's Mansion House before deciding to get something to eat up-town. They heard a shot when they reached First Temple and Main Street and saw men running in different directions. Two of the men came towards them. Entering a gate and crouching down behind a fence, they caught a glimpse of them as they passed.

They also saw another man at close quarters. Baker said he knew all three and the next day of the trial he identified Blythe and Morris as the two who passed by him and Mr. Toms, the policeman as the third man. He said Blythe wore a beard and moustache and was trying to conceal a long knife or sword under his coat as he ran. He knew Blythe because he had bought vegetables from him at his store opposite the Revere House where he had also seen Morris. Toms he had met at his shop where he had a pistol repaired.

When asked why he did not give this information at the time of the murder, he answered because he was fearful of his safety.

In rebuttal, the defense proved that no performance was given the night of the murder, the fence he hid behind wasn't built at the time, and Blythe had shaved his face and had no beard at that time and showed other discrepancies in Baker's claims proving his accusations were false.

Butterwood, the other witness, alleged that an attempt had been made by some person unknown to bribe him not to testify but he bombastically protested to the court and those present that he was not for sale. He said he heard the shot and a cry of "Oh, God, don't murder me." and when he saw two men running towards him he jumped over a pole fence and hid among some current bushes. He recognized the men as Alexander Burt and Brigham Hampton. At the time, he didn't know their names so didn't report seeing them but since that time he had learned who the men were.

In rebuttal: A. Burt was at home playing checkers with several friends from 9:30 to 12 o'clock. The murder occurred a little before midnight.

Mr. Hampton in 1866 was a partial invalid. His physician, Dr. J. S. Ormsby testified, "Could not have run a block." The trial lasted until Saturday Dec. 23rd. Judge McKean, in summing up the case, Alexander Burt was discharged and the others committed to wait the action of the Grand jury.

Margaret laughed when she saw John in his black and white striped prison suit when she went to the City Hall to visit him on Christmas Day. He wasn't alone. There were at least one hundred other supposed offenders mostly Mormons similarly dressed. Proof that the anti-Mormons in their fanatical zeal twisted and distorted the law.

John was not released until April 30th 1872. The court of last resort reversed Judge McKean's ruling relative to the manner of drawing and empanelling jurors, thereby invalidating nearly all that the crusaders had done during their 20 months misuse of power. All of these Mormon men were set free.

John was proud of Margaret, the way she had taken care of his business and attended to his affairs while he was imprisoned, just as she had done while he was in Southern Utah. He was home less than a year before he was called out again.

Chapter 14

Brigham Young received an optimistic report for possible settlements along the Little Colorado River from the exploring party returning in March. He immediately called 250 colonizing missionaries to move south as soon as the weather permitted.

Only a few more than a hundred got underway before the mission was abandoned. The arid, rocky land made travel difficult and seemed impossible to tame and cultivate. Leaders of the Church proclaimed such uninviting territory was actually a blessing, for there the Saints could settle without fear that anyone else would try to take it away.

"If there be deserts in Arizona," said George Q. Cannon, "thank God for the deserts. The worst places in the land we can probably get, and we must develop them. If we were to find a good country how long would it be before the wicked would want it and seek to strip us of our possessions?" Saints of this persuasion looked upon the hardships as challenges and the mission as the will of God to strengthen the Kingdom.

John was one of the first group to leave with the Horton D. Haight Company. Others followed, as the members were able to obtain the means to go. Traveling was slow with the loaded wagons and it took over three weeks before they reached the Big Colorado River at Lee's Ferry April 22, 1873.

The water was low and those who had horse teams to pull their wagons were able to drive across the river but the other teams had to be unhitched and driven across. With much work and sharing teams, most of the wagons reached the other side.

The work didn't stop there as the men made a wagon road out of a horse trail. The company went on, stopping at Willow Springs, a place by the Little Colorado where the water was good and the grass better. Here a large group of missionaries caught up with them, which increased their numbers to about 100 men and boys, five women and one child. Their leader was Elder Day.

Men were sent to explore the area around the Little Colorado River. They searched for a suitable place for a settlement, going as far as 136 miles up, down, and around the river but were unable to find one. A hot and discouraged people gave up. The feed for the animals was gone and the river itself seemed to be drying up. The Day Party was first to leave, and after Brother Haight took a vote, some of his people started homeward with them.

President Haight and those who would go with him, John was one, moved camp a few miles to the Moabby where they remained until the end of June. This was near Moenkopi, a village of friendly Indians and here John met Ira Hatch, an Indian Missionary who was visiting his children. The Hopi Chief Tuba and his wife Pulaska cared for them.

"What are his children doing here with the Indians?" John asked a settler who seemed to know Ira.

"Because his wife, the mother of these children was an Indian, part Paiute and part Navajo."

"Ugh! What kind of a marriage was that?"

"He was told to marry her by President Young through Apostle Rich. So he did."

"Brother Rich, who came south for General Conference, went to Santa Clara where Hatch was living, and asked him to meet him at the Gibbon's home. The Gibbons were raising this Indian girl, Maraboots, and had added Sarah as a first name. When asked, Ira said he was willing if she was. Sarah was asleep. Sister Gibbons woke her up and she said, yes, she would marry him and since Brother Rich was leaving at sun-up, she got dressed and Apostle Charles C. Rich married them that night. She was only 16 years old.

After the wedding, she went back to bed and he went home to the Fort where he told, Amanda Pace, his wife of only a month about the marriage. She wasn't very happy about sharing her husband and the one room at the Fort with a second wife, but they became good friends."

"What happened to his first wife?" John was curious.

"She died at child-birth and the baby soon followed." The man continued, "You'll like Ira." He then went on to tell John about Ira. As a missionary along with Jacob Hamblin and Thales Haskell, Ira had worked with the Indians all over the Southwest, from Las Vegas Springs to Fort Defiance. He had learned many Indian languages and was a valuable guide. Living among the Hopis also called Paiutes, they came to love him and he them.

Her father, Spaneshank, the son of a Navajo Chief, was taken prisoner in a battle with the Paiutes and since he was a chief's son, they treated him as such and he married a Kaibab Paiute, Chief Kanosh's granddaughter.

When his wife died, he wanted to return to his people, but he had two children, a boy and a girl. He could take his son, Peokon, because he would be a warrior.

If he returned with his daughter without a mother, she would become someone's slave so he gave her to his good friend, Ira Hatch. She was a young girl and with no way to keep her, he gave her to the Gibbons to raise

This marriage saved Ira Hatch's life.

The grass was getting scarce at Moabby and the group decided they could stay there no longer. On the 30th of June they started back reaching the Colorado River between the 3$^{rd}$ to the 5$^{th}$ of July. The other company with Brother Day was still crossing the river here at Lee's Ferry. They were using a large rowboat with two oars, taking the wagons to pieces and making two trips to the wagon, which was very dangerous, considering the swift current in the middle of the river. The river was very high at the time and the driftwood passing by, made it all the more dangerous.

Swimming across, the animals were driven a few at a time. The new comers helped the remaining wagons and people to get across. Then they started to cross in the same manner.

President Haight took charge. They not only worked all day but a good portion of the night by the aid of campfires built on both banks of the river. About noon on the 7th of July everything was landed safely on the other side. Then President Haight released his mission to go home, telling them to scatter along the road for water and grass and to go to their homes where they could help our people there.

John didn't feel good about going back home without completing the thing Brigham Young had asked them to do. He and a few other missionaries with the same reasoning stayed near the ferry, waiting to hear from President Young. Belatedly, he did send word to the struggling company of missionaries that they were to stay in Arizona and he made clear his belief that no matter what the obstacles were, a company of determined Saints could establish a successful outpost.

With the consent of President Young, John L. Blythe built a real ferry to be used at this crossing. For the timber he had to go over a hundred miles to the Kaibab Forest and even with help, this wasn't an easy task. When finished it was 20 by 40 feet, one that could hold two wagons, loads and teams.

John D. Lee launched this barge that John built, October 15,1873. It was in this boat the James's. Brown party crossed in 1875 and a

119

larger migration to the Little Colorado in the spring of 1876 including Johnny, John's son. John Blythe was not around to see these crossings. He was appointed Bishop and President of the Arizona Mission on Dec. 28th, 1873.

By January 20th John had visited the missionaries in Kanab and in the Johnson Settlement and the others on his list. His family moved to Kanab when John went with the Haight Company waiting to join him so Margaret and the family were ready to go with him when he left on this mission.

The missionaries were to build a fort and establish a settlement near Moenkopi, on land that Chief Tuba had given the Church when he visited President Brigham Young. The men consulted together and concluded to start about the first of February, weather and roads permitting. This settlement would include John's family, and thirty other families who were called to settle on this land. The company leaving Kanab consisted of forty-six individuals; thirty-one were men, four women and eleven children. The men included Ira Hatch who President Young had added to John's list.

John sent a letter on March 13, 1874 to Brigham Young and George A. Smith who were living in St. George, saying the company left Kanab the seventh day of February and arrived at the river the evening of March tenth. All were safe, although they had very severe weather on the journey.

"On February the 28th, after we had crossed the summit of Buckskin Mountain and had gone a little ways, we found Brother James Jackson, the son of Colonel Jackson, nearly frozen to death. He had been living for several months at the Ferry and had gone back to Kanab to get food and the necessary supplies to last him through the winter, when we met him between Kanab and Johnson's place he had to leave his light wagon, the snow being too deep to bring it over. He returned to our camp on the afternoon of the 20th at Navajo Wells, stayed over night and got more provisions and started on horseback for the Ferry. He was in good spirits and the weather clear and pleasant.

"We were busy building a 14X16 foot rock house at the wells where we also sunk another well and rocked it up and we claimed the land for a herd ground using James Lewis's name of Kanab. We placed it in the care of Bishop Stewart and James Lewis for the benefit of the Mission and the Kingdom.

"In the storm that came up the next day, Brother Jackson lost his way on the mountain. When he reached his wagon he was so benumbed that he could not build a fire so he crept into his wagon and had remained there in his bedding until we found him. He had bread and cheese and some wine in the wagon. When he heard us coming and in fear that we would not see him with every thing covered with snow, he crawled about two blocks on his hands and knees to meet us.

"After attending to his comfort and examining his situation, I inquired if he would like to be sent to St. George to his father. He preferred to be taken to the ferry where he claimed he had a little home and said Sister Emma Lee would take care of him.

"He manifested great faith in the ordinances as we administered to him and seemed to have great faith that he would get well. Although everything that could be done for him was done, he died about four hours after reaching here.

"Brother O. M. Allen was also very poorly on the journey, but he is recovering fast since we arrived here and is walking around. The weather here is warm and pleasant. The boat is all- safe thus far and I will do the best I can to secure it before the high water.

"I have not seen John D. Lee yet. We found Emma and children all well and alone with the exception of a miner who is lying sick with a sore foot. It has been running a half-pint of matter per 24 hours for several weeks. He is asking to get to Beaver to receive medical treatment at the governments expense. Sister Mangum is now nursing him.

"Brother Jacob Hamblin spent one night at our camp at Navajo Wells on his way back to the Moabby to meet again with the Indians and we let John Everett and three more men of the Company go with him. They were all mounted and had one pack animal. They went by the Paria and Brother Jacob agreed to come back and meet us at the ferry. But instead he has left a few lines in pencil stating that he thinks we had better wait until we hear from the Oraibis and the Navajo Indians.

"We think of taking some of the horses and going by the trail to the Paria Settlement and pack down a little of the tithing supplies. Our seed potatoes froze which were underneath our beds. The season has arrived here when the land ought to be prepared and our seeds and vines and trees put in soon.

"I have consulted with Ira Hatch and the few brethren that are with me and we have concluded that if there is no news from Brother

Hamblin or anyone across the river we will saddle up our horses and with Ira Hatch as Indian interpreter, we will cross the River. We will make our way to the Moenkopi and ascertain the facts and the feelings of the Indians and if the way seems to be open, we will return for our wagons and outfits.

"I shall endeavor to use every precaution I can for the safety of all. Brother Mangum and his wife and family from the Paria settlement came here intending to remain and raise what they can until the Fort at Moenkopi is built and the way open for the women and children to go over on this Mission."

The next letter to President Young was written April 8th at Moenkopi said that all those at the Mission who accompanied him were well and safe. " They arrived at the Oraibi farm on the 28th of March.

A few days after he had last written to him, Brothers Jacob Hamblin and John D. Lee and the four Brethren, whose who had gone over the river with Jacob as guards, the men he understood who were to help build the fort and work with the Indians, said they had enough of the mission and would now go home. One was John Everest of Kanab, a stonemason and the only one of them who had any knowledge of the business. The other three were from the Paria settlement."

John had supposed that Jacob Hamblin would return and stay at Moenkopi, but he was also going back to Kanab and said he didn't know when he would be back.

John asked him if the way was clear and safe for the company to go. He considered it was, although some of the Navajo Indians were a little riled and mad but he did not think there was any particular danger. He said he had made another appointment to meet the Navajo Indians in company with Ira Hatch in 10 days. They were to meet at Moabby, John Lee's place, when all of the Chiefs would be there.

Previous to Jacobs's arrival at the ferry, Ira in company with two others went to Paria for supplies and did not arrive in time to fill the appointment and with Hamblin in Kanab; no one met with the Indians. This disturbed John as he was moving the mission to Moenkopi. Jacob Hamblin had made two trips to talk to and pacify the Indians and John didn't understand why the Navajos were still upset with the Mormons. This was apparent for when they reached Moenkopi there was not an Indian on the place. Tuba and all the Oraibi Indians had taken to their old stronghold when they found the

Navajos were threatening vengeance on the Mormons for killing their braves.

Until the winter of 1874, the Navajos carried on a peaceful trade with the Mormons. This was changed suddenly when a party of four young Navajos went to the east fork of the Sevier River to trade with some Ute Indians who were camped there. On the way home, in Grass Valley, they got caught in a severe snowstorm that lasted for three days. They found shelter in a vacant shack belonging to a Mr. McCarty. He did not belong to the Church and considered the Indians as savages. Somehow he learned these Indians were on his property.

These young Navajos while they were waiting for the weather to change became very hungry and killed a small calf belong to McCarty and were caught in the act of eating it by him and a few men he had gathered. He and his friends killed three of them and seriously wounded the fourth with a bullet passing clear through his body.

The wounded one escaped, leaving every thing behind, his pony, food and the traded goods. After enduring excessive hardships, he made his way across the river and it was thirteen days before he arrived among his own people.

Telling the story of what had happened, and since the killings had taken place in Mormon country, where the Navajos naturally supposed they were among friends, the deaths were blamed on the Mormons. This stirred up the Indians and for revenge they were ready to kill all the Mormons who were on their side of the big river.

When President Young heard of it, he requested Jacob Hamblin to visit the Navajos and satisfy them that our people were not a part of it. Feeling that this affair, without great care, might bring on a war, Jacob started at once for their country to fulfill his mission although he was just recovering from an illness that kept him in bed for over a week.

# Chapter 15

On the way to Moen kopi, between Bitter Springs and Rock Pools, four Indians on horseback approached them, Chief Ketchene, two braves and a squaw. John signaled the company to stop. Ira rode up to his side.

The chief demanded to see Jacob Hamblin. When he found he was not with the company he expressed great wrath towards him -- angry with Jacob for not keeping his appointment.

The Indians went with them as they traveled to Rock Pools. The squaw who was brought by the Indians as an interpreter could only speak a little Spanish so was no help as such. Ira, who understands the Navajos talk very well, did understand, as well as John and the other men, that when Chief Ketchene found Jacob he was going to take his scalp.

Ira explained as best he could to the chief what he knew of the situation and tried to defend Jacob. The talk ended by Chief Ketchene demanding Ira and John, the Mission President, meet with him and other chiefs as well as the friends of the three dead sons and the wounded one in ten days at Peokon's Camp. John and Ira agreed to meet them at the appointed time.

The Indians asked for meat saying they were very hungry. The men killed a yearling steer and gave it to them. To the relief of the entire company they took the beef and rode away.

When the missionaries reached Moenkopi they found the Hopi settlement completely deserted.

Ira said, "Tuba and all the Oraibis have taken to their old stronghold when they found the Navajos were threatening vengeance on the Mormons for killing their friends."

He was right as Tuba and three of his companions came to their camp the next day. They welcomed the missionaries and were glad to see them.

They offered their huts for them to live in until they could build better. Margaret hearing of his offer started moving into Tuba's little house and the other women and men started emptying their wagons and moving into the other huts.

Chief Tuba explained, "I don't think many of us will be down here this season as we have a good deal of snow and we will be able to raise a good deal of corn up near our stronghold."

The Indians showed them where they could plant their gardens, using their land and water which otherwise would go to waste this year.

You could feel the love Tuba and Ira had for each other. Chief Tuba was a peace loving man and the Hopis or also called the Oraibi Indians were not a warring people. They defended their rights but found no joy in killing and scalping other men. They planted and preserved foodstuffs for their present and winter needs. This was part of the reason the missionaries were sent here to teach them better ways to get more use from their farms and land. John was the first to bring irrigation to them.

Before Tuba left he told Ira he and some of the others might want to come and live beside them and learn more about the Great Book. In just a few days Tuba and a few others came down. Tuba lived with the Blythes.

Although they found the place Jacob Hamblin designated for the fort, the few men who were left on this mission decided to wall up the spaces between the huts for defense rather than spend their time trying to build the fort. However they cleared, plowed, and planted the land that was adjacent to the proposed fort. In this area there was a big spring, almost as large as the Hopis spring. Tuba told them it belonged to John D. Lee, sold to him by Jacob Hamblin and if they planted anything using his water he would claim the produce and to be sure he would take it from them. This left no water for the Mission. Tuba said they could have water from their spring, all of it this season. Then next year all the water his people could spare.

This didn't stop Margaret. As soon as the mission ground was ready she planted the peach trees first and then the other fruit trees she brought from home. She planted grapevine starts and helped the men put in a nursery of about a half-acre of the choicest fruit seeds. These too were brought from home. She had John find a way to get water to all of them through his irrigation project.

On April 2$^{nd}$, John and Ira Hatch along with Tuba as their guide, started out to meet the Navajo Chiefs. The next day they found a Navajo who could talk the Oraibi language so that Brother Hatch could understand. He agreed to pilot them to Peokons, the meeting place and to be their interpreter.

"I don't think it was by accident we met him. I think he was sent to be sure we were coming." Ira said to John.

And to confirm his idea, the Navajo told them he was sent as a messenger to bring Ira and the Company Chief back with him and if they didn't come the Navajos would kill every one at the mission.

Being released as guide, Tuba soon made ready to leave and Ira knew he would not be going back to Moenkopi but to his stronghold. Hugging Ira and John and with their expressions of thanks sounding in his ears, Tuba eagerly left the men.

"That took a lot of courage for him to offer to guide us." John said.

"It was only for his love and respect for me that he even considered taking us. He did it although he knew he might be killed in the process."

"Why are they so frightened of the Navajos?"

"Well, for one thing the Navajos had a habit of stealing their children, and selling them in Mexico as slaves for horses, guns and ammunition. A small band would come galloping through their village and each Indian would reach down and snatch a child up, like a hawk getting its prey, then passing on without missing a hoof beat leaving shocked and grieving parents."

When they came to the place where young George A. Smith was killed, the guide stopped them for a rest. He seemed pleased to see Ira's reaction of guilt and grief.

"What's the matter?" John asked.

"They killed him right here!"

"Who?"

"George Smith. He was just a young man. I told his father I would take care of him when he let him go on this mission with us and I let him down!" Remembering made tears stream down his face.

"His Father gave him two things, a fancy pistol and a beautiful horse. Oh, he was so proud of them! The Indians took them, too!"

"How did it happen?"

Ira told John, "In October, 1860, we were asked to go and live a year among the Moqui Indians. I had been in their village before and now we were to teach them more of our ways, learn their language better so we could teach them about their forefathers from the Book of Mormon. A request from these Indians had been made to Brigham Young.

"I have never been on a mission when we were so well supplied. Seven of us men, Jacob was our leader, two young Indian women, Sarah, my wife and Eliza, Jacob's adopted daughter. They were to teach the squaws sanitation and better ways to cook and preserve their foods. With us we had a Ute Indian, Enos, who knew their language and of course young George who had persuaded his father to let him come.

"We had many pack mules to carry our supplies, food and ammunition. We even had a boat on a wagon for crossing the Colorado River, which became such a trial we had to abandon it shortly before we reached the River.

"Although we had prayers night and morning we all seemed to feel an evil influence hanging over us as we neared the river but we crossed it without our boat and had no problem until we climbed the steep hill on the other side of the river and after traveling over the parched terrain, we ran out of water. The nearest water hole we were depending on was dry.

"The next day, four older Navajo men met us and told us we were not to go on or we would be killed. They told us to follow them to Spaneshank's Camp where they were from, there we could get water and be protected, but his camp was 15 miles out of our way. We knew our animals couldn't make it and the other water was much closer.

"Traveling over the sand dunes, Sarah and I took pity on our poor horses and decided to relieve them of our weight and walk until we reached the water.

"All of a sudden amid war-hoops and flying sand came painted Navajo Warriors galloping out of a ravine. They startled Sarah's horse and he broke away from her. Then one of the riders rode along side of Sarah and tried to lift her up on his horse. I saw what was happening, jumped on my horse, and rode along side of him and slapped him hard across his face with my riding whip. He dropped Sarah and the Indians rode away, vanishing as quickly as they had come. Sarah said the warrior who tried to take her away was her brother, Peokon.

"Bless the four Navajos who stayed with us for they showed us a place where we could stay up on a mesa. One man could guard the only narrow entrance and he could see if anyone was approaching long before they could reach the entrance. The water was down below.

"Before our train and people were able to reach our stronghold, the Indians started gathering in around the waterhole. The four Indians along with Jacob and Enos talked to their chief and men giving the missionaries time to get through the entrance and safety.

"The Indians wanted guns and ammunition. Saying if we gave this to them we could go on our way. Jacob told them we would trade food and supplies with them but we could not give them guns and ammunition and with a promise we would trade with them the next day the Indians left.

"We kept the entrance guarded without need and all enjoyed a peaceful night.

"The next day a large number of Indians came to trade. They brought beautiful blankets and beaded moccasins and furs. While Jacob and I who knew the Indian ways were trading, some of our men took our horses from our camp to water them.

"Young George went with them. Coming back to camp George's horse pulled the reins from his hand and headed back to the waterhole with George running after him.

"The men with the other horses didn't see him go, but when they reached camp and found he had not returned with them, the two men went back after him but it was too late.

"The Indians who were by the water hole admired his horse and his pistol. When they asked, he trustingly gave them the gun so they could hold and examine it close up. The last Navajo he let see it quickly spurred his horse around George and shot him in the back with his own gun. Then he dismounted, pulled George's buckskin shirt up over his head and his companions shot four arrows in his back. When the two men from camp found him, the Indians, his gun and his mare were gone. He was still alive.

"They took him back to camp where the arrows were removed and the girls cleaned and bandaged his wounds and made him as comfortable as possible.

"Because of this, the company agreed to leave early in the morning, hoping the Indians seeing them going back and away from their camps, would let them go in peace. We realize what they really wanted was our guns and ammunition.

"Planning to travel fast, we made our packs as light as possible and left our heavy equipment behind. The four Indians who stayed with us helped us pack and offered to travel in the rear of our train until we were out of danger and also lead us to Spaneshanks.

"When we left in the morning we put young George on a mule in a saddle we made for his comfort with Brother McConnell sitting behind him to hold him and guide the mule. He was in much pain and kept pleading with us, as we were getting ready, to leave him there and let him die.

"We left as quietly as we could and traveled a mile or so before we were alerted. About twenty Indians were trailing us and coming on fast. We pushed our horses and mules as hard as they would go and were on the level part of the red sand dunes when they were right behind us, just out of pistols reach. We could hear the wounded boy's cries and pleading for us to stop, but we couldn't.

"They were right on top of us when one of our pack mules went crazy, left the train and started bucking and tail spinning around in circles. His antics made the Indians stop and stare at him. Then from his actions the pack he was carrying opened up and the trinkets and beads and other bright objects flew out from it, spreading them over a radius of a quarter mile. These were things we had taken for gifts. The Indians got off of their horses and started gathering them up. One found a small metal mirror that reflected in the light, which drew a number of Indians to it as they prize a mirror very highly. After spilling his wares the mule came back to his place in the train and acted as though nothing had happened.

"As soon as we felt it was safe we stopped, but young George had died. We wrapped him in a blanket and found a place off from the trail where the Indians couldn't find him. We put him between two large rocks and covered him with smaller rocks then tried to make the spot look more natural by putting a little brush on top of the rocks.

"With heavy hearts we moved on to Spaneshanks Camp. He greeted us with open arms and was happy to see his daughter again.

"Enos, the Ute Indian, told us that on the second night after we arrived, Peokon came to his father and wanted him to give up all the missionaries that they might die to pay for his dead warriors who were killed by the Mormon soldiers. Spaneshank refused and Peokon left cursing his father.

"I couldn't understand why Peokon thought Mormon soldiers had killed his men until later when I found out the soldiers who killed his warriors probably came from Camp Floyd which is a military base just south of Salt Lake City. At the time, they had been in the area. That is why the Navajos were hostile toward us.

"Did I tell you when Sarah asked George to describe the Indian who shot him, she felt that he was her brother Peokon? Now we are going into his camp. Yes, I am afraid. It will take another miracle for us to come from there alive."

They reached Peokon's place about nine the next morning and by noon the Chiefs started to gather. In the afternoon the large Council meeting place was filled. John and Ira were ushered to the far end of this windowless Hogan, the opposite end from the door, just as Jacob

Hamblin and the Smith brothers had been. They sat cross-legged on the dirt floor. The only light was from a fire burning brightly in the middle of the room.

"Is Peokon here?" John asked Ira.

"Yes, he is the one sitting next to Chief Ketchene."

The smoking commenced. Then the old Devil who killed Doctor Whitmore at Pipe Springs and made such a sweep of his stock, entered and pointed at John and Ira. With a fiendish grin he crowded in and took a seat in the already filled room saying he had come to listen, not to talk.

Ketchene did the principal talking to John through the two interpreters, Ira and the Navajo guide. He related the murder of the three Indians at Circle Valley of which two were his sons and of the extreme suffering of the one shot through the body and of the thirteen days it took him to reach home. Swimming across the big river and trudging through the snow without food or even a blanket to keep him warm. But he, Swiftwind, made it home to tell the sad tale.

The young brave was brought in the hogan, his shirt was lifted so the men could see the wound where the bullet past through his body. It was a pitiful sight causing the boy much pain.

Ketchene said, "The Mormons did it." and the Council Chiefs agreed.

John and Ira tried to convince them that the Americans, not the Mormons shot them, that their Mormon Chief and the people were sorry when they heard of it.

Ketchene asked, "What difference is there between the Mormons and the Americans?

For you look alike and you dress alike. We have seen Americans eat and sleep and live with Yogott's family."

"The name they give John D. Lee." Ira whispered to John.

"And the last time Jacob came to see us he had two Americans with him so you must be all the same."

John told them the difference was we, the Mormons, believed in and worshipped the Great Spirit.

They asked how it was that Jacob had not returned with the horses and cattle he had promised.

John replied, "We did not know as he had not told us of promising them."

After trying for a length of time to convince them that it was Americans who had taken the Mormon land and kept their cattle there and they were the ones who had killed their young men, the Indians made a proposition to settle it if John and Ira would join with them in making a raid over into that part of the country. As Brother Hatch knew the trails he could guide them and show them the men who did the deed and let them, the Navajos kill these men. Then they would make a clean sweep of all the horses and stock in that section of country.

John and Ira gave them to distinctly understand that they would not comply with their proposition, saying, "The Mormons were Peace Chiefs and did not allow their people to kill or steal."

This reply kindled their anger and all of the Indians showed their hate and some of the Peokon warriors started crying for blood.

One Indian came over to John and passed a sharp knife across his throat and when he did not flinch, he cut off some of the buttons on John's coat and then passed the knife across his throat again trying to frighten him. This he repeated until every button was cut off of John's coat but John showed no sign of fear.

Then Ketchene asked if they had come for them to use them up, as they had not brought the horses and cattle to comfort the friends of the dead and wounded.

"Jacob has lied to us so often and you must be lying when you said that you did not know of the demand that was made of the Mormons. 100 head for each man killed and 40 head for the wounded one, one half to be horses and the other cattle. The spirits of the dead men tell us that their blood must be atoned for - so their friends and relatives might not suffer."

Then Chief Peokon made a lengthy speech stirring up the feelings of the Indians very much and said he wanted to cut their throats. He asked John through the interpreters what he thought of that.

He replied, "We have no fear. We know the Great Spirit and trust in him."

Ira held his breath for he expected his brother-in-law to do exactly that which he was threatening to do. He felt it was to get even with him for cutting his face with his whip, which left a scar that could still be seen in the flickering firelight, making his face look almost inhuman.

Chief Ketchene quieted the Navajos and asked John why they had come to their country, whether they were driven there.

He answered, "We came by special invitation from Tuba and the other Oraibis, to live with them as friends and to teach them many things concerning their forefathers that have been revealed by the Great Spirit to us." And told them of the many advantages they might derive if they would behave themselves toward them and not demand unjust things but live in peace and be friends with them.

His words had no effect on the Navajos, but they did cut their demands a little, the same amount of horses but fewer cattle. They added the horses their men were riding and the six horses they got trading with the Utes and the red blankets and the other things that belonged to their dead and wounded men. Plus Peokon wanted the white horse with the black left ear on which one of the dead men tried to escape, to remember them by.

These demands John wrote down to please them and agreed to send their demands to the Mormon Chief. They gave John and Ira to understand the horses and cattle must be delivered by the 13th of June or John and Ira must return if the answer was unfavorable. "If you do not come, we will kill every man, woman and child at the Moen kopi and any other white man who crosses the big river."

On the other hand, they promised to be their friends and give them all of the Oraibis land in return for bringing the horses and cattle.

Again John protested as to the injustice of their demands, insisting that the Mormons did not kill their sons.

And again Peokon aroused the Indians against them. He shouted, "Kill them now! They will bring us nothing. Scalp them and cut their throats and bring peace to our hearts!"

Then some of the Council, the older Chiefs, stood up for Ira, saying, "He came as an interpreter and his squaw is Chief Spaneshank's daughter. You would not kill our friend, our brother. He need not die. Let him go."

Chief Ketchene spoke, which silenced the other chiefs, and pointing to John said, "We will roast him over these coals and his cries will comfort the hearts of our kindred dead and Ira can go and tell his people what we do to the Mormons who kill the Navajo!"

When told what the decision was, John mildly said, "Brother Ira, tell them I want to pray to the Father of us all before they put me on the coals."

"Let him pray." Chief Ketchene replied, "He claims no fear. When he is on the fire, we shall see whether he cries or not!"

John and Ira knelt down and John's prayer was one of forgiveness and love for these dark-skinned brothers. He prayed that they might see the light and know who their friends were. He asked for those who were sorrowing for their lost sons to be comforted. He asked the Lord to bless them with food that they and their children would not know hunger, and to bless them with peace and prosperity. The prayer ended and John asked if he should disrobe.

Peokon asked Ira what John had said and Ira repeated in Navajo the words of John's prayer. When Ira finished it seemed that dark Hogan was filled with light and a breathless silence reigned for about five minutes, then the Chief Ketchene told two men who were by the door to get John's and Ira's horses and saddle them.

When they were brought, Ketchene said to them, "I believe your hearts are good and you are our friends but our young men are crying for blood. Get on your horses and go straight home. Don't stop or turn to the right or left for if you do these men will kill you. Now go!"

It was morning. For more than twelve hours they had been held captive under the shadow of death.

John came back with a bad cold and felt poorly. Margaret told him to let everything go and get into bed, but he insisted there were things he had to do that just couldn't wait. Margaret said sadly, "Wouldn't it be something to escape the Indians just to die now from chills and fever?"

John went to bed.

# Chapter 16

John wrote to President Young along with telling of his experience with the Navajo, he sent the list of demands the Navajo Chiefs wanted to compensate for their killed and wounded braves.

He told him the deadline the Indians had set for the horses and cattle to be delivered was June 13th and if the Mormon Chiefs refused John and Ira were to go to Peokon's camp and tell them so.

"I feel and realize the powers of darkness are fighting and contending this mission with a force and power I have never seen or felt or come in contact with before. At the present we are but six men in number. Except for the protecting care of our Heavenly Father, we and our families, our animals and outfits would soon be used up by those Indians as all hands would not make a good cattle guard, but our trust is in the Lord God of Israel. We believe His servants have sent us on this Mission and my council to the Brethren is to be of good cheer and redouble our diligence and faithfulness.

"We will continue to prepare and cultivate every foot of land we can and raise all we can to sustain both man and beast until we hear from you."

Earlier in March, John D. Lee also wrote a letter to Brigham Young blaming Jacob Hamblin for making the Indian problems worse. He felt that Hamblin's actions would result in destroying the mission of Bishop John Blythe and Company at Moenkopi stating that Jacob had lost all of his influence among the tribes.

Jacob and John Lee never could get along with each other. Their personalities clashed. Jacob was soft-spoken, humble and obedient to the Church Leaders' council, while Lee was described as arrogant and opinionated, however optimistic and charitable.

This letter to President Young was written three days after one of their disagreements.

When Jacob and Lee met at Lonely Dell, John Lee found fault with everything Jacob did dealing with the Navajos. He told Jacob the chiefs said it was 27 days when they were to meet. So it was 27 days not 25 as he claimed and it was a definite commitment Jacob made when he told the son of Ketchene he would meet with the chiefs in ten days at my place."

"You said you would bring Ira Hatch but neither of you showed up." He continued, "Remember, I was with you when we were on our way to Paria. We met Ira Hatch. You told him of the appointment you made with the already infuriated Natives. You asked Hatch to fill the appointment, saying you had special business in St. George and Ira replied, 'If you made an agreement to meet the Navajos you had better do so yourself as I have as much as I can do to fill my own appointments.'

"This is another breach of promise which only served to aggravate and increase the indignation of the already offended Navajos," Lee contended.

"You claim true friendship with them, that they said they would never hurt you or your family. We were meeting in your hide-out at Moabby, why didn't you pacify them?" Jacob asked.

"I wasn't home."

"That's right! You were with the miners hunting for gold."

"And in that terrible blizzard I almost lost my life." Lee shuddered remembering, then continued, "But don't forget I saved your life when Chief Ketchene's son asked you to meet his father, the two of you alone, to talk things over. You were about to go but I told you it was a trap and all he wanted to do was to kill you and take your hair?"

"Jacob, you don't use any sense! When the chiefs came and you were not there, they felt they had been injured, insulted and mocked with impunity. Ketchene said you would not be a captain to them any more. Why didn't you tell them you didn't want to meet with them instead of lying like a dog? Now they have become so enraged that they are almost beyond control."

When John Lee felt Jacob was treating his views lightly, he added, "An agreement is an agreement." and all present, the miners and the members agreed with Lee.

Jacob answered, "I am the Apostle to the Lamanites and I run that 'shebang' and not you!"

One word brought on another until both parties got quite warm. Lee had the last word before Jacob stormed out the door.

"Great Apostle Hamblin, by your betrayal you have ruined the Mission at Moenkopi!" And added so those present could hear, "He that seekth to exalt himself shall be debased, but he that humbleth himself shall be exalted."

On receiving John Blythe's letter President Young called men from Round Valley through Kanab to go to the aid of the missionaries at Moenkopi. "Bring everyone home from the Moenkopi. Leave the Navajo alone until they know who their friends are," were his instructions.

How grateful John and Ira were when a platoon of 50 mounted men arrived to guard them and take them home. John R. Young was their leader and Jacob Hamblin came with them. He asked Brother Young to wait four days while the Missionaries were packing and getting ready to leave so he could go and visit the Moqui Indians about forty miles further on. This he agreed to and Jacob left taking Tom Chamberlain along with him.

After they had their wagons packed, Margaret had John dig up two of the peach trees she had planted to bring back home. (The trees never reached Salt Lake as she gave them to Emma Lee to plant at Lonely Dell.}

John objected to this until Margaret asked, looking over her hard work and the sprouting seeds, "Do we have to go?"

"Of course we do!"

"But I'11 leave my garden and trees," Margaret lamented, never realizing the true danger they were in.

On the morning of the fourth day when Jacob was to return, a runner came and told Ira and John the Navajo were planning to meet Jacob on the trail and kill him for not keeping his word and meeting with then. Ira got John Young to pick ten men with the fastest horses. They had to hurry to reach Jacob before he came to the place where Ira felt they would attack. It was about a twelve-mile ride and they had to push it to be on time. Jacob rode out on Old Satan, a big sorrel mule of Bishop Esplin's. It wasn't very fast but good traveling over the harsh land he had to cover.

As the men reached the top of the rise over the place of the supposed attack, they could see Jacob and Tom coming over the opposite rise and into the trap. They shouted to tell them of the danger, but Tom and Jacob thought they were being greeted and started rushing down the hill toward the place where the Indians were hiding. Tom was in the lead as Jacob's mule was not a fast runner.

The Navajo thought they had Jacob and let out a war whoop. Old Satan, frightened by the piercing cry, bucked and stampeded and Jacob had to hold on for dear life, grabbing her mane with one hand and the saddle horn with the other. The riders met them at the bottom of the gully and the Navajos veered off. When they rode up, Jacob was back in his saddle and with thanksgiving they returned to Moenkopi safely.

After Chief Hastele and other Navajos, along with an Indian agent and interpreters went to the place in Grass Valley where the shooting of the Braves took place, all were satisfied as to the truthfulness of Jacob's and the missionaries' account of the killings. Chief Hastele said he would so report to the other chiefs. The matter was finally settled the 21st of August 1874 at Fort Defiance. From this meeting both the Mormons and the Navajo came away satisfied. Peace was again restored along the Colorado and east of it so Brigham Young renewed the colonizing along the Little Colorado River.

John D. Lee was at the ferry when the Blythe party crossed the Big Colorado River. He showed John Blythe the papers that had been filed giving Emma the sole right to the ferry and its location. Lee said they were making out pretty good collecting the tolls for the river crossings.

"I usually get food and other goods rather than money which makes living here more comfortable. And do you know many of my passengers would rather part with their goods than with their money."

"I guess you don't need the money. I heard that you and the miners found a rich deposit of gold out near the San Francisco Mountains."

"Just rumors. I had my fill of mining when I went with them on that ill-fated trip. I was never so glad to get home in all my life! Oh, no, we found nothing and we almost froze to death. After that experience, I would rather choose to suffer poverty and affliction with the people of God than to enjoy the pleasures of sin with the wicked," Lee answered.

That Fall Lee left the river and went to the southern Utah settlements. His purpose was to talk to the Prophet and see if he could be reinstated as a Church member, to visit his family in Panguitch, and get some needed provisions. He was disappointed when he was unable to see the president. His clerk said Brigham Young's time was filled with those already waiting to see him and advised him not to wait around, as he wouldn't have time for him.

John D. Lee then went from St. George the few miles to Washington where he still owned a home and some property and while there Brigham rode up in his carriage. When Lee went out to greet him, the father who had adopted him years ago, neither got out of his carriage nor embraced him and Lee felt their cold relationship as Brigham spoke looking down from his carriage seat.

"I have been told that you associate with gentiles. You play cards with them. You eat and drink with them and you swear as they do, using the name of Deity in every other sentence. A stranger that did not know you couldn't tell you from a gentile by your talk, manner and conversation. I'm sorry to hear you have changed so. Once you were a faithful man and sought the interest of God's kingdom. I could trust you to do anything on earth that wanted to be done. I hope these reports are false."

Lee replied, "Your informant must have little to do. As far as my associating, eating and drinking and playing games of cards with gentiles, that I don't deny, but as to cursing and going back on the Church, that I deny. My situation at the ferry compels me to associate more or less with outsiders and I can't see any harm in that."

"John, you must be careful and stand by your integrity." Brigham Young blessed Lee, then drove on leaving Lee disappointed and discouraged.

When Lee went to visit his family in Panguitch, he was recognized and arrested for his part in the Mountain Meadows massacre and taken into custody by William Stokes, a Deputy U. S. Marshal. He was held in jail at Fort Cameron in Beaver. Here the trial was to take place, but with the difficulty in securing witnesses, the case didn't come into court until the following summer. The jury finally selected consisted of eight Mormons, three Gentiles and a 'Jack' Mormon.

Eighteen years had elapsed since the massacre at Mountain Meadows and during this time, John D. Lee was the only white man who admitted and was known to be present when it happened.

Many factors came into play to bring about this horrible affair. The atmosphere was that of war with Buchanan's soldiers on the march to Utah to 'quiet the rebellion' or to annihilate the Mormons as some of the army felt they were ordered to do. The members south of Great Salt Lake had their fervor generated by the eloquence of George A. Smith as he told the Saints to store and horde their grain and other supplies as they may be in need of every morsel of food before this war was over.

Jacob Hamblin brought five Indian chiefs from the southern part of the territory to Brigham Young who pledged their support to help the Mormons rather than the 'Mericats' since there was also a threatened invasion coming from California. The Indians returned without Jacob as he stayed to marry another wife.

The ill-fated Francher Party let a small group known as the Missouri Wild Cats join their train. Many of them were single men, without cattle or families and other responsibilities. When the members refused to sell any of their grain or food to the Francher Company, these Missourians who renewed the hate they had for the Mormons when they were in Missouri, started threatening and irritating the Saints at each settlement from Fillmore to Cedar City.

The fear of an army again driving them from their homes, the rehearsals of past sufferings and indignities, and the often-repeated vows to avenge the blood of their martyred Prophet had set the fires smoldering even in the calmest heart. Those Saints who had suffered the expulsion from Missouri and remembered the massacre at Haun's Mill could barely contain themselves when hearing these comments and the mocking of their religious beliefs.

They boasted of their participation in the murders and outrages that were inflicted upon the Mormons in Missouri and Illinois. They bragged about using their women in Missouri. "No different than polygamy," one said. They made jokes, being sure the members could hear about the things the Saints held sacred. "Where is your Bitch-shit?" another would laughingly ask at each settlement.

When they said they would return with a proper army and then the Mormons would see who would use their grain and food, that is, if they were alive to witness the plunder, some of the settlers felt they were declaring war and that this threat should be handled by the military which was already organized to fight the advancing army.

These Missourians definitely flamed the fire that resulted in the massacre. However, the irony of the situation was that some of these men who said and did the most to agitate the Mormons, being miners without families or cattle herds to care for, were impatient to get on to California and left the company before the massacre.

These men and others of the Francher Company threatened to destroy the town of Fillmore, tearing down fences and destroying other property. When the people in Paragonah were unwilling to sell of give them any food or grain, they took their frustrations out on the next town, Cedar City. Here they broke down the barricades, invaded the town and stole corn and other supplies from the Bishop's storehouse and turned their cattle and stock to graze on the planted gardens. When the people tried to drive them away, they recklessly fired at the members. Because of this, the members at Cedar City held no love or concern for the Francher Company.

Returning home from meeting with President Brigham Young, the Indian chiefs following behind the Francher Party suffered their own abuses from this company. When the emigrants supposedly poisoned the spring at Corn Creek, where some of their people died and many became very ill from drinking this water, the chiefs started gathering the warriors from the different tribes feeling surely these were the Mericats they were to fight. They were encouraged by the settlers who gave them guns and ammunition, thinking the Indians were going to be the 'Battle Ax' for the Lord.

To add to the Indians frenzy, ten of their braves died after eating the meat from a dead beef the company herders had thrown to them. It had been poisoned with the same poison they had used to kill the wolves and other predators that were following their herds.

John D. Lee living in Harmony could see the gathering of the tribes and knew they were up to no good. As their Indian Farmer, he felt partly responsible for the actions of these Indians, yet he knew the sentiment held by his friends and neighbors. He asked the advice of his immediate military superior, Major John M. Higbee, who then asked Major Isaac C. Haight at Cedar City, whom in turn asked Colonel William H. Dame stationed at Parowan.

His answer was that the military would do nothing to help the emigrants as he had other concerns at the present time. He told Lee, "If we attack and kill the Indians in defense of the emigrants, it would be little less than suicide. You must be well aware of the exposed condition of the Southern settlers."

By this time hundred of Indians had gathered. Coming with painted faces and in full war regalia, they were ready to attack the Francher Company who was now resting at Mountain Meadows where their cattle and other stock had good grazing.

The first attack came as a surprise and the camp suffered injuries and even a few deaths. They quickly brought their wagons in a circle, set about to make a trench to protect them when firing on the Indians and set up a good defense plan. Now the Indians were losing their men as they continued their raids.

A Chief and some of the warriors came to John Lee and insisted on help from the Mormons. "We were told we could soon kill all of our enemies without any of our braves killed then we could have all their cattle and take them to ease the pain of our dead. Now the Mericats are strong and kill many of us. You come and fight with us."

These were not the words they used but Lee got the message and when he hesitated, they added if they didn't come now they would kill Lee's family and go on the warpath against all of the Mormons.

To appease the Indians, Lee rounded up a few men and with

painted faces they joined the Indians in their assaults on the Francher train being careful not to shoot directly at the men who were shooting from the wagons so any resulting deaths could be blamed on the Indians.

Major Haight sent a message to Brigham Young telling him of the rumors going around and asked for his advice. He sent James Haslam an express rider with his letter who happened to leave the same day the Indians began their attack. Haslam arrived in Salt Lake about noon on the 10th of September and immediately gave the letter to Brigham Young. On reading it, he quickly wrote an answer and asked James if he could undertake the return Journey without delay. He said he could and Brigham said, "Go with all speed. Spare no horseflesh. The emigrants must not be meddled with if it takes all of Iron County to prevent it. They must go free and unmolested."

Although he had just finished a hard journey, he left immediately. Arriving in Cedar City on the 13th, Haslam gave the letter to Major Haight. When he read the letter, he shed tears and cried, "Too late! Too late!"

All members of the Francher Company except seventeen small children had been killed.

Men were called out by the military through Major Haight to help at Mountain Meadows. Some were told they were to bury the dead as the Indians had killed all of the emigrants and some were told of the orders Colonel Dame had given. They were to help the Indians to save their own skins and were not told of the plan that had been devised to exterminate the company until they had reached the Meadows. Many of them felt they were there as part of the army fighting to defend their rights and that this plan had been sanctioned by the Church.

After the Franchers were driven out of Cedar City, a meeting was held. The agitated members were ready to fight and destroy the wagon train. A way was suggested but the cool-headed ones argued against it and it was voted down. Some decided to encourage the Indians to do their work for them.

After the first day of fighting the Indians, at night and under the cover of darkness, three men left the Franchers pinned down wagons and galloped north toward the settlements to ask for help. When they reached Pinto, one of them, young William Aiden was shot and killed by a white man. The other two men quickly turned their horses and escaped.

Having no desire to return to Mountain Meadows, they by-passed the Franchers wagons and lit out for California. However, the two men never reached the Vegas Springs before they were ambushed and killed by Indians.

On hearing about the killing of Aiden and fearing the complications resulting from his death, Majors Higbee and Haight went to Parowan to confer with Colonel Dame. When this meeting ended, Major Haight said, "But you know what the council decided."

Colonel Dame replied, "I don't care what the council decided. My orders are that the emigrants must be done away with." These words were relayed to John D. Lee.

Lee finally convinced that he was doing what had to be done, accepted the decision and helped to make the plans for the execution. He was to decoy them from their wagons with a promise of protection and conveyance to a place of safety.

Lee tells how the people in the camp welcomed him as their deliverer. How trustingly the women and children came to him. They accepted his terms, laid down their arms and came out from their stronghold. The small children who were too young to talk were put in a wagon that led the procession. The women and other children were separated from the men walking behind the second wagon which held their wounded. The men followed walking in single file. Each unarmed emigrant had beside him an armed Mormon 'guard'. Major Higbee, on horseback, was in command. Absent were both Major Haight and Colonel Dame.

When the wagons were well in front of the men and the women and children following closely behind the wagons were out of sight of the men, a signal was given. Each of the armed men shot the man walking beside him and then sat down so those who had missed their target or those who could not find the heart to kill his assigned man let the Indians finish the job.

The women and older children were left entirely for the Indians. When the shots rang out, the Indians who were hiding in bushes on both sides of the road where the wagons had stopped, came out and with their blood-curdling war cries, pounced on their victims, killing them with knives and hatchets. It only took a few minutes to complete the massacre. Lee and the driver of the wagon supposedly killed the wounded that were riding in the second wagon.

What a shock awaited the men who had participated in this wholesale murder when they saw the blood and carnage surrounding the dead bodies. They gathered together and sat stunned, unbelieving they had caused this horrible human destruction. They made a pact of silence, swearing among them they would never reveal those who had taken part in this terrible affair.

The Indians were having a field day, looting the wagons and taking the clothes off of the dead. Some were gathering the cattle, horses and mules and dividing them among the tribes. Many of the wagons were destroyed until the Mormons put a stop to all of it and sent the Indians on their way, taking the loot they had already gathered. One chief left with only shiny cooking pans dangling from his saddle, enjoying the sound of their banging together as the horse took each step.

The settlers cared for the small children who never saw what happened to their parents until the government by an act of Congress returned them to their friends and relatives in Arkansas.

It was reported to Brigham Young that the Indians had killed all of the Francher Company and John D. Lee gave the same report when he talked with President Young who wept over their fate. For several years the facts relating to the tragedy were unknown, but gradually the truth leaked out and an investigation was made of the affair. Lee was excommunicated from the Church and action was also taken against others, as the truth became known. Some like Lee went into hiding and some left the territory, changed their names and became model citizens in those states.

At Lee's first trial the prosecuting lawyers influenced by the anti-Mormon political climate that had invaded Utah were determined to prove the Mountain Meadow Massacre was planned and carried out as ordered by Brigham Young. They were unsuccessful as they couldn't find a reliable witness and in their efforts to do so, were rather unconcerned whether John D. Lee was guilty or not. The eight Mormons on the jury voted for his acquittal and the other four members voted guilty which made a hung jury.

Lee was sent to the penitentiary in Salt Lake City. Here Margaret along with Johnny and his intended future bride visited Lee and asked him if there was any message he wanted to send to Emma. Johnny would be passing over on the ferry on his way with the Allen Company who was to settle by the Little Colorado River.

"Oh, yes!" John Lee replied, "Tell Emma to collect the ferry tolls in money when ever she can and send them to me. I am here without a cent and a little money would bring me better food and better treatment. Please tell her I am desperate and tell her I send my love to her and all my children."

Johnny promised he would and they left.

Ellen, Johnny's girl friend, had coaxed him to take her to see John D. Lee the evil murderer she had heard so much about when she heard Johnny was going to see him.

She was disappointed. "He didn't look like I expected him to. My father said he was the devil himself. He looked like an ordinary man. Are you sure he cut the throats of two women?"

"No, don't believe all you read and hear. My folks say he is a generous, kind-hearted man. He was in charge of the Indians who attacked the company so he gets blamed for the whole massacre."

In February Johnny left Ellen, his beloved, and they promised to write. If he found this new settlement to his liking, he would come and get her and there they would make their home.

Lee was released on bail of $15,000, May 11, 1876 and a friend, William H. Hooper became surety on his bond. He visited his families and took care of what he could to restore his business. He saw the treatment and abuses his wives and children were suffering from those who had once been his friends, but he enjoyed the freedom he had from being away from that horrid jail. The place was one of stink and filth in the common sleeping room, filled with lewd profane talk of some of the inmates and smoldering hates that resulted in violence and barbaric cruelties. Yet he knew he would return to face a second trial in three months.

His sons tried to persuade him to cross the Colorado and go down into old Mexico. He would not go. His word had been as good as his bond for too many years to change now. To run away would admit he was guilty and that he would not do. Right up to the end of his second trial he felt sure he would be exonerated

It was plain at the beginning that the prosecution had changed their target since the first trial. When on giving the opening statement they said the Mormon Church was not on trial and the only man to be considered was John D. Lee. They would dispose of his case first, and consider others if and when theirs should come up. The question before the court was simply: Did John D. Lee commit murder at the Mountain Meadows? Did he not on his own responsibility, plan and execute this mass killing in defiance of the orders of his superiors, and in contradiction to the accepted teachings of his church with regard to the shedding of blood?

The first witness was Daniel H. Wells who had come to Beaver from Salt Lake to be present. At the time, he was the commanding officer over all the military in the entire territory. He admitted he knew Lee and said Lee did not hold any official position in the military in 1857. He also said he felt Lee had considerable influence over the Indians.

The second witness was Laban Morrill who stated he had never been at Mountain Meadows but knew of the message sent by Major Haight to Brigham Young from Cedar City. At the same time Joel White was sent to deliver a message to John D. Lee at Harmony that said, "Manage the Indians. Hold them in control and keep them from molesting the emigrants until we get word from Brigham Young."

Joel White said when he met Lee, he said, "I don't know about that." After he heard the message. The prosecution used this to prove that Lee had acted in opposition to the wishes of the local military.

The fourth witness was Samuel Knight, the driver of the second wagon. He testified Lee was walking between the wagons. His wagon was carrying the wounded, three men and a woman, as well as the arms, supplies and gear from the camp. He said he was so busy holding his team when the Indians attacked those walking behind him, he didn't know for sure what did go on, but thought Lee had killed the woman by striking her with the butt end of a gun. He had no idea whether or not others had helped with the killings. Under pressure, he did admit the Indians jumped out of the brush and started killing people. He was not too positive, but it was his impression that Lee killed that one woman.

Samuel McMurdy, the driver of the first wagon that held the children, said Higbee had called him to bring his wagon and come to the Meadows and after he arrived, John Lee ordered him to drive up to the camp and into his wagon were loaded the children. His team went first and walked fast, so fast that it was quite far ahead. Lee ordered the halt. He did not see Lee strike anyone with a club or other object, but he saw a woman fall. Later he thought he saw him draw a gun and, shoot two or three in the wagon behind his. He could not recollect the names of any that were there except Higbee and Lee.

"You did not help to kill anyone?"

"I had nothing to do with it at all."

"Then you did not raise your hand against anyone at that time, or do any of the emigrants?"

"I believe I am not on trial, sir."

"I ask if you refuse to answer the question.

"I do not wish to answer."

McMurdy said he did not know whether everyone was killed or how many children were saved but the prosecutors got what they wanted from his testimony. Lee had killed at least one person.

Nephi Johnson came from his hiding place to testify although many thought he would never show up. One was the Sheriff who said, "He will never come in. He has been in hiding too long himself. He would be afraid to come in." Just then he appeared and was introduced to the Sheriff, "I don't believe I ever saw you before," he said to Johnson who replied, "No, you have never seen me, but I've seen you many, many times."

As a witness, Johnson would tell them nothing of the happenings at the time of the massacre. He claimed he had gone up the side of the hill to catch his horse and saw the massacre at a distance. Yes, Haight had ordered him to the Meadows and he had gone to Lee for directions. He could not remember any names of the men who were there except John D. Lee, Klingonsmith, the one who was first to break the oath of secrecy when he testified at Lee's first trial. Then there was Bateman and Hopkins, men who were now dead.

Johnson was on the witness stand for some time and when pressed as to why Klingonsmith, Haight and Higbee all stood back and gave Lee control? He answered, "He acted like a man that had control."

"Did he not have control?"

"I can't say."

"Did you not think at the time that John D. Lee had absolute control of everything there?"

"He acted like it."

Now the Lawyers had what they were looking for. Lee and only Lee was responsible for all that happened at Mountain Meadows.

The seventh and last witness was Jacob Hamblin, by now well known as a frontiersman and Indian scout with a reputation for honesty. He had not been present at the massacre at all and so had no oath of secrecy to keep.

He began by saying he went with his Indian boy the next spring and gathered up the scattered bones and buried them. At Fillmore he met Lee as he was returning home and Lee was on his way to report to Brigham Young. Lee told him of the massacre and he insisted that it had been carried out according to orders. Jacob claimed Lee told him there were two ladies who were hiding in the bushes, found by an Indian Chief, who had escaped the first massacre, and the Indian killed one and he killed the other.

The attorney insisted that the story be repeated with more detail. Did the girl cover her face? Did she cry out? Did she get on her knees and promise to love and serve him all of her life if she were spared? He went on and on with the dramatics and had complete control of his audience. How old were the girls? Were they very beautiful? Always he came back to the statement Jacob had made that Lee confessed he had killed one woman and the prosecution added that he had thrown the girl down and had cut her throat.

By the time the lawyers were through with Jacob Hamblin, the people in the courthouse were in a state of horror and shock. They were ready to believe the worst.

Through it all Lee sat facing the court in silence. He called no witnesses, made no defense. After an hour the jury, which was made up of ten Mormon men, brought in the verdict: 'Guilty of murder in the first degree. '

He had been betrayed.

He wrote to Emma at Lonely Dell, "Old Jacob Hamblin, the fiend of Hell, testified under oath that I told him that two young women were found in a thicket by an Indian Chief, who brought the girls to me and wanted to know what was to be done with them. That I replied that they were too old to live and would give evidence and must be killed, that I then cut her throat and the Indian killed the other girl. Such a thing I never heard of before let alone committed the awful deed. That old hypocrite thought that now was his chance to reek his vengeance on me by swearing away my life."

He appealed to the Territorial Supreme Court with no results and was taken back to the scene of the Massacre and executed by a firing squad on March 23, 1877 almost twenty years after it had happened.

## Chapter 17

The sixty-four days it took John A. Blythe to get to his designation was full of problems and pleasures. His Mission started February 3rd 1876. That morning he said good-bye to his girl, Ellen, promising he would be back to get her if everything worked out to his liking then they would make their home in Arizona. That is, after they had a big wedding and send-off in Salt Lake City.

The next morning he picked up his partner, Theodore G. Angell, and when they finished packing their wagon the young men were eager to start their mission. As the young men started on their way, they were given farewell hugs and best wishes and with smiles their families let them go.

"What, no tears! I'11 bet you are glad to get rid of us." John remarked.

And his sister, Lizzy shouted back, "We sure are!" And they made faces at each other and laughing, they parted.

It was dark before they reached Lehi and John found the team, two small mules, insufficient for the trip. The road was slippery and hilly around the point of-the mountain and the poor mules had to strain every muscle to pull the heavy loaded wagon as far as Lehi.

John and Theo sent word by telegraph to Salt Lake and John was determined to go no further and wait there until another team came to go with them. Receiving no word from home by noon, Theo talked John into going on to American Fork and while there, Theo's father, another Theodore Angell and Heber Searle brought them another team. Then they went on to Provo where they spent the night.

In the morning, John made a few purchases, spending $8.25. These were grain and stakes for the animals, an ax, a table knife and fork, since he forgot to pack them. Then he bought a long whip. That was after both John and Theo had fun practicing making it "crack" which came about quite naturally to both of them. They would use the whip to encourage the teams to try harder when it was rough going or when they were in a tough spot, responding to the sound of the whip "cracking" rather than its sting.

Even with a double team, they had to stop three times to let them rest before they reached Salem getting there shortly after dark. Here they spent the night. They did cover 15 miles.

Next the team struggled through snowdrifts and slippery mud and nine inches of snow was found at Santaquin that made the going slow.

They spent that night at the first ranch they found south of Spanish Fork.

At daylight with numb fingers, John greased the wagon wheels to keep them turning, afraid they would freeze up tight if they weren't kept lubricated.

The road was no better all the way to Nephi, which made traveling hard on the team. The men didn't find traveling much easier than their animals. With raw winds and blowing snow and the cold penetrating through their entire bodies and trying to ward off frostbite in the hands and feet and then shivering from the cold during the nights.

They did have two nights since they left Provo when they slept in warm beds. One was in Brother Pyper's home in Nephi where they were treated to his kind hospitality. The other was at Fayette where the settlers went out of their way to feed them and their animals and found them warm, comfortable beds.

Even with the cold air burning their noses when they breathed, they didn't seem to despair. They were young and eager for adventure and full of dreams for the future. These they shared with each other. John planned to get married in a year from this June. Theo wanting to be settled on some land of his own and have herds and flocks and a place of security and safety to bring his future bride, that is, when he found her.

"I wonder why they had us come on our mission in February?"

"So we'll be there in time to plant our crops." Theo answered.

After Nephi, they moved on to Taylorsville and on the 11th, the night was spent in Fayette. When two exhausted men and their used-up teams arrived here, the whole town took pity on them and treated them royally.

The road from Taylorsville had been extra hard and heavy with its drifts, ice and mud. Once the team became so bogged down the men thought they would never get them out. They tried, but found now was no time to use the whip. It took all the added strength the men gave them before the team finally pulled out and were moving again.

Hating to leave the comforts had in Fayette, they left at nine in the morning, repeating their thanks to those who had been so kind. One more night was spent with members in Salina, who treated them very well. Then they forded the Sevier River, had a dry noon and arrived in Richfield just before sundown Sunday night.

Here their leader received them. Captain William C. Allen and were introduced to other members of the mission. Some of them John and Theo had met before and all had stories to tell of their trials traveling to meet here in Richfield.

Four companies, each of 50 men and their families were organized and called by Brigham Young to start separate settlements in Arizona along the Little Colorado River. Their leaders were, Lot Smith, Jessie O. Ballenger, George Lake and William C. Allen. The 50 were divided again in trains of 10 with a Captain leading each train. John was fortunate to have Brother Allen also Captain of their 10 wagons for he was very thoughtful and considerate of his men. Although most of his train left early Monday morning having rested over the Sabbath, he suggested John and Theo make Monday their day of rest and they readily agreed.

John wrote a letter to his girl and a postcard to his mother. Sister Allen made them a batch of bread and John had two of the mules forefeet pared down and re-shoed but he and Theo rested most of the time.

After fording the river, they arrived in Monroe about one in the afternoon. Here they caught up with the Lars Jensen Company from Spanish Fork, who wanted them to stay and travel with them, but Theo wanted to go on, hoping to catch up with the Allen train. Because it was growing dark they made camp within a half mile of the summit between Monroe and Marysvale. The next morning they unloaded their wagon and carried everything to the top the last two hundred yards. They had it reloaded by noon and reached Marysvale about 3 pm. In Marysvale John found a letter waiting for him from Ellen.

"Too early to stop now." Theo said, so they loaded up with grain and hay and left.

They did catch up with their train in Circle Valley and here Lars Jensen's ten caught up with them. They all stayed over a day because they had good grazing for their animals. The first found along the road.

Deer tracks were sighted. John and Lars went deer hunting but came back empty-handed, so they used up their ammunition shooting at a target. John hit the target many times and decided he was now as good a shot as his father.

If they thought the way was rough getting to Richfield, they hadn't seen "nothin'" yet. The wagon trains started up the canyon and at the first fork of the river, they crossed on solid ice. When they came to the second fork, they had to chop the ice away before it was safe for the wagons to cross. This took four hours before all the wagons reached the other bank. While they were working, two men fell into the icy water.

" For those men the Sevier River lives up to its name." John mused.

"It lives up to its name even if I didn't fall in," added a tired Theo.

Still winding up the canyon they reached its head and camped for the night. It snowed four inches during the night and it snowed all the way to Panguitch where the snow was already over a foot deep.

John ran across an old friend, Don Clayton. His brother, Heber had them dine with them after they put up their team with the Order. Heber said there were 125 families living the United Order. Also the name of Panguitch was an Indian word meaning "fish".

They bought hay and grain from the Order and that day only traveled two and a half miles since the roads were so heavy with snow. Reaching Hillsdale, they only made five and a half miles the next day. On the way they had to brake and put rocks in front of the wheels to keep their wagons from slipping over the dug way. The next day they did a little better. They made it to Mammoth Creek, all of 8 miles.

A near tragedy happened on the 24th. Before they made the 6 miles to Little's Ranch they climbed to the top of the basin. Two wagons could not make it to the top. Theo took a team down to help. John stayed with the other wagons blocking the wheels to keep them from slipping back down the hill. After the first wagon was brought up and John and Theo were preparing their team to go after the last wagon Brother Maulstrom offered, "Here take my team and give your team a rest."

They did and were soon back with the other wagon. As John and Theo returned the team and were about to hitch it to Maulstrom's wagon, the wagon was pushed back just enough to start moving over the crest of the hill. It gained momentum and shot down the steep incline on the other side of the mountain, turning over and over losing its load before landing right side up.

The soft snow kept the wagon from breaking up into pieces and they had plenty of help gathering up Maulstrom's scattered tools and goods and reloading his wagon. Even the sacks of corn hadn't split. The wagon had landed within a few yards of a road the company would pass on their way down the mountain.

As the men trudged up the hill returning to their wagons they thought it was a miracle they had witnessed. No one was hurt or killed and nothing was damaged.

"Maybe we should take all of our wagons down that way. It would sure save us a lot of work." Theo commented.

They continued down the canyon. After doubling teams and much hard lifting they finally got to Long Valley at Glendale. Here again John knew the family with which they stayed, Sister Brinkerhoff and family, a widow and a daughter of old Hawk.

"Hawk? That's a strange name." Theo commented.

"Oh, he was called that or more often 'Hawk-eye' because he had this uncanny way of knowing where the Indians were hiding or could almost see through trees and bushes and tell where lost or stolen horses or cattle were. But it didn't do him much good. He was killed by an Indian."

John stayed another night. He sold a gun, bought 600 lbs. of corn and wrote a letter to Ellen, but wished he had waited another day. Then he could have told her about the curious thing he saw in Orderville - a live calf with a double head, three eyes, two on the sides of the head and one in a crease in the center of the head, three tongues in two mouths.

He found friends here and the boys went to the Leap Year dance and they had a gay time. No, he didn't dance with anyone as pretty or sweet as his Ellen.

So happy to meet with his old friends, Spencer, Bishop, Hoyt, Asey, Esplin and Stellar who were now living in Orderville, he wanted to stay another day, but Theo wanted to go on.

Still filled with the spirit of fun had the night before, John stayed to visit with his friends while Theo went on, three miles to Mt. Carmel and John was glad he stayed as he had a very pleasant time.

"All work and no play makes John a dull boy." He told Theo trying to justify his staying over.

"Well, you played all day and you're still a dull boy." Theo laughingly answered.

John met Theo and the wagon train one mile the other side of Mt. Carmel where they left the Rio Virgin and cut across the hills southeast of Kanab. Here they had to double up their teams again to pull the wagons up the dug way and they camped for the night five miles from Mt. Carmel.

Continuing over the hills to Kanab, they arrived there a little after dark. Big drifts of sand had slowed the wagons the last two days.

Kanab was familiar to John, having stayed there with his mother, sister Elizabeth and Bobby his adopted brother, while his father went with the Haight Company exploring the land along the Little Colorado River.

He was happy to see Levi Stewart, the Solomon's, the Rider's, Brother Nathan Adams, B. Riggs and he went to church with Sister Bunting and family. He enjoyed visiting and getting his fill of home-cooked meals during the five days Captain Allen waited for the arrival of his other missionaries as this was another gathering point. Here John and Theo were assigned to another train, captained by Brother Adams.

Before they left they repacked their wagon, leaving a plow, harrow teeth, a shot gun and ammunition, a wad cutter, two boxes holding their extra clothes, a side of bacon and other things reducing the weight by about 500 lbs. These they left with Brother Rider.

John went to mail his letters at the post office. He was given the mail, a large packet of letters and a large packet of newspapers for Lot Smith's missionaries who had gone ahead. He didn't realize how homesick he was until he saw the newspapers.

"I wonder if they would care if I opened this package up and found out what's happening at home?" John asked Theo.

"But when will you find time to read them?" Returned Theo as they had already started on their way. John sighed and tossed the newspapers behind him.

After traveling 12 miles the wagons stopped at Johnson's Run, giving John a chance to go visit the Johnson's. He stayed with the family all night and returned to the wagons about noon and wished he had stayed longer learning Captain Adams decided to lay over another night.

Their next challenge came on the road at the foot of the Buckskin Mountain. It became very muddy. In some places, knee deep to the teams, making heavy hauling and slow going.

In the morning, starting at eight o'clock and after going a half-mile they doubled their teams in order to go any further. Ed Petty doubled with John and Theo, taking their wagon four miles. Then they thought it best to go back after Petty's wagon. Theo and Ed went back taking the little mules and Ed's team.

About nine that night, the men returned riding Ed's mare. They came for the other team having had no success.

Next morning even with the extra team and John's help they only moved the wagon a hundred yards. The exhausted men with worn-out teams gave up. John and Theo were about to head back to their wagon when Captain Adams and Brother Maulstrom came along side with a couple of teams to help them. With two more teams it was still "nip and tuck" to get the wagon along and it was three in the afternoon before Ed's wagon was brought up to theirs. Some of Ed's load was then transferred to John's wagon. After catching up with the other missionaries, they found the roads no better. The train only covered five miles that day.

On the other side of the mountain, it was dark before they arrived at Rock House Springs and made camp. Here they caught up with two other companies and because of lame teams, Captain Adams had his men lay over for two days.

On Saturday, the third day, the horses were all right, but Adam's mule was still lame. They decided to go on anyway and traveling through heavy sand they reached Jacob's Pools.

Although it was Sunday, they traveled to Soap Creek where the water was very bad, but the scenery was interesting with large rocks held up by very slim bases. Like giant mushrooms with a stem as part of the original rock or as John described them, "Like turnips standing on their tails." It was hard for Adams to hold any kind of religious service as the men left camp to explore these unusual formations.

By Tuesday they reached the Big Colorado River at Lee's Ferry. John left the company and walked to Lonely Dell to visit Emma, John D. Lee's wife, a delightful person, and one with charity and compassion.

Emma knew hardships as few Pioneers did, having crossed the plains with the ill-fated Martin Handcart Company. About a fourth of this Company of 562 individuals was buried in shallow graves along the way. During a severe snowstorm, fifteen members died in one day. Most of the deaths resulted from illness aggravated by exhaustion, freezing, too little food or a combination of all three.

Emma and her friend, Elizabeth Summers, sailed from England and through the Perpetual Emigration Fund, their $45 each would bring them from England to Zion. Half of the route would be accomplished by pulling a handcart, furnished for them at Iowa City. Thousands of the Saints from England and Wales successfully used this method to reach Zion, but fate had other plans in store for the Willie and Martin Companies.

As the last group of Saints leaving Liverpool that Season, when they reached Iowa City to pick up their handcarts, they found the supply of handcarts and tents completely exhausted and had to wait while these were being made. The Willie Company, who had sailed weeks before the Martin Company, was still waiting for the rest of their handcarts to be built.

With haste these handcarts were thrown together. Unseasoned wood was used which resulted in causing many breakdowns and the company had to stop while they were being repaired, slowing up their progress. Some of them had to be abandoned completely, which added weight to the other carts. These further delays resulted in the food and supplies furnished for each company and carried in accompanying wagons, to be used up long before they reached Utah.

When the Willie Company was finally outfitted, the leader, James G. Willie, agreed to take some of the Martin Company along with him since his company was much smaller than Martin's. Emma and Elizabeth were among those chosen to go with them.

Reaching Winter Quarters August 19th, they were warned that the company couldn't get through to Zion before winter because of the long wait for their handcarts, but the optimistic and eager Saints voted--shouting, "On to Zion! On to Zion!" Later many sorely regretted this decision.

Their problems increased and by the time they reached Fort Laramie the train of heavily loaded handcarts was moving very slowly. The average time to reach the Valley was 100 days. Captain Willie knew they were way behind schedule and in order to move faster, he asked everyone to lighten their load.

Much cold weather clothing and bedding was left behind. Checking the carts, he asked Emma to leave the big, heavy, brass kettle she was carrying in their handcart. Since it was filled with all of her personal possessions, she refused.

This argument ended with her sitting by the side of the road on top of her kettle as the procession of handcarts passed her by.

After begging her to change her mind, Elizabeth left sharing their handcart with another family, but Emma still had her precious kettle.

Knowing the Martin Company would be coming she worked for the Colonel's wife there at the Fort for her keep while she was waiting. Her wait was over ten days. The Martin Company was having as many problems as the Willie Company only more of them. Walking and sweating under the hot sun of August, coats, blankets and other warm clothing was removed from their carts to lighten their loads.

When they came to the fort, Emma teamed up with a 17-year-old boy who was slight in stature but physically strong and a pleasant companion. She did her share and more, pulling the handcart. One time they added a sick mother and a newborn baby to their load.

An early winter caught up with them in September bringing suffering from the cold and an added burden to their travel. The streams they crossed were icy cold and anything that got wet quickly froze. Some had toes and fingers painfully frost bitten. Elizabeth Summers lost most of her toes from getting them frozen during this terrible weather while she was traveling with the Willie Company.

Emma took good care of her feet. When she came to a stream, she took off her shoes and stockings, hiked up her dress and outer wear and then carried her 17-year-old partner who weighed little more than a hundred pounds, across the water on her back. She returned and brought over their handcart then thoroughly rubbed and wiped her feet and legs with her wool neckerchief, put on her dry stockings and shoes and was ready to move on. So neither of them suffered from frozen feet as some members of the party did.

Heavy snows encountered along their way and the dead and dying found the company moving at a snail's pace. With little time for ceremony, the dead were buried in shallow graves with rocks piled on top of them to keep the pack of wolves, which were seen following the train, from digging them up.

Most of the treasured linens the ladies brought along and the bed sheets and blankets were used as burial shrouds.

Coats and other clothing were taken from the dead and gratefully received by the recipient. Even Emma removed the coat, pants, and shoes from a dead friend knowing he would have given the "shirt off his back" if he felt someone needed it more than he--and someone did.

One bitter cold day, a grief-stricken mother pulled off the wool shawl that covered her head and shoulders and tenderly wrapped it around her dead little girl before the baby was laid in her tiny grave. After a short prayer, her father added, "May she rest in peace and Heavenly Father, protect her little body so she will not be disturbed or molested by man or beast."

The sobbing mother returned to their cart, since she could not bear to see her little one covered with dirt. As soon as she was out of sight, the father picked up the baby, removed the shawl and carefully put the baby back in her grave. As he finished covering the grave, he wondered if he did right. What would his wife say when she saw the shawl? With misgivings he walked behind her and gently placed the shawl on her head and over her shoulders. Instead of scolding him, she pressed his hand and thanked him.

Early snows lay deep upon the mountains and every muscle was strained as they struggled and climbed pulling and pushing their handcarts. Icy streams had to be crossed. Floating and broken ice cut legs and places became slippery causing many falls and injuries. One man broke his leg and after it was set and crudely braced, he was determined to pull his handcart, but had to give up after trying. His leg was frozen before he reached the Valley and he had to have it amputated. He walked with a crutch the rest of his life.

While they were traveling along the Sweetwater, missionaries passing on their way home to the Valley, saw their pitiful plight and on reaching Salt Lake told Brigham Young about the condition of both the Willie and Martin Handcart Companies.

He immediately formed a relief party, gathering generous donations of food and blankets from his followers and sent these relief wagons on their way.

President Young also sent two men in a light wagon as messengers to let the companies know help was coming. When they reached the Martin Company, the ravine looked like a cemetery with all its newly dug graves. The survivors were so overjoyed on see the wagons a surge of energy swept over them and they went out to meet the Relief Party.

They looked like a collection of near skeletons. Emma was down to half her weight. The Relief Wagons had to take their gathered Saints over seven hundred treacherous miles before they entered the Valley. The Martin Company didn't reach Great Salt Lake until the end of November.

Emma said if she ever got warm again, she would never complain of the heat.

Now, here she was living where the extreme summer heat baked and blistered bare feet after walking through the hot sand for only as little as ten minutes.

When her husband brought her here, where the Paria and Colorado Rivers meet, it was barren and it appeared that no man had lived here before. Jacob Hamblin had suggested this place as a hideout for John D. Lee. Her husband left her to set up camp as he went to get more supplies and his other wife. As she started to get things together, a fierce windstorm came up, whirling hot sand unmercifully at her and blew her camp completely away. After the wind calmed down, she gathered up what she could find and started making camp all over again. With work, perseverance and much help, she finally had a good shelter that she often shared with the sick or weary traveler. This she called Lonely Dell. Her greatest complaint was being left alone for months without seeing anyone except Indians.

Emma greeted Johnny with a warm welcome. He gave her the message from her husband John D. Lee and she had him stay for breakfast and dinner. When he got back to the ferry all of the wagons had crossed over so the man at the ferry took him over in a small rowboat.

John was so impressed with the scenery he had passed through, he wrote to his friends telling them it would be well worth their time to come and see this strange and beautiful country. He advised them not to make the journey in winter, though, but in late spring or summer. He wrote, "You would see sights beyond your wildest dreams," and he couldn't wait to show Ellen this romantic country when he brought her down in June.

Because the next stretch of land would be dry and sandy, at Navajo Wells they filled barrels with water for their animals and again at Limestone Tanks. Here the water was caught in holes in the rocks and they took their teams to drink from them, but had to carry their buckets almost a mile to fill their barrels.

Sunday they stayed at Moabby - an oasis in the desert owned by John D. Lee, but his favorite wife Rachel was not there. She had gone to Salt Lake to stand by her husband while he was in jail. Twelve wagons of the Dayton Company were camping there, as were some missionaries who were working with the Indians at Moenkopie. These missionaries were invited to do the preaching at the Sunday services. This proved very interesting to John as he heard the part his father and mother played in making Moenkopie a safe and productive place for them, the present Missionaries.

"It's a beautiful spot. Sure wish our mission could be spent here." John remarked as they left in the morning.

"Nah, this place doesn't need missionaries. Lee has already made a home and ranch here. Didn't we agree to give one year of our time to help members settle along the Little Colorado? You might say ours is a work mission."

"But at the end of the year we can choose to join the settlement or be released, and go home. Right?"

"Yah-but, let's just wait and see."

On Tuesday they saw the Little Colorado River for the first time. It was about the size of the Jordan River in Utah, but the water was not clear. It was red and muddy.

"Look," Ed Petty said who was often with John and Theo. "That water is rising. I'll swear it's a couple of inches higher than when I first looked at it. Watch the bank on the other side, it's still rising!"

By dark they estimated the river had raised at least 14 inches, running over the banks and early in the morning when they left camp, the water had dropped at least 8 inches. They had witnessed the rivers flood pattern, which destroyed their dams and crops more than a few times during the next two years.

Following along the Little Colorado, they came to jet black lava formations and then saw the spectacular Black Falls. It was a beautiful sight. Red muddy water dropping about twenty feet from different spots along its 75-foot width. Below the falls the river could not be used to water the stock so the men had to take their animals over a mile to the Sandstone Tanks and water them in buckets, dipping the buckets in the pools that had formed in the rock crevices.

After traveling fourteen miles, they found the Grand Falls, which is composed of several small falls and a larger one. Water drops about 40 feet to the lower or large one and then again the water falls 50 or 60 feet into the river.

John would be sure to show Ellen these falls when they were on their honeymoon.

Traveling on, they came to the first crossing of the Little Colorado where two companies were camped. After a little trouble and a great deal of noise, by two in the afternoon all of the wagons were on the other side.

Laughter, fun, music and prayers were shared as all three trains lay over on the other side of the river. Then all the wagons rolled on together.

When they camped by a clear, snow water stream that flowed from the San Francisco Mountains, they found the old Butterfield road. The one used by the early settlers of California and among the cottonwood trees they found deer tracks. Three men from Adam's Company, Walker, Christensen and Ed went deer hunting. Walker killed one.

The next day, Captain Adams and John went deer hunting. They saw a few signs but didn't spot a deer. The wagons kept moving about 15 miles that day and the hunters caught up with them when they camped for the night. Walker was the better hunter since he shot another one the following day.

Progressing up the river, they met James Brown, president of the Indian mission, on his way back to Moenkopie. He was the guide for the first companies and said Allen's Settlement was thirty miles up the river where the trek had ended. When he heard John Blythe was with the Company, he asked Captain David E. Adams where he could find him. Adams pointed John out. Brown rode up to him and questioned, "John Blythe? You're much younger than I thought you would be."

"You must have me mixed up with my Father. He was the president of the mission at Moenkopie."

"Oh, of course! Ira Hatch speaks so highly of him. Your father is a fine man - fearless and firm in the Gospel. You should be proud to carry his name."

With a smile John said, "Guess I do have a name to live up to."

"Indeed, young man, indeed." he said as he left, anxious to be on his way.

Reaching the Sunset Crossing a little before noon and planning to lie over until morning, Theo, Ed and John took a raft two miles down the river to see the boys at Lot Smith's Camp while Walker and some of the other men went deer hunting. Walker brought back another deer.

Lot Smith didn't approve their visiting and told them so. He felt they were hindering the work of their friends, Alf Derrick, Wm. Hardy, Heber Brewer and Isaac Emery. To prove him wrong, they pitched right in and visited while they worked. They were back in camp by sundown wondering if Captain Allen would be as strict as Lot Smith.

The next day they crossed the river, which took a few hours. Then they traveled over some very good land and on Sunday, the ninth of April, they finally arrived at their destination. Dan McAllister and George Butler came out to meet them as President Allen was up the river exploring.

In the evening all of the Allen Company that had arrived had a meeting. John was asked to say something for the Adams Company. Again he was embarrassed and made his remarks very short.

The next morning, he was sent to work on the large log building that would be used as a dining hall and for storage. It was started the week before. Brother Dayton, the overseer, proposed they add a rock kitchen as an addition to the hall. President Allen set John to work as mason and to build this kitchen and its chimney.

With a little help to get started and a few instructions, but with no experience as a mason, he wondered if he would ever get this 12 by 14-foot kitchen built.

The first day his progress was slow. The second day he had the walls up all the way around three feet high. On the fifth day he had the walls and chimney completed and with George Butler's help, got it ready to roof. While the men put on the roof John plastered the inside and when it was finished, he felt he had become a pretty good mason.

Chapter 18

In the afternoon, after finishing the kitchen, John drew his quarter section of land. The number was "1". He was pleased with his good fortune until he found his land was far away from the buildings that they had just completed. President Allen started numbering from the far end. He had the land around their proposed settlement surveyed, divided in quarter sections and numbered. Each man had a chance to draw a number, as it was thought this was the fairest way to distribute the land.

All were happy with this arrangement except John Bushman and Nathan Cheney who had plowed the land near the proposed buildings and had it all ready to plant.

When the suggestion was made to use this land for a common vegetable garden, planted and cared for by the Company and for them to receive credit for the time they spent plowing and each would receive his own section of land by lottery, they were satisfied.

There was quick work in the way of settlement at Allen's Camp after the first wagons stopped at this chosen spot. Immediately Jacob Miller started building a house and in two days Brothers Bushman and Cheney had their plows all set up and started turning the soil. Members under the competent leadership of Captain Allen did their part to make this settlement a pleasant place in which to live.

Peace, harmony and brotherly love characterized all the settlers at Allen's Camp from the very beginning. It was small wonder John wanted to bring his Ellen to live here in this friendly atmosphere.

John wrote to his parents, "It is all United Order here with no beating around the bush. We give in everything we posses and our labor, time and talent. We try to live as Christ taught and I've heard very little grumbling or complaining. Every morning at the sound of the triangle, we assemble to pray and sing and we do the same every evening. We found eating together was a problem because of our different hours spent doing our assigned jobs, making it almost impossible to get us all together at the same time. I like it this way. Sister Adams sees I get fed and I do chores for her in return."

The naming of the settlement "Allen City" was something else. The Saints had two choices, Allen City or Ramah and when the voting was counted there was a tie. Although those who were in favor of 'Ramah' accused the other side of cheating, since they worked with the undecided, promising them favors. "Scandalous!" claimed the Ramah supporters expressing themselves without ill feelings.

To break the tie, they put both names in a hat and had a three-year-old boy reach in and pick one. He came up with "Allen City", but later this name was changed to St. Joseph, in honor of the Prophet, Joseph Smith. Within the year it also changed location, a few miles east and up the river.

Here they built a stockade fort and houses inside of it. John spent days working as a mason and as a mason's helper. John and Theo were proud of the stone house they built for themselves. This happened later in the year.

John's assigned work was varied. Besides doing work as a mason, he took his turn doing night and day herding, plowed many fields and planted wheat and corn and did any other job he was asked to do. He started working on the dam in April, gathering rabbit brush and cutting logs, then hauled, carried and shoveled tons of rock and gravel to the dam site. He dug; it seemed to him, miles of ditches, working on the main ditch that took the water from the dam to the fields and the smaller connecting ditches.

Water, the essence of survival for Allen City, had to come from a dependable source so a dam was built across the Little Colorado River about one and a half miles above camp. The water held could then be used as they needed it to irrigate their fields of wheat, corn and vegetables. An all out effort was made to quickly build this dam. As many as twenty-seven men and eleven teams were put into action each day. Hills of rock and gravel fortified the logs and brush that was used to start damning up the water. This backbreaking work was finished near the middle of May and the first water was turned out to run down the ditches May 13th.

The labor force was then changed to plowing and planting. They divided the work into two shifts, early morning until noon and the other working in the afternoon.

The young men who were called as missionaries, did much hard work to help the permanent settlers found their city. The United Order wasn't run Puritan style - rather each member knew what the Church standards were and was left on his honor to live by them. This led to a feeling of freedom, responsibility, and self worth among the people and an optimistic, easy-going group made up the Allen Company.

Pleasures, fun, and entertainment weren't lacking, either.

The young men bathed and swam in the dam, hunted deer, rabbits, ducks and wild turkeys and whenever they could find an excuse, some went over the river to Lake's Camp to visit their friends and the families with eligible young ladies. Birthdays were noted, although some of the men and women, too, were so tired they slept all during their own party. Humorous stories were told and good-natured teasing when 'goofs' were made.

The musicians among them organized a dance band, mostly made up with fiddlers, and four singers sang together making a barber's quartet. For his part, John played tunes on the washboard and shrill, whining songs with his saw and Brother Cluff's violin bow.

Celebrating the 4th of July began at three in the morning with small firearms saluting the camp. The gunshots went on until sunup. Games of competition were held, shooting at a target, jumping, wrestling, and throwing quoits and less strenuous games for the women and children.

In the evening a dance was held under the front bowery that was enjoyed by all. Several of the boys from Obed, Lake's Camp, joined them and were introduced to a Miss Jarvis by Brother Wm. Creer. Miss Jarvis was Theo, dressed as a lady by Sister Adams and she acted as his maid. Both of them played their parts to such perfection, they completely fooled all of the boys from across the river, just as the young men at Allen's had planned, since all of the Obed men were eager for an introduction.

Sister Adams had no trouble borrowing a lovely dress to fit Theo and found a small pillow to put in the proper place, but finding a pair of ladies shoes big enough to fit his feet was a problem. She finally found some.

She worked with his hair and interlaced it with ribbons and used some of her precious white cake flour to powder his red, sunburn nose.

Seeing him after the disguise was finished, John claimed, " His own mother wouldn't know him. He looks like a genuine lady!"

He even fooled many of the members at Allen's Camp.

"She has a dress just like your best one." One man was heard to say to his wife.

Miss Jarvis was the center of attention, surrounded by young men who didn't see the Missionaries laughing behind their backs. Finally Miss Jarvis consented to dance with Brigham Stowell and the next dance was promised to Doxey. The dance was half over before the

Lake boys saw something was wrong with Miss Jarvis. She was so awkward dancing and Brigham declared to Doxey, "You can have her. She is so clumsy and she has calluses on the palms of her hands worse than mine."

The loud laughter coming from their hosts made them realize they had been fooled, but took their embarrassment in good sport and some carried on the fun by dancing with Theo and laughing at his less than graceful movements.

A few days later, Brigham Stowell, Doxey and two other young men came back over the river and told the young missionaries three of their saddle horses had been stolen by some Mexicans who had just passed their camp herding many horses and going south to the Mexican border. They asked John and Theo if they would ride with them after their horses. President Allen gave four of the young men permission to go.

Crossing the river, the eight men started galloping after the horse thieves.

However the young men who had been fooled by Miss Jarvis had planned to get even. When they saw these Mexican horses pass their camp they planned to pretend they had stolen three of their horses. They hid the horses about five miles from their camp in a little valley where they couldn't be seen until they came right upon them. Here they hobbled the horses and left them with some feed.

When they brought the Allen men to this spot and planned to tell them it was all a hoax, their horses were gone! Only the hobbles were left where the horses had been. The riding horses were never found.

It started raining Saturday evening the 15th of July and rained all night. Early in the morning John woke up to the cry the river was rising. When he got up the water was spreading over the land, having risen above its bank eighteen inches or more. John went up to the dam and found the water ditch overflowing. He shut down the head gates to protect their fields. The water was running over the dam in torrents.

In the evening the water was still rising and began rumbling with the washing of gravel. Then the next day, the members feeling it was an answer to prayer, the river lowered about a foot. That evening it rose again, but was down again in the morning.

At 3pm, John was back in camp and began to write a letter when the alarm was given. The river was rising again. He rushed outside and within two minutes the water had risen over three feet and washed away their dam.

From the time the first wood passed the camp, in less than half an hour all of the logs and other wood that composed the dam was seen tumbling down the river. The members watched and saw all of their hard work building the dam pass by in front of them. Many of their gardens were washed away. At one place the water had spread over 300 feet. The flood damage was estimated at a $3000 loss.

A temporary water ditch was dug connecting the river to the main ditch so they could water their crops and the members decided to build the dam again using a stronger reinforcement and a higher dam to hold more water. Again, this second dam was washed away.

Allen City, later known as St. Joseph, experienced the washing away of eight dams before one was built strong enough to hold back the sporadic, raging Little Colorado River waters.

On August 4th, John repaired his gun, answered Ellen's most recent letter and prepared to leave in the morning with three other young men for Pleasant Valley. Here they were to locate claims for Allen City. This valley was in the San Francisco Mountains between Allen City and Prescott. They had a hard time finding it.

Traveling three days after leaving Sunset City, Lot Smith's Camp, Joe McMurrin and John went ahead of the wagon and climbed the highest point around to look for Pleasant Valley and the best way to get there, but failed to see the valley. They arrived in camp two hours after dark rather discouraged and very tired and thirsty, having kept up a steady and rapid walk nearly all day.

At daybreak, Alma Iverson and John climbed the mountain peak west of their camp and again were unable to locate it. However, returning they found a fine spring in a little hollow. Following the stream running from the spring, Iverson got ahead of John. John met the boys with the wagon and they set up camp by this little stream, but Alma was nowhere to be found. It was after dinner before he came stumbling into camp.

In the morning after it stopped raining, John went out to try to find some game. While hunting he came to some wagon tracks that led through heavy timber. Here a road had been blazed. He hurried back to camp and soon they were following the road he had found. It took a north direction, which surprised John.

Camping when it got dark, they reached Pleasant Valley about 11 o'clock in the morning. Coming in from the east side, Mormon Lake appeared to be a meadow because most of it was covered with cattails and rushes. Alma Iverson who was traveling about a half-mile behind the wagon saw a big cinnamon bear. He ached to shoot it, but didn't dare, as he had no one to back him up if he missed and the bear came after him. As soon as he told the men when he reached camp, four of them went after bruin, leaving Joe McMurrin in camp to get supper.

When they got to the place where he was last seen, they found he had left the area. Having walked all day, no one felt like scouting around after him.

They were very disappointed as they went back to camp as they really expected to get that bear. The valley was surrounded on all sides with good pine timber. The only strips of dry land were on the northwest and south sides. Five springs were found on the west side and one more towards the south. Deer and antelope were abundant.

They set about doing what they came for and the first day cut a couple of sets of house logs and laid four foundations. About noon, Westover left camp to get a deer and came back with one. John and Iverson saw five deer that had come down to water and went after them but came back empty-handed.

Many logs were cut to build five houses and eleven foundations. The men worked hard and steady yet found time to do a little hunting. Westover and Iverson took the team and wagon and went to the northeast end of the valley to the place Iverson saw the bear. They came back the next day with that big cinnamon bear. Log cutting and house building was forgotten as all hands took part in jerking old bruin.

On August 18th, when the men came back to camp after working to put up a house on the other side of a spring which had been claimed. They saw the claim would run out in three days and if the claimant did not come by before then, they would have the right to the spring.

"Oh, oh, guess we lost that spring." John said when he saw three strangers in their camp, thinking they were the rightful owners.

He was wrong. It was a sheriff, his deputy and a man who stole $6,200 in gold coin from two sheepherders who were at this north spring at the time they were robbed. They brought him to show them where he hid the money. He claimed he could not remember and after hunting for three days they gave up and left.

A few days afterwards, five men who said they were hunters planning to get their winter supply of meat, stayed in their camp for a few days. Although they went out every day, they never returned with any game.

The boys started wondering. "They are hunting, all right," Pete observed, "For the gold coins." To confirm their suspicions, when a flock of wild turkeys was spotted and all the boys went out after them, two of the men joined them. John shot one as did McMurrin, but the hunters were experts with their guns and brought down six turkeys, which they gave to the boys and to their relief, the four men left their camp the same day.

They had another visitor, a Mr. Casey, who said he was the brother of the two men who had been robbed and asked if they had seen anything that looked like a good hiding place for the thief to hide the money. When they asked about the claim he didn't seem to know anything about it. Andrew "Lucky" Rogers found the $6,200 a few years later.

The young men finished their work, put location claims on each of the buildings using their names and others from Allen's Camp and were glad to be on their way home.

The first part of September, John and Alma Iverson went back to the valley with J. Clark and W. M. Whipple. They cut, hauled logs, and completed building the houses where the first foundations were put in. This took more than two weeks. These claims appear to have been sufficient to hold the ground until John W. Young needed it in 1878 in connection with his railroad work.

Mormon Mountain, Mormon Lake, and Mormon Dairy were the names given to this area. Lot Smith established a dairy September 1878 up in the pines. 48 men and 41 women from Sunset and Brigham City, a settlement near Sunset, were at the dairy caring for 115 cows and making butter and cheese and seven miles south of Pleasant Valley was the site of the first sawmill on the Mogollon Plateau.

This mill was first erected about 1870 at Mt. Trumbull, in the Uinkaret Mountains of northwestern Arizona. It was built to cut lumber for the new temple at St. George, Utah, which was 50 miles to the north. Then in 1876, the Church Authorities gave this mill to the struggling Little Colorado River settlements. Taken down in August by the head sawyer, Warren R. Tenney, it was hauled into Sunset in September and was soon re-erected by Tenney and the men from these settlements. The sawmill was placed in the pinewoods near Mormon Lake. It was soon turning out 100,000 board feet of lumber

John was one of those called to rebuild the mill. He was sent to the mill site shortly after he returned from Pleasant Valley. McMurrin and Clark went with him, leaving on Friday the 13th.

"Why don't we wait until tomorrow?" Joe suggested, "I've had enough bad luck to last me the rest of this Mission."

"Ah, Joe, you aren't as superstitious as the Zuni Indians, are you? Come on, we are all ready. No reason to stay and the sooner we get there the sooner we'll get back."

Joe was riding his own pony. Blythe and Clark took a wagon furnished by Allen City. When they arrived at the mill, the three of them met twenty men who were working at the mill. These men came from the different settlements; five from Allen City. Theo was one. All were in good health and since the new comers arrived on Sunday, the work had stopped and they found the men resting.

"We're getting there - just a little more to be done. Of course we'll need to cut logs for lumber and bring them here so they can start sawing logs as soon as it is ready." Theo explained.

Besides working on the mill, John went hunting for the camp. He was also sent to check out trees he felt would make good boards. He brought back an antelope and a wild turkey.

"Where are the deer? I didn't see a single one." he asked Brother Tenney.

"If you were a deer would you stay around here with all these men and the noise we make. We've scared them away."

The next Sunday the camp was all excited. Joe McMurrin went out to hunt for his horse early Saturday morning and had not returned. All hands except the cook and Clark, who was ill with pine fever, went out to look for him. They hunted until sunset with no success. When they got back to camp, there he was having come in about an hour before the men returned, explaining:

"Well, I hunted and hunted but didn't find my horse. Before I knew it, it was dark and cold. I couldn't make a fire. I didn't have any matches. So I walked and I walked. I was afraid to stop for it was bitter cold and I was afraid I'd freeze to death. When it became light and warmed up a little, I could walk no further, so I curled up in a sunny spot and slept. When I woke I found my way to camp."

Wednesday, Joe McMurrin and Clark left with the wagon for Allen City. Clark, because he was sick and Joe taking him, hoped to find his horse on the way. Friday, ten of the men left for their homes.

For the next two weeks, John worked on the mill or cut and hauled logs. When their food supply was nearly used up, Theo, John and F. A. Olson started for Allen City on foot. They had no horses and Joe had taken the wagon. Leaving at nine in the morning, they reached Rock House Station about four the next morning having traveled 38 miles. The first 30 miles to Sunset Pass was without water and as they walked, they became very thirsty, suffering severely for the want of water. Olson was the worst off. About a mile from Sunset Pass, he folded up and swore he could not go another step.

"We are almost there. Be like a horse. Smell the water and run for it." John suggested.

"I can't! I can't move."

"Neither can I. Guess I'm not a horse." Theo answered wearily.

John and Theo, as worn-out as they were, each got on one side of Olson, put their arms around his waist, his arms around their necks and dragged him the final mile.

Drinking all the water they could hold, they went on, walking the eight miles to Rock House Station.

"What have we got here?" asked Brother Gallenger as the boys, reaching their goal, dropped and tumbled over each other.

Brother Gallenger and Brother Towbridge were spending the night at this station and were on their way to the sawmill with a wagon loaded with flour and beef and other supplies.

The twelve hours the boys stayed here, they were fed and drank much water. Being refreshed continued on their way since they were fortunate in getting a ride on a buckboard for fifteen miles--almost to Cottonwood Station. Walking again, they reached their destination at three in the early morning, having traveled 70 miles in less than 48 hours.

"I think that's a record." Theo said and he, John and Olson were proud of their accomplishment.

The people made them feel very comfortable. They heated water so each of them could have a hot bath, using the same water in a round tub. Olson was first, John second and Theo last. Hot water was added for both John and Theo.

"How do you expect me to get clean bathing in all your dirt?" Theo asked.

"Quit complaining," John answered. "It isn't every day you get to bathe in hot water and it sure helps stiff and sore legs."

The three were given time to relax before they were assigned other tasks. John wrote five letters. While he was resting, he went into the shoe repair business, fixing a number of shoes as well as his own buckskins and acted as the dentist's assistant, holding the heads of Olson, Theo and James Truman as Jerry Hatch pulled their aching teeth.

The Christmas Season was a lonesome time for the missionaries. Although Christmas services were held Christmas Eve and John McLaws, the postmaster, had them over for a fine dinner, they gathered together at Clark's place wishing they were home enjoying the things that were going on there. Then they started feeling sorry for themselves. Listening to their sad laments. Theo stood up and went to the door.

"I can't take any more of this," said Theo as he went out the door. He rode to the Baradosa Ranch owned by Mexicans and came back with a bottle of moonshine and shared it with the boys. Then they thought the world was all their own until about three in the morning.

The next morning John felt awful, he had a splitting headache and he could hardly move. He felt guilty and resolved he would never drink again, no matter what! His resolve was strengthened when he and Frank Grey were asked to go after a load of lumber leaving at nine that morning.

They arrived at the mill Saturday afternoon and because Sunday was the day of rest, had to wait until Monday to load their four wagons taking on about 3,500 board feet.

It was the next Saturday before they returned to Allen City. A part of two of those days was spent hunting for their animals that had strayed away from their wagons.

As soon as the wagons were unloaded, Theo, Joe and John McLaws took the wagons and started after another load of lumber, taking five wagons and eight spans of animals.

President Allen, who had gone after his family, returned January 9th. While he was gone, five houses were built, and John worked on all of them. He started with his own, hauling two loads of rock and he and Ted Olsen built the chimney. After the walls were up, John McLaws made the doors for him. For the roof he went over to the marshes near the Obed Camp and gathered a load of rushes and flags with which he covered the roof then finished by spreading a load of dirt over them.

Theo shook his head. "I don't think Ellen will be too happy to live in that house. Remember she is a city girl. She's used to finer things."

"It will only be temporary. I'11 build her a beautiful home as soon as I can."

With President Allen came another family planning to settle in Allen City. Then in the middle of the month, three more families arrived, the Skousens, the Despains and the Borups. With these new arrivals, the prospect for John and Theo to go home soon brightened.

"That day cannot come any too soon for my purposes." John told Theo and he sat right down and wrote a letter to the Salt Lake 3rd Ward Bishopric, the Ward he and Theo were representing on this Arizona Mission. He asked Bishop J. E. Weiler if he would arrange for them to pick up their needed supplies from the tithing and Bishop's Storehouses as they traveled back home. He also asked his father for $10 to pay for any other expenses.

During the first part of February six missionaries were released to go home from Allen's Camp, Alma Iverson, Charles Hansen, Dan McAllister, Joe McMurrin, Theo and John. All were eagerly preparing for their return trip. John was the most eager of all, planning to return with his Ellen.

On the 6th they went over to Obed to a surprise dance and had a tip-top time and the next day Allen City gave the boys a farewell party. Small gifts of remembrance were given to the missionaries. John had a clothes box made and the members almost filled it with wedding gifts for Ellen.

John Phillips with his wife and child joined the missionaries when they left for their homes on the 8th. John found the going much easier and the weather much better returning from the way it was coming. At the Ballenger's Camp, Dan Davis and John Egbert and family joined this little train.

When they came to the road leading to Moenkopi John got a mule and left the wagons and went there to see the place and some of his acquaintances that were living at this Missionary Post. The people were putting in crops and he saw some of the fruit trees in bloom that his mother had planted. He stayed the night. Trying to catch up with the company, he left in the morning. He passed through Moabby and Willow Springs without stopping and overtook the train camped on the divide.

After they crossed the Big Colorado River, they camped at Lonely Dell and John visited Emma Lee.

"The jury found him guilty." Emma said when John asked about her husband, "and he will be executed in a few days," she sobbed. "I know he never killed anyone. They are just using him as a scapegoat. Why don't they shoot the men who did kill the people? Here, read this letter he sent me."

After John read the letter Lee wrote to Emma he asked as he shared her grief by hugging her, "How could Jacob Hamblin say such things?"

"And they said I would have to give up the ferry. Only giving me ten days to move out."

"How could they? You have papers to prove ownership. They can't just kick you out!"

"With my husband's conviction, I lose all my rights."

John left this visit wishing he had never heard this sad news. She gave him a pair of moccasins for his sister Elizabeth.

The next night was spent at Soap Springs and the following night at Jacobs Pools and Friday at House Rock Springs. Saturday they camped on the Buckskin Mountains. They traveled on Sunday and nooned at Navajo Wells where Dan Davis ate a poison plant he thought was the same weed his mother collected for greens. It made him very sick so they immediately gave him some salt and warm water, which gave him relief and by evening when they stopped at Johnson's Settlement he was in his usual state of good health. Monday they reached Kanab and camped in front of John Riders. Here they spent nine days.

A dance was given in their honor and a group of local actors entertained them with a good play. "Almost as good as one they would see at the Salt Lake Theater." The boys commented.

Most of this time John worked for Brother Rider. Dan and Joe went to Long Valley to get grain for their animals, as there was no extra corn found in Kanab. Some of their cattle and horses strayed and were not found for three days. The weather became cold and it snowed a little.

John heard that Levi Stewart, one of the founders of Kanab, died. He only lived six months after he lost his whole family in a fire that engulfed their home.

One more night was spent at the bottom of Hurricane Hill. Then on to St. George where John met his father as was prearranged. He was there for the dedication of the new temple and where the April Church Conference was held.

John stayed at Brother J. D. McAllister's home. He was the president of this Stake of Zion, and Sunday he attended the last sessions of conference, which were held in the Temple.

When the meetings ended and they were filled with spiritual food, John was anxious to start for home but his father wanted to stay and visit with his friends and acquaintances from Arizona and Southern Utah who were also attending Conference.

"I can't wait to see Ellen. Have you seen her lately? How is she?"

"You didn't know! She was married on Valentine's Day!"

John couldn't believe what he was hearing. Ellen married! It couldn't be! She was his. They had an understanding!

"No! No! You're wrong! She promised to marry me!"

"She didn't write and tell you?"

"No! One letter said she didn't want to live in Arizona. She thought Salt Lake would be a better place as it had more advantages. I wrote right back and told her we would live wherever she wanted to, but I thought our place was in Allen City as the people were so wonderful."

Now there was no hurry for John to get to Salt Lake City. His father visited his friends.

John Jr. wrote in his journal: "All is lost!"

After a few blank pages he wrote:

The St. George Temple is a plain but elegant structure and will cause a person to feel a reverence when they enter the building for the purpose it was erected.

The town of St. George is about a mile square and has somewhere in the neighborhood of two thousand inhabitants. The streets are regular and lay parallel to each other, east and west. The sidewalks are nicely shaded by various kinds of shade trees. The dwellings in general are small but neat with a vineyard and an orchard surrounding each little home. Giving the whole town at a distance, the appearance of one vast orchard, spotted here and there by a little cottage. The houses, gardens, streets etc., all appear so neat and clean that the first impression is of the apparent enterprise of the people.

The only building of much importance, except the Temple, is the St. George Tabernacle. This is a large one-story cut stone building with a spire on the east end of it in which is a large clock that gives the people of the city the time of day.

# Chapter 19

On the Sunday John and Theo reported their mission in the 3rd Ward, the Ward they represented. The congregation went right along with them as they were telling of their experiences. They shared their hardships and laughed at the funny things that happened. Things that weren't so funny at the time, but now John and Theo could laugh at them, too. Their talks were filled with youthful enthusiasm and the members enjoyed the meeting.

A number of people came up to them after the meeting to shake their hands and wish them well and a small group of girls stood near by looking at them but not speaking to them.

Theo nudged John. "That one can't seem to keep her eyes off of you. She's not bad looking either."

When John looked at her, she bowed her head then looking at him blinked her eyes, smiled and quickly turned her head.

"Why doesn't she look at me like that?" Theo asked.

John retorted, "I'm better looking!"

"Ho! Ho! Ho!" laughed Theo.

The next Sunday, John Jr. was speaking in his own Ward without Theo. It was harder to speak to the members here who knew him and to make matters worse, Ellen and her new husband were sitting in the congregation. He couldn't see a friendly face as his father was not there and his mother was sitting at the piano to accompany the singing.

Although he used the same talk he gave in the 3rd Ward, the congregation seemed dead. There were no looks of sympathy for his trials. No laughs when he told them about Miss Jarvis or how the boys from Obed tried to fool them, how it backfired and they lost their horses. He could hear the babies crying and the old spinster Campbell sisters and their friend who always sat on the front row, talking to each other seemingly unaware that John was speaking.

Three giggling boys didn't help either, since he thought they were making fun of what he was saying. They weren't laughing at him, but at a mouse that was on the stand running between the legs of the three members of the Bishopric who were sitting behind the pulpit. Then they saw it disappear under Margaret's skirt.

John sat down with a sigh and was glad when the congregation began singing the closing hymn. Suddenly his mother stopped playing the piano, the chorister stopped leading and the singers stopped singing one by one and all eyes were on Margaret who jumped up and gave her skirt a vigorous shake and out flew the mouse landing on one of the Sister Campbell's lap.

She jumped up and screamed, dropping the mouse on the floor. The dear little ladies around her also stood and screamed and held up their skirts, one with unexpected energy landed standing where she had been sitting and there was much confusion. The frightened mouse almost stood still wondering which way to run.

One of the giggling boys caught the mouse by the tail and holding it at arms length in front of him ceremoniously marched down the aisle and out the front door.

John Jr. didn't know if a closing prayer was said or not. In the all the excitement he left through the side door.

Margaret found John slumped in a front room chair. He looked like a balloon with most of the air leaked out.

"I'm so sorry John, but I couldn't stand that thing running up my leg." She apologized.

"I'll never set foot in that place again!" he said through tight lips.

"But it wasn't your fault. Your talk was good! I'm proud of you and all you did on your mission."

He didn't change his position but sat there smoldering in his shame.

With extra zeal, he pitched right in helping his mother and father in every way he could, but when he was resting, he was so depressed and his mother missed his happy, optimistic, old cheerful self.

When Sunday came around, John Jr. would not leave his room. It was the same the next Sunday. His father tried to talk to him, but he wouldn't listen. He offered to outfit him so he could go back to Arizona.

" I can't go without my Ellen. What would people think?"

Finally he was convinced to attend Church in the 3rd Ward and on the first day he went, one of his friends said, "I heard about the mouse that added spice to your homecoming." He tried to laugh with his friend, but it wasn't easy.

Elizabeth was going to be married. While her brother was away, Thomas H. Mitchell had courted her. Many prophesied her future husband would go far both in business and Church-wise. Margaret and John felt she was getting a prize.

He was friendly and out-going and had a way of lifting up the self-esteem of every one he talked to by making them feel important. Yet he was deeply spiritual and had reverence for holy and sacred things. He loved life and had the faith to follow his dreams and most of all he loved their Elizabeth.

He was the oldest son of Benjamin T. Mitchell and his seventh wife, Susannah Houston. His father was a stonecutter by trade. In Nauvoo, his father worked on the temple by day and stood guard at night to keep their enemies at bay. Along with Parley P. Pratt, he surveyed Salt Lake City in the fall of 1848. He cut the stone and helped build many of the important buildings in Salt Lake, including ZCMI and the beautiful City and County Building. He supervised the cutting of granite for the Salt Lake Temple. He was called to go to St. George and he and his older sons who had learned the trade from him, worked on the temple there. He was now the second Bishop of the 15th Ward.

Many parties were given for this popular couple but John Jr. was found at few of these until Josephine, the girl who flirted with him when he first talked in the 3rd Ward, took him in hand.

She was an excellent dancer and witty and full of life and a fun companion, but she was not his Ellen. When she realized he didn't plan to marry her, she dropped him and gave her attention to any eligible young man who came along.

While she was dating him, she did succeeded in getting him to attend church meetings in both the 13th and 3rd Wards and resume his old friendships.

The first thing he knew about it was when Bishop Weiler called him into his office saying he wanted to talk to him. Josephine was pregnant and claimed that he was the father. John was outraged and vehemently denied it.

"Haven't you been her constant companion for months now? You've been seen at Church and at all socials with her. She says you are the father and I believe her."

John was too angry to answer and he stormed out of the room.

Next his father talked to him. "I'm told Josephine is going to have a baby and you are the father."

"I'm not the father. I never touched her in that way!"

"Even if you're not, why don't you marry her anyway? She's pretty, full of life and energy. She would make a good wife."

"I told you, I am not the father and I wouldn't marry her even if I was!"

"Why not? It would save both of your reputations. And if she didn't please you, you could find another girl and marry her, too."

"What kind of marriage would that be? I don't love her and I could never trust her!"

His father gave up.

Next it was Josephine's father who approached him and he brought her along. When her father asked her in front of John if he was the father, Josephine said "Yes."

"You lie!" John exclaimed facing her.

"Who is the liar!" her father shouted back. "If you don't take responsibility for your actions, I'll see you land in jail!"

His sister, Elizabeth, asked Johnny about it, too. Josephine had come to her and asked for help.

"Now everyone knows and thinks I'm guilty." He decided after questioning his sister and found she had heard it from other sources too.

The Bishop of the 13th Ward, his Ward, came to see John Jr. at his home three times, but each time he had conveniently "just stepped out". The third time, he left a request for Johnny to attend "Bishop's Court" which would be held for him the following Thursday.

He didn't go. "They have already decided I'm guilty." was his excuse.

"No, John. You would have a chance to tell them you are not the father."

"Oh, no. They would just excommunicate me for something I didn't do."

"They would believe you. They know of your honesty and integrity." His mother argued, but it did no good.

His mother and father were the only ones who believed him.

Josephine became the wife to a sweet old man and had a baby in seven months. John thought this prove he was not the father as he had insisted, since he had stopped dating Josephine a little more than nine months before this baby's birth. It made him bitter, blaming the Church instead of the persons who had not believed him.

At the next April Conference, John L. Blythe was called on a mission to Scotland and was to leave April 30th and Elizabeth was married earlier in the month. Margaret was so busy preparing for the wedding and for her husband's leaving she wasn't aware of her son slipping away from the Church or realized his new friends were sons of apostate members. She justified his not attending the 13th or 3rd Ward meetings but was pleased when she saw him in the Tabernacle congregation at General Conference.

Her husband left in high spirits. He felt with Margaret, John and God's help everything would be well cared for at home while he was gone.

He stopped in Pittston, Pennsylvania to visit relatives and old friends. The gifts he intended to give them were shipped on to New York by mistake and he had to mail them back when he reached the dock where his ship was anchored.

Margaret's problems began as soon as John's train pulled out. The clerk in their Produce store came to her and said he was quitting his job. He had never worked for a woman and he didn't intend to start now. Maggie complained that her house was too small, with her three children, the adopted Robert, who she insisted he live with her to be company for her son Charles, and the girl she had to help her take care of the children and her house.

Two farmhands were asked to settle in other towns. Johnny was staying out late at night, sleeping in late and not taking care of his usual household chores or working in the fields like Margaret expected him to do.

"Why don't you get off my back?" He complained when Margaret tried to get him to change his ways.

Then he found her, the girl of his dreams. She was a singer and had an engagement in Salt Lake. It started as a dare by one of John's friends. He had the nerve not only to talk to her but also to invite her to a dance. It was not a Church dance, but a City affair. He couldn't believe his good luck when she said yes, much to the displeasure of her aunt who was her chaperone.

It was love at first sight for her, too. Her aunt couldn't do anything to change her mind when she told her she was going to stay in Salt Lake and not finish her tour. Her aunt pleaded and begged. Reminding her she was giving up fame and fortune by not appearing in the other cities she had arranged for her concerts.

Johnny brought this pretty little Italian girl, Louisa Christmas, home to meet Margaret and told his mother he was going to marry her.

"How long have you known her? Just a few weeks?" His mother asked when she got him alone. "You say you love her. How can you be sure? Marriage is so important, John, think about it. It just isn't right! Wait a while and let her finish her tour and see if you feel the same way then."

"No, we love each other and we are going to get married, now!"

"But she's not a Mormon, John. She's a foreigner and a gentile, I forbid you to marry her! It just isn't right!"

"You can't stop me!"

She continued to try and reason with him. Margaret and her son had their first real argument.

Margaret found solutions for most of her problems, but Johnny's problem she had to share with her husband who was now in Scotland.

On receiving the letter, he sat right down and wrote a letter to his son asking why he would ever want to marry some one outside of the Church when there were so many lovely Mormon girls he could choose from. He also asked how he was going to support her and where he expected to live. "Surely you have no thought of living with your mother?"

Johnny's answer was, "I love her, father, and I am going to marry her with or without your blessing. It won't take me long to be qualified as a schoolteacher. As you know, I am good in reading, writing and arithmetic."

"For a wedding present, I would like your five acres, the land south between State and Main Street. Give me this and I won't ask for another thing. There I can build a permanent home, like the one Thomas is building for Lizzy."

His son had answered all his questions and John wrote back, "This is a hasty and premature decision. If you love her, wait until you can take her to the Endowment House and there marry her for time and all eternity. Honor your Priesthood then you will be happy. This is no time to add to the burdens of your mother. She needs your help. Pitch in and meet the responsibilities of life fair and square and not shrink from honest labor. Forget about school and raise grain and other crops to sustain my families and others."

And Johnny's answer was, "We were just married by the Justice of the Peace and we are very happy." And he asked again, "Can I have those 5 acres?"

A letter from Margaret came at the same time. She told him John and Louisa were married and he had his heart set on teaching school. Which was just as well since he hadn't been much help ever since he met the girl. "It will please him if you give him the five acres."

Very disappointed in his son, he wrote, "Under the circumstances I give you the liberty to choose to qualify for teaching. As I value our relationship as father and son more than houses and lands, the 5 acre lot is yours."

# Chapter 20

Land and was sighted May 26, 1878 and the steamship anchored near Queenston. A smaller ship came alongside and received the mail and the passengers for Ireland. Of these were two of the six Missionaries who were shipmates during the voyage. All six shared the same cabin, the former ship's hospital. John and the other four were taken ashore at Liverpool, England.

What a relief to be on land, out of that crowded stateroom. Here some of the missionaries had been seasick and were unable to leave their beds most of the time. John suffered again from scurvy. This illness developed during the long trip taken around Cape Hope, South America when he was sailing from New York to San Francisco, allured by the discovery of gold. The lack of fruits and vegetables in their diets left many of the passengers suffering from scurvy. John never fully recovered from this lack of Vitamin C.

The missionaries went to the Millennial Star Office. Here Brother Bull was printing Church material. Brother A. F. McDonald, the president of the Scottish Mission was also there.

After breakfast and after receiving some good counsel from the Brethren who were there, John put up at the Temperance House. He had the afternoon and the next day to see the sights in Liverpool, visit a museum, an art gallery and St. George Hall.

That evening he went by steamboat with Elder Kippen and President McDonald to Glasgow, Scotland.

Whenever Elder Kippen and John got together something unusual happened. Anxious to start their Missionary work, they found the busiest street corner in Glasgow and held their first street meeting. The first either of them had ever held or witnessed. John started out with prayer, then Elder Kippen started shouting, "We are the missionaries from the Church of Jesus Christ of Later Day Saints." When no one passing paid any attention to them, he cried, after the manner of a revivalist preacher, "Oh, ye perverse and wicked generation! Repent and be baptized!" Still they had no audience.

Then John started, "We are Mormon missionaries from Utah, with a saving message." They were stared at but no one stopped.

John felt inspired to sing a song, so he began with an old-time favorite, one his mother taught him. Elder Kippen knowing this religious song joined in and the people started to gather. John was able to tell them who they were and how the Gospel was restored in these latter days. As he talked the crowd grew but they assembled themselves quite a distance apart from the Elders seemingly not wanting to appear interested in what John was saying.

When he finished, Brother Kippen bore a powerful, sincere testimony.

The Elders then began singing another familiar song, one that needed soprano voices. Without thinking neither of them could reach the high notes, they started the singing loud and clear but when they came to this part of the song, they sang the notes as high as their voices would reach then there was complete silence. There was no sound coming from their lips, just an embarrassing silence. Then when the song came back within their range, they continued singing to the end of the verse. They gave each other a knowing glance and stopped singing but the group of people started singing the next verse and gathered in closer to the Elders, and sang with them until all the verses were sung and left with a warm feeling toward the Elders and each other.

President Walker warned John and Elder Kippen, "Coal miners were a proud and private people and ready to pick a fight with any stranger." They planned to go house to house to get the miners to come to a meeting that evening. He also suggested they stay close together when they were in that part of town.

The Elders had poor luck as the women at home continually closed the doors in their faces. Then they met this one lady who seemed very interested. She invited them in for tea and asked them to stay until her husband returned from the mines. Then they could talk to him.

During their conversation, John found she and her husband were relatives to the miner who had been killed a short time before and John who was there at this time had impressed her with the words of comfort he gave the grieving wife.

When the man came in the door the coating of coal dust on his face didn't hide his displeasure seeing two men in his home. Finding they were Mormon missionaries he stormed into the kitchen calling them all kinds of dirty names and they were ready to run when he came through the door carrying a large butcher knife in his hand. The last words they heard him say were, "Ye can'na steal my biddy!"

They ran as if their lives depended on it – which it did - and gradually outdistanced the knife-carrying husband and when the road divided, John ran one way and Elder Kippen took the other road. When John looked back he saw the man standing at the crossroad trying to decide which one to chase.

There were no new investigators at the meeting that night only two very tired and thankful missionaries.

One Sunday morning when the two were walking up the road to Brother Walker's house where they were going to hold meetings, they aroused a dog. He started barking and jumping up and down hitting the fence trying to get out.

"I'm glad he's behind that fence."

"So am I! He sure looks furious!"

Just then his master came out of the house opened the gate and sicced the dog on the Elders. Having walked two hours and too tired to run and seeing no safe place to go, they stood still, facing the dog who was coming at them full speed. He got within a few feet when Brother Kippen stepped forward threatening the dog and started barking. The startled dog stopped dead in his tracks, turned around and with his tail between his legs returned to his master.

"I didn't know you could bark like that." John said in wonder and relief.

"Neither did I," was the Elder's reply.

During the time John served on his mission he seldom had a companion to work with. He was assigned to labor in Ayrshire because he had relatives living in that area. He was to work out of Kilmarnock, but before he went there, he took the train to Muirkirk and received a hearty welcome from his brother Charles and his wife, Agnes. He visited with his sisters Margaret and Jane who were living in Strinrar. Both had Marshall as their married name. Jane was a widow and Margaret was married to John, who was a tailor and they had a lovely, well-educated family of seven girls and three boys. In both homes he was treated royally.

John Blythe must have looked rather shabby after his long journey from home because Charles had his boots half-soled and his brother-in-law, the tailor, had his son measure him for a new suit. John insisted he pay for the choice material of dark blue wool he would be using and for his work.

Twice John went to church with his brother and Agnes and had cause to remember both meetings. At the first meeting, the minister let a man speak to the congregation who had just returned from Utah. He said he had joined the Mormon Church before he left for Great Salt Lake. When in Utah he had renounced his membership because of its strange and foreign teachings and he desired to return and be accepted back in his old church and religion.

The second time the meeting was held in a smaller church. His brother thought John would be better accepted here. Although he was not a member, John felt his brother favored this church. A traveling evangelist gave the sermon with much zeal and enthusiasm, tickling their ears then ending with the suggestion their love of Christ could be shown by opening up their pocketbooks for the work of God. John saw his Sister Jane sitting up near the front.

When the Services ended, Jane motioned for John to come and sit by her so they could visit. He barely sat down when the evangelist came over to them and asked what they wanted. Were they in trouble? Did they need help?

When Jane said, "No. He is my brother from Utah and we just wanted to visit."

"The preacher asked, "Are you a Mormon?"

John said, "Yes."

"Do you have more than one wife?"

"Yes, two." John was going on to explain that he was a missionary but the evangelist didn't give him a chance.

He grabbed his coat, stood him up and asked how he dared to enter their church - a lustful, sinful, and dirty man. The minister came to see what the trouble was and when told he was a Mormon, they each grabbed him and not too kindly walked him out the door. John's first thought was to fight back, but remembered he was a servant of God.

Jane told Charles and Agnes who were waiting outside for him how he was treated. Charles wanted to go in there and tell them off. John said he would rather he didn't, but he wasn't stopped. He stormed through the door, found the minister and his aid and said, "That Mormon is my brother. He is not lustful, sinful or dirty and you of all people had no right to treat him like that. For this you will not see me or any of my family in this kirk again and you will never get another farthing from me!" And he departed as quickly as he entered.

While visiting Charles, John wrote a letter to Daniel, his brother in Australia and was surprised to hear Charles had not heard from his oldest son who had also gone to Australia, for three years.

"Don't you write to him?" John asked.

"We had a little disagreement when he left and he needs to write to me first."

"But don't you wonder how he is doing? Whether he is alive or dead?"

"Aye."

"Isn't he in Melbourne with Daniel?"

"I think so. He had my other son leave me and left me with no one of the family to help me run my business. That was three years ago and now I have no family."

"I'm writing to Daniel and I'll include a letter to your sons."

John did, but Charles refused to sign it or add to John's letter until John told him he knew from what Daniel had written that Charles Jr. was married and had children. Then Charles broke down and wrote a few lines to each of his sons.

That's how it started, along with Agnes bringing out John's mother's Bible, which had been in her desk for years. His Mother had carefully recorded her own family's history and the birth, marriage and death dates of her parents and grandparents.

Seeing these, Agnes sighed "And we don't know anything about our own grandchildren."

John added, "And they don't know anything about their grandparents or great-grandparents."

The ice was broken and Charles agreed with Agnes. Their grandchildren should know about them and when Charles was sold on an idea, he never did anything halfway. He and John went to every source they could find to gather the names of their kindred. Cousins should know cousins and their progenitors as well as their grandparents and great-grandparents, he decided. Many were the family groups they copied of their immediate ancestors and in-law's extended families.

John wrote to his brother Daniel in Australia, requesting him and his relatives to get up a correct genealogy of our kindred in Australia and send it to him. Saying he and Charles would gather up all they could in Scotland and preserve them for the mutual benefit of our offspring. On the return of this information, Charles never lost track of his sons and grandchildren again.

The 'Law' genealogy on his mother's side seemed to fall into John's hands. One cousin had been keeping and gathering family records for 42 years and to reach Ebenezer Law's place, another relative, John took off his shoes and stockings and walked over Carntable Hill and through the moor and the fragrant heather to Moss Bank farm. Here he was given records of his ancestors and also some of his wife, Margaret's ancestors, too, which were many generations. From these two relatives he received hundreds of names. At the time, little did John know in about ten years he and Margaret would be doing the temple work for many of these names in the Logan Temple.

A Mr. Mitchell, an agent of the Glasgow Protestant Layman's Association, challenged Elder McDonald, President of the Scottish Mission, to a debate.

Subjects: Is salvation wholly a work of God? Mr. Mitchell will affirm, Mr. McDonald will deny. 2nd, Do the scriptures of the Old and New Testaments sanction a plurality of wives? Mr. McDonald will affirm, Mr. Mitchell will deny.

The President asked John to occupy the Chair on his behalf. It was to be held in the Larne Hall. It would seat up to 600 people. His letter said, "It is not the victory I'm after in the discussion, but the opportunity to place before the people the truths of heaven and a correct knowledge of God and His laws".

John accepted. Replying, "Although I do not approve of debates and prefer a more modest way of declaring the truth of the everlasting Gospel, I feel satisfied in your ability through the blessings of our Heavenly Father to prove clearly the points at issue. And do some good thereby in endeavoring to silence the clamoring tongues of those who oppose the work of God."

John invited both Charles and his brother-in-law, John Marshall to come and hear the debate. Charles came.

President McDonald's rebuttal of 15 minutes to Mr. Mitchell was well done but poorly received by the audience. And again his 30 minutes contending the plurality of wives and sanctity of marriage was well proved by the scriptures and the rest of his lecture was very convincing.

Then Mr. Mitchell used I Kings, Chapter 11 to prove his point. "The Lord said unto the children of Israel wives will surely turn away your heart after their Gods." And added, "Solomon had many wives and they did turn away his heart after other Gods. And Solomon did evil in the sight of the Lord. The scriptures say many wives are evil in the sight of the Lord. Therefore you Mormons with your many wives are sinners and evil."

Then he poked fun at his opponent, acting out a supposed conversation between McDonald and his wives. This got a good laugh.

John wished Charles hadn't come to hear the debate.

John was pleased when he received the new pilot blue wool suit his brother-in-law, the tailor, made for him. That is, until he tried it on. It was way too small. Disappointed he asked John Marshall to come and see for himself what a poor fit it was and he also complained about the poor sewing as the stitches broke open under one sleeve when he tried on the coat.

The tailor told John to send it back and he offered to return the money he had paid for the suit, which John readily accepted.

During his mission, John was never invited to the Marshall's home again, but he thought nothing of it since Charles often brought his sister, Margaret, along with him when he visited John. Neither did he realize how much his letter hurt his brother-in-law for he was proud of his work and felt it and he had been insulted.

Originally John Marshall planned this suit as a special gift for his wife's brother from America. Then John insisted he pay for his suit, which took away the joy of giving a gift. Still he did his finest tailoring and was careful with the details and styling. Then to have it thrown back in his face!

Also John never realized he was responsible for the ill fit as he was measured for this suit when he first got off the ship. Since then he had put on considerable weight and was now wearing heavier clothing, too.

Because of this, John never had a chance to fully acquaint John Marshall and his family to the true Church and its teachings.

Charles hospitality was just the opposite. John was always welcome in his home. He and Agnes made John promise to spend Christmas and the New Year with them. Charles often took him to John's appointed meetings if they were in the area, although he never attended any, and to the train when he traveled longer distances. He told John not to lack for anything while in Scotland as he had plenty.

A letter from his wife, Margaret, said grasshoppers had invaded the Valley and had eaten most of the wheat and alfalfa he had planted before he left. Because they had also eaten most of the other crops the harvest would be poor. She would sell half of the pigs and some of the stock in order to pay their debts.

This was the bad news, but her letter contained good news, too.

Louisa had joined the Church and in September she and Johnny were going to be re-married in the Endowment House for time and all eternity.

At the close of his mission and before he left for home, President McDonald rented Larne Hall and had Robert Brown print 500 fliers that he and the missionaries widely distributed throughout Glasgow and the adjacent towns. He hoped to acquaint the public with Christ's true church and its teachings. He felt these fliers would stir up some interest among the people. They read: Mormonism revealed! Is it Christ's Church or the Devil's? The date, time and place followed and ended with "Everyone welcome, no charge."

On the day of the meeting, John, who was to be one of the speakers, had a terrible headache. He could hardly hold up his head. John and two of the Elders were staying at Brother James Houston's home, which was near Larne Hall. After administering to John, the Elders left for the hall to see if every thing was ready for the meeting as they were asked to do by President McDonald.

Sometime later, Brother Houston came to John who was lying on the bed and said, "The Elders have been gone a long time. Their food is cold. I'll go and see if they need my help. The Hall must be in a terrible condition to keep them this long."

John thanked him and turned over hoping for sleep, which did not come. More than an hour passed and none of them returned. John, his head still hurting and in much pain walked to Larne Hall to see what the trouble was. When he opened the entrance door, he was struck with the force of evil so strong that the power of darkness almost overcame him. He saw the three men lying on the floor and would have thought them dead if he hadn't seen an army of fiendish looking evil spirits surrounding them. They were gloating, smiling and nodding to each other. Some were gleefully laughing, pointing their fingers at the three fallen Elders.

With all the energy he could muster from his weakened body, John raised his right arm and in a loud voice commanded the evil spirits to depart in the name of our Savior and he saw them growing weak and looking dejected as they left one by one. The men soon aroused and John's headache was gone.

That evening John and President McDonald were able to clearly present the principles and beliefs of the Church of Jesus Christ of Latter-day Saints. The other Elders bore mighty testimonies as to the truthfulness of this, the Gospel as restored by the Prophet Joseph Smith to an audience of about 400 people. From this meeting came eleven baptisms.

John was to meet Charles on Market Day in Ayr. He and Elder Milne went to Ayr the day before, trying to find the only three members of the Church who lived there, but had no luck. While searching John found his wife Margaret's Aunt. She was old but cheerful and clear of mind and they could see she was living in dire poverty. So when they left John slipped a large coin in her hand. "She would have given us tea, if she had some to give us, a bed, if she had one." John observed thinking of her graciousness.

They went to the eating-house and after paying for their dinner they didn't have enough money between them to pay for a nights lodging and didn't know what to do. They made it a matter of prayer and while they were eating Elder Milne found a slip of paper in his pocket. It had the name and address of a family living there, which were relatives of Church members living in St. George, Utah, Elder Milne's home town.

This family welcomed them, gave them supper, a bed for the night and breakfast in the morning in exchange for news of their Utah relatives but refused to hear about their religion.

When they met Charles he had Margaret, John's sister, with him. He took them to a teahouse where they had a good visit. Then Charles invited the Elders to his home in Muirkirk and took them by train. Here the Elders stayed eight days.

Anxious to convert Charles, they talked much about the principles of the Gospel and most of the time Agnes was quietly listening. Yes, he could see the right way to be baptized was by immersion, but he did not feel it necessary for a remission of his sins. "I'll be judged by how I live my life and no baptism can change that or make me free of all my sins." He insisted.

Finally Charles got out of patience and said, "I hope I will be preserved from ever being entangled with such a gospel." and he never did join the Church.

Agnes was impressed by what she heard and the next Sunday when they held a meeting in Glen Buck, she brought two of her sisters to hear the Elders speak.

Charles drove them up to within a quarter mile of the place where the meeting was held. Left them and took his team to the Arch Green Farm and waited there until he decided the preaching would be over.

After a good meeting the Elders were able to distribute some tracts. Mrs. Blythe and her sisters had listened very attentively, which pleased John.

On parting, when the Elders left Muirkirk, Charles told John, "Although I was nippy at you with the tongue in regards to your religion, still there is affection in my bosom for you that will only cease with death."

John, as promised, was with Charles and Agnes during Christmas and the New Year. One of Agnes's legs became very swollen and at her suggestion John administered to her, asking God to cure her leg. She later wrote to John stating, she had made up her mind if her leg had been cured through the blessing she would have been baptized in the face of every opposition, but it did not get better. Her leg got worse.

John was asked to visit Brother Gibson the president of the Irvine Branch that had the largest church membership of any place in John's mission area. Brother Gibson was not sending in his reports or the contributions he received from the Saints. John was told to set apart a clerk to relieve him of this duty. John knew William Gibson was well versed in the Book of Mormon and the principles of the Gospel. He had heard him bear a strong testimony to its truthfulness a number of times.

President Gibson greeted John with warmth and enthusiasm and told him how much the membership was growing, "by leaps and bounds" as he expressed it and the rented hall was almost filled for Sunday worship, which he held each week.

John asked why he hadn't turned in his reports and contributions.

"I spend all of my time doing for the members and the growth of the Church. I have no time for book work."

"I know how busy you are so we will set apart Brother Wilson, one of your members, to act as a clerk to help you. He will be responsible for keeping the records and sending in the monthly reports along with the tithes and offerings to the Mission President."

"Records and reports, yes, but I will take care of the finances." Brother Gibson replied.

"The money given by the members needs to be carefully recorded. This would be one of Brother Wilson's duties, giving you more time to do your church work."

John wondered, and then asked, "You haven't been using the tithes and offerings for your own private use, have you?"

"Yes," was the reply, "and rightly so. I do more for my congregation than any minister in these parts. They get paid. Then why shouldn't I?"

"You know we don't have any paid ministry in the Church of Jesus Christ of Latter-day Saints. Remember King Benjamin in the Book of Mormon? He was a religious leader of thousands yet he refused the gold and silver offered to him for his support but labored with his hands to take care of his needs."

"The money isn't yours. It belongs to the Lord. Do you have any of it left?"

"No I don't. I thought I was doing right. I spend all of my time doing the Lord's work and I needed money to take care of my family."

"It seems to me you are trying to run the Branch all by yourself and neglecting your family. Let the members help you. You know the Brethren and Sisters. Give them the positions they are best fitted to do. Like King Benjamin, work to support your family and if you do this you will still find time to serve the Lord, and if you are earning money, you will be able to pay back the money you spent."

"I'll do this," Brother Gibson agreed. "When I can, a little at a time."

The next month and then again the second month the Branch clerk said Brother Gibson had given him none of the money collected from the members. Brother Gibson was relieved of his Office.

John was asked to take charge of the Irvine Branch until another president was appointed, since William Gibson had been excommunicated for setting up his 'Mormon' Church known later as the Gibsonites. He had rented another hall and had persuaded about two thirds of the members of the Irvine Branch to join him.

Because of this, John not only held the usual Sunday meetings in Irvine, but a weekly meeting for the Priesthood members and also organized a Sunday school with Francis Gibson, the brother of William Gibson, as President.

"I can't understand how your brother who had such a firm testimony could leave the Church and set up his own church. Do you know why? Was it money?" John asked Francis.

"It was his wife who insisted he do this. Of course it was for money. She said, "With his silver tongue he will have an income much larger than he was getting from the Branch tithes." He loves to feel important and now he can do and teach what he wants." Francis added.

"He came to me wanting me to join them, but I told him I already belonged to Christ's true Church and I tried to persuade him to give up this idea, but it did no good. I wish I knew as much as he does about our Church's doctrine. He knows what's in the Bible, the Book of Mormon and other scriptures and things I don't even understand."

"What good is all of his knowledge? He has exchanged his testimony as well as lost the gift of the Holy Ghost for a little money. I feel sorry for him."

"So do I," Francis said sadly.

John found the three members in Ayr that he and Elder Milne were unable to locate the last time they were in Ayr. They were James Drysdale and family, who were cold and indifferent to John and the Gospel when they first met, but after John spent the afternoon talking to them, their faith was kindled and they went down to the sea to be baptized. Brother Drysdale, his wife and oldest son were re-baptized and three of their other children were baptized and were made members of the Church of Jesus Christ of Latter-day Saints.

The next day the Drysdales invited their neighbors and friends into their home to hear the Elder's message. The spirit was strong and John felt his words were well received. Later John was told there were other members living in Ayr. He arranged a Conference for these Saints. The president of the Mission brought Brother Nibley and other area Church Officials to address the Saints and they organized a Branch in Ayr.

This conference was such a special event the member's children were kept home from school so they could go to the meetings and have the privilege of shaking hands with the Mission President and the other men representing the Church. The women prepared sumptuous meals and brought out their finest tableware to serve these honored guests.

Now, meeting together each week, the members felt that they were not alone sharing and defending their religion. James Drysdale thanked John for bringing the Gospel back into their lives.

Returning home, John felt his Mission in Scotland had been a success except he had not fulfilled the wish of his heart. Not one of his father's family or their children had been baptized.

A few years after returning from Scotland, John was called on another mission. He was to be the President of the Australian Mission.

He could hardly contain his excitement. "To Australia!" He repeated to Margaret. "Now I can see my brother Daniel. A dream come true!"

Every thing at home was running smoothly. His farms were well cared for. His Real Estate business was bringing in enough money to pay all of their expenses. All members of his families seem to be happy and content. Yes, this was the time to go, he decided.

Margaret agreed saying, "And I'll take care of everything here the best I can."

John quickly gathered up all the things he thought he would need, said good-bye to friends and family and left for California. There he booked passage on the first ship he found going to Australia.

His letters written to Margaret and family from Melbourne, Australia, were few and far between. The first letter said he finally arrived safely and how good it was to stand on solid land again. He didn't suffer from Scurvy this trip as the Captain put many limes on board the ship. These were small green fruit, which were cut in half so the passengers could suck the juice from them.

The next letter told of visiting Daniel, a happy reunion although Daniel's health was poor, and he saw his sister Ann who lived near Daniel and all of their families came together for a big party.

Next he wrote about Charles' two sons. Both had large farms, large beautiful homes and cattle and large flocks of sheep. They call them 'mobs', not flocks of sheep. The sheep were controlled and herded by a few well- trained dogs. The dogs were gentle with the sheep, but not to strangers as John found out when one bit him. They owned gold mines and most of their wealth came from these.

When Margaret read this she wondered if John would forget his mission and go mining for gold. She knew the answer before she read it. He wrote, Charles sons had little time to visit, which is just as well as I am here to spread the Gospel not to visit.

He wrote about the strange animal he saw. It didn't walk or run. It only hopped. It had a pouch or pocket across its belly where it carries its young.

They were told about meeting some of the original natives of Australia whose skins were black. They were not like our Indians. They had been cannibals but didn't practice this any more. For this John was grateful, as missionaries were likely to be eaten.

He wrote about his missionary work, wishing he could be in more than one place at the same time and wishing he had more missionaries to help him spread the Gospel. "We find many people here anxious to hear about the Church and its teachings. This place is truly already to harvest.

And the last letter said he was on his way home.

## Chapter 21

John sat back in his old chair. It was so good to be home. It was empty now. Maggie and Margaret's children were grown. He was ready to sit back and let the rising generation continue the work of building up Zion. He was so weary. The trip back from Logan to Salt Lake had taxed him more than he thought. He looked at Margaret as she cleaned the house arranging things for his comfort and his books and journals so he could reach them. It was so good to be with her again, away from Elizabeth's noisy children and his older sons, Charles and his adopted son, Robert, who were going to school there in Logan.

Where had his life gone? So much had happened without him. Most of his children were married and had given him grandchildren. Maggie seemed to be content in her new home. Forty years ago he was in California. He wondered what would have happened to him if he had been without Margaret's constancy and love. He would probably still be in California defending his mines, making more and more money – and living a hardened and empty life. How sweet the gospel was. He really must write a final testimony for his posterity.

John reached for his most recent journal. When he opened it, he saw it wasn't his writing and called, "Margaret, whose journal is this?"

"Oh, it's Elizabeth's," she said taking it from John. "They must have thought it was yours when they brought your things from Logan. It's her history. She wrote it when she was there with you."

"Will you read it to me? I'm sure she won't mind. We were reminiscing about our experiences of long ago. I guess she wrote them down."

Margaret began, "I am Elizabeth Ann Blythe, the daughter of John Law Blythe, married to Thomas Mitchell. I want to write a little about my life because I believe we women, mothers and wives, don't get the credit we deserve for our part in settling the West. Mother and I were pioneers and suffered more hardships than our husbands as many of the pioneer women did, but to read the history of the Western Movement, you would think the men did it all by themselves.

I was born on New Year's Day and mother made me feel each New Year the world was celebrating my birthday. I was raised by some remarkable parents. Strong in their faith, they imparted their testimonies to me. So it was easy for me to gain a testimony of my own.

Maybe I was spoiled a little being the only daughter mother had around, but I couldn't see it that way. She sent me to the best schools available, Mrs. E. Cook's was one of them and when I was older, the University of Deseret. Knowing I liked to sew, she saw I was taught this art by a professional, Phoebe Sloan. Besides dress making, she taught me to make buttonholes and this skill was one of my specialties.

We moved from California when I was less than two years old and along with the Church and the people in the Thirteenth Ward, the Salt Lake Theater played quite a part in my early life. Father had the money but we never lived in a mansion. He was a thrifty Scotchman always doing for others and the Church, but often forgetting his own children. Well, I can't say that for at mother's insistence he paid for my singing lessons, my piano lessons and I even took lessons in elocution. (I wanted to be an actress like Hannah Marie.} I went to operas and plays and learned to enjoy classical music and Shakespeare.

You think my life was soft? Well, it wasn't. I had to do everything for myself and a whole lot more and practice, practice, practice. That's what my folks made me do and not only on the piano either. When my brother was learning to play the violin, even the dogs howled when he practiced. Thank heaven, mother let him quit taking lessons. That was about the time one of our hired men broke his violin when he accidentally stepped on it. Was it on purpose? I think so.

My brother John thought I was a nuisance because I liked to follow him and his friends around. Sometimes I did even after they thought they sent me home. I would stay behind them and see where they went. Like the time I almost drowned in the Millrace. I hadn't learned to swim yet and the boys took me by the shoulders and tossed me in the deep water with my clothes on. They threw me in because I saw them swimming naked where no swimming was allowed because of the danger of getting caught in the water wheel and I told them I was going to tell father.

The first time I came up after hitting the water, I tried to yell for help but only "Hell" came out before I went under again—and knowing 'hell' was a swear word and I'd get my mouth washed out with soap if I swore, the only thing I said when I came up for the second time was a big explosive "Pah" so my brother couldn't tell the folks I swore. About this time Johnny jumped in after me and saved me from drowning.

Then there was the time when I was four years old and playing with my doll across the street from a saloon. I saw a man who was drunk stagger out of the swinging door and lay his head on the hitching post. He was followed by another man who drew his gun and shot him in the head. When I saw this I screamed at the top of my lungs and the man turned his gun on me and shot. The bullet whizzed past my head barely missing me. Did I ever run for home! For a long time I never told my parents because I wasn't supposed to be playing there in the first place.

One wintry day when my brother with some of his friends climbed up the hill to the top of State Street to go sleigh riding, I was with him. It was quite a climb but coming down the hill was so much fun. Traveling at full speed, we could almost make it to our place on Second South when the Eagle Gate was open. The first time we went down I was lying on John's back and the ride was exciting. When we climbed up to the top of the hill again my brother said he didn't want me to ride on his back.

He wanted to go down alone.

"You can't leave me here!" I shouted. "I'm going to ride on your sled." Before he knew it, I laid on his sled and started down the hill all by myself. Oh, it went swift but I was good at guiding and could stay in the wagon tracks where the snow had turned to ice.

I was having fun, not caring what my brother was thinking up there on top of the hill, when of all things there was this wagon crossing the road right in front of me. I had to turn sharply to run under the wagon bed between the wagon wheels, but I made it and got stopped in a snow bank on the other side of the road.

I looked back knowing it was a close call. I saw the woman's face was white. The man got down off the wagon and came over towards me. I waved and said, "Hi! Father! Hi! Mother!" cause that's who they were.

Johnny got spanked for letting me go down the hill all by myself.

I wasn't very old when we moved to Rhoades Valley. I worked hard there as mother's little helper. I fed the chickens and gathered the eggs. You would never think of finding a Rattlesnake in a chicken coup but I stepped on one when I was gathering the eggs. The first thing the snake did was coil up, shake his rattler and strike at me. It happened so fast and I was so terrified I didn't move and he bit my leg but I was lucky, this one time my father was near by and heard me screaming. He killed the snake, cut my leg with his pocket- knife where the snake bit me and sucked out the poison.

Mother said he saved my life. I had a sore leg for a while but I didn't die. That's the only time I've been bitten by a snake and I've seen many of them since then. Guess I was saved from dying a number of times when I was growing up.

When I was attending Mrs. Cook's School, four of us girls, class mates, decided to go on a picnic up the canyon. Although it was the last part of February and way too early for Spring, the weather had been warm and all of the snow had melted in the valley. We had our ponies. Mine had just been given to me on my birthday and I wanted to show him off. Carrie couldn't go unless her brother went along with us. For my part of the food, I brought bread, cheese and my favorite dried fruit, apricots.

It was sunny when we left but when we reached the mouth of the canyon the weather changed and it started to snow. We about decided to forget our picnic and go back home when David, Carrie's brother, said he knew of a cave close by and there we could make a fire and have our picnic inside the cave.

This sounded exciting but before we reached the cave we were in snow about six inches deep and the snow was coming down fast. Then right in front of us on top of this rock, we saw a Mountain Lion who jumped down from the ledge and frightened our horses. My pony lit out just like crazy! Before I could get him to stop, I bet he had run more than two miles. Was I ever scared! I didn't know if that Cougar was following us or not. I didn't know where I was because everything around me was white and covered with snow. It did stop snowing but not before it covered my horse's tracks.

We were lost and I was cold because I didn't wear a heavy coat. I tried to find my way back but after going a few feet I was afraid I was going deeper into the canyon. When I stopped trying to find my way out and my pony stood still, everything was so very quiet the only thing I could hear was the horse breathing. I stopped crying long enough to pray. Oh, how I prayed!

Since everything was so still, I don't know why I didn't hear him. This big Indian riding a horse seemed to raise right out of the snow. I was too amazed to be frightened and I thought I was seeing things until I saw two dead rabbits hanging from the side of his saddle.

Without saying a word he took the horse's reins from my hands and led us through the snow back to town.

When we reached the outskirts of the city and I knew my way home, he gave me back the reins. I asked him to come to my house and my mother would give him something to eat. He refused pointing to the rabbits and said he had to go. I handed him my picnic sack holding the cheese and apricots. He smiled, turned his horse and left.

I could see my father, David and two other men riding towards me. Since David and the other girls had returned home and reported me missing, they were coming to look for me. Did we girls ever have a story to tell Mrs. Cook!

When I was sixteen my father was appointed to take charge of a branch of the United Order organized in Salt Lake City. I helped him keep the records and that was a job in itself. I made shirts for the boys and men and dresses for the women and if that wasn't enough I worked in the silk factory, unwinding the silk threads from the cocoons. That was careful, exacting work. I made ladies dresses outside the Order because I had a reputation of making beautiful gowns. I couldn't keep the money I earned. It had to be given to the Order.

I was sure glad when the Order dissolved about two years later. When it was first started there were thirty-nine members, some with their families, who signed up. They met mostly in our old house at Second South and State. Here they gave their report of the hours spent and the kind of work they did. Prayers were said and food was served and more than a few slept there and made it their home.

This United Order had a mixture of nationalities. Five members were born in Scotland, thirteen born in Denmark, twelve in England and three came from Sweden. One was born in Calcutta, India and one came from Castilla, Spain. Then there were four born in the United States; one in California, one in Illinois and two in Utah, towns of Manti and Morgan. We needed a few interpreters but all were trying to learn and speak English. I was surprised how the Gospel seemed to envelop us bringing all of us together as a family.

Our farm was at Millcreek and we gathered our fruit from the 3$^{rd}$ Ward orchard. Mother assigned the women their tasks and helped them learn some new skills. She was always cheerful and encouraging and much loved by the sisters. Father with the help of Brothers Heber Searle and Neils Neilsen planned and rotated the work for the men.

There were a few who left the Order before it was disorganized. Joseph Waters was one. He made ladies slippers, men's shoes and boots, so we were sorry to see him go. He said he was leaving for Spanish Fork in search of a wife as he had not found one here. Some blamed me for his leaving since he had asked me to marry him and I said no, because he was too old and not very handsome. This branch of the United Order failed like all the others leaving my folks poorer but wiser, my mother said.

Margaret stopped reading and asked John, "Are you awake?" and when he said yes, she said, "She hasn't written anything about our experiences at Emma Lees and the ferry or Moenkopi. I thought she would write about that. Now she's writing about Thomas. Most of this you know." She continued reading.

I was so much in love with Thomas when I married him. To me he was just perfect and so handsome with his red hair and you should have seen him when he was wearing his fireman's uniform. I wish I had a picture of him with his metal helmet and all. He was a hard worker and loved his children. He was so patient with them. He seldom punished them when they did something wrong or naughty. Rather, all he needed to do was to look disappointed or talk to them in a calm, quiet way so they could understand what they did wrong and how to change their ways. I think he got this trait from his mother.

I can picture him now holding Huey, our first baby, in one arm or over his shoulder while stirring the gravy with his free hand when I was busy putting the food on the table. He was good around the house and usually milked the cow and slopped the pigs. He loved beautiful things in and around the house. When we were first married and when they finished building our home, he said it looked incomplete until we planted flowers, lawn and trees in front of it.

I wanted to make and hang the drapes and curtains for our windows before Christmas, but instead I made four dresses. Do you know why? The Christmas present my father sent us ladies from Scotland while he was on his mission, was fifty-two yards of black dress material and since I was the seamstress, I was to make the dresses for my mother, Maggie, Louisa and myself. I would have rather he sent me a picture book showing interesting places in Scotland, like he sent Maggie's girls or even a policeman's whistle like he sent the boys and men. Anything except yards and yards of black cloth.

"Why did he send black?" I asked my mother. "Why not blue, or white, or brown, or any color except black? Did he think we were going to someone's funeral or we were in mourning?"

"Elizabeth, don't complain." Mother said holding up the cloth at the end of the bolt. "Look at it. It is beautiful material and I'll be happy to have a Christmas dress made from it. He sent pins, spools of black thread and these Betsy Ann needles. You couldn't buy any of them here. I'm sure it wasn't easy for him to gather up all of these gifts. He was so thoughtful. Appreciate them."

I did when I saw the fruits of my labor, all of us wearing lovely stylish gowns. But why black?

Life was pleasant while we lived in our new home and we shared many fun times with Louisa and Johnny. We both had three children and were doing well financially when our husbands learned of a rich valley with few settlers just beyond Fort Duchesne in the northeastern part of Utah. Here they felt we could do much better by opening a store and bringing much needed supplies to those people living in this area.

In a short time we sold our homes to buy the merchandise and the outfits to carry it to Ashley Valley, Uintah County. That is, after John and Thomas checked out the place for this ambitious enterprise. They rented a large building owned by an old timer Jake Workman as a temporary place for our store.

Quite a caravan left Salt Lake City. Wagons loaded with merchandise, furnishings for our new homes and covered wagons for the comfort of us ladies and our six children. Mother loaned us some of her farm hands to help us with the wagons with a promise we would send the men back as soon as we reached Ashley Valley.

We traveled over much hot desert to get to our new home. The roads were poor when we could find one and we often had to make our own where there were only trails to point the way. Once we ran out of water before we could find a stream. Our children were suffering from the heat and begging for a drink. Thomas found some canned tomatoes we were bringing to sell. Oh how good the juice and the tomatoes tasted and they quenched our thirst. Ever since then whenever my children get real thirsty they ask for juice from a can or bottle of tomatoes.

We hung up rag rugs and blankets to separate our living quarters from the store and barely had things organized when we had our first robbery. This gang of dirty, rough looking men robbed us at gunpoint.

One held his gun on Louisa and me who with our children happened to be in the store at the time.

Ever since I was four and had a gun shot at me when I was playing near that saloon, even a gunshot triggered fear throughout my whole body and now a gun was pointed at us and I was petrified. Huey, my six year old hid behind me and Pearl clung to my skirt. She and my youngest child sensing my fear started crying.

Then Louisa and her children started to come over to us but the robber saw her and yelled, "Don't you move or I'll shoot!"

She quickly pushed her children out of danger behind the rag rug into our living quarters.

Next he shouted, "Keep those brats quiet!" but Elizabeth and the baby cried all the louder.

Then little, petite Louisa ordered this ruffian who was guarding us, "Put away your gun. Can't you see you are frightening the children?" and much to my amazement, he did.

Our husbands couldn't do a thing to help us. They were busy gathering up the supplies apparently from a list they were handed and had more than one gun pointed at them.

After our guard holstered his gun, Louisa seemed to change. She straightened up and with a regal air walked right past the man who had been holding us captive and went over to the center of activity, grabbed the list from Thomas and turned to the gunman who seemed to be the leader of the gang and said, "We don't let merchandise leave the store without being paid for."

He holstered his gun, reached into his pockets and turned them inside out to show he had no money. Seeing this, she handed him the list saying, "Here sign this for receiving these items and we will put them on your bill."

He did, then the gang gathered up their supplies and left. We couldn't read his signature but that same gang never robbed us again nor did they ever pay their bill.

Before long our new store was built and with large letters, 'Blythe and Mitchell Mercantile' printed across the front announced our business. We celebrated feeling we had reached our goal.

We were in our new quarters just a few months before Louisa became ill and died. Her sudden death was a shock to all of us. My brother John was devastated. He blamed himself for her death.

"Why did I bring her to this god-forsaken country, far from doctors, medicine and help!" he lamented. He didn't care about anything and refused to be comforted and I wasn't much help mourning over the loss of my best friend.

Louisa's aunt came to her funeral and John didn't object when she wanted to take his two daughters to raise. No, she couldn't take the boy since she was a spinster and she said she knew nothing about boys so John A. Blythe Jr. was added to our family. Oh, how mother grieved over her son and the loss of her granddaughters.

People started settling Ashley Valley and as the town grew so did our business. The men made many trips to Salt Lake to get merchandise to restock the store. Sometimes Thomas would let me accompany the wagons so I could visit mother.

Father was in Australia as the mission president, having been called by the Church on a South Seas Mission shortly after he returned from Scotland. Again mother had the responsibility of taking care of his affairs as well as Maggie's family. She was also running a dairy in Taylorsville. I don't know how she did it!

Buildings sprung up all around us. The saloon was too close and John started visiting it. A bank was built and was robbed almost as often as we were. Many were the men who warmed themselves around the pop-bellied stove that heated the store and I had Indians, soldiers, ranchers and travelers eat at my table. I enjoyed cooking and visiting with our visitors.

You always knew when the ranch-hands received their pay. They came to town, visited the bar, imbibed freely then they would ride through the town whooping and shooting their guns in the air or at any stray chicken that happened to be in the street. At these times, I would cling to Thomas or anyone else who was nearby because I was so frightened when I heard the gunshots and to this day I hate guns.

With the rapid growth of Ashley Valley, Thomas decided we needed a post office. He petitioned the government for one and they made him the Post Master and the Post Office was set up in our store. Then Thomas asked Washington if the town itself couldn't be named to designate it from the whole of Ashley Valley. Again the Government answered his request and sent him a list of names to choose from. Vernal was the name he picked and after other members of our town agreed to his choice the town was officially named Vernal. The name brings back good and bad memories, the bad outweighing the good.

Schools were poor and I supplemented my older children's schooling by teaching them reading, writing and numbers at home. I also saw to it that they attended church every Sunday, although our meeting house was made of logs, hot in the summer, cold in the winter and the rough benches would put slivers in your bottom if you didn't sit quietly. I was active in Church, in local and civic affairs and was often asked to plan our May Day celebration and our Christmas programs. I thought up unique ideas and decorations, which seemed to be enjoyed by all.

Two children, a boy and a girl, were added to our family before I noticed a change in Thomas. During this time we had great luck in hiring good, honest, competent men and women as clerks and helpers to keep our business growing. With John's 'I don't care' attitude and with Thomas feeling everything was running smoothly without him, he joined John and spent many hours away from home gambling and often visiting the saloon.

When Thomas took a few drinks his personality changed entirely. He became mean. He found fault with everyone and everything. I didn't know him when he was like that. He didn't seem to know what he was doing, but he had to have his own way. One time he came after me with a gun and I think he would have killed me if he had found me. I thought it would have been better if he were more like John who was often drunk but pleasant and friendly before he reached that stage.

I don't know if this change came about as a result of too much prosperity but both men acted as if there was no limit to their wealth and were constantly gambling with their money and the things they owned. One day we found our freight wagons belonged to someone else. Our business was even lost before they quit.

We lived in Vernal four years before tragedy struck again. I had a business all my own, a millinery shop. I couldn't make ladies hats fast enough to keep up with the demand. I'd left for Salt Lake to get some more supplies but never reached the Valley before I was met by mother with the terrible news. Huey, my ten- year-old son was dying, having been drug by a horse.

Mother went with me and to get back to Vernal the fastest way we could, we went by train to Price, Utah, then by light buggy the rest of the way. My oldest son was still alive when we got there, but never regained consciousness before he died a few days later. My son, Thomas Houston Mitchell Jr. was buried alongside Louisa in the Vernal cemetery.

How did it happen? My husband won this untamed horse while gambling and after having taken a few drinks insisted Houston take the horse to the stream to water him. Huey not wanting the horse to run away, tied the rope around his hand and wrist so he could lead him, but the horse had other ideas and started running down the road dragging the boy behind him. A neighbor saw what was happening and was able to stop the horse, but it was too late to save Huey. He was severely injured.

I was so unhappy at Thomas I was ready to leave him right then, but I was pregnant and waited until my sixth child was born. Thomas couldn't forgive himself. He quit drinking, became his old self and did everything he could to please me, but I couldn't forgive him.

Father came home very ill when he returned from Australia and was unable to do any hard work. Knowing father, I'm sure he was a good mission president, but he felt he had been a failure because he was unable to convert and baptize any of his close relatives, his favorite brother Daniel, or either of his nephews, Charles's sons or any member of their families.

When father visited Daniel in Melbourne he found him unable to walk or talk having had a stroke just before father reached Australia, but Daniel recognized his beloved brother John and held him with his good arm and cried for joy at their reunion. Father was at his bedside when he died and signed his death certificate. Father was grateful that he was able to see him before he died.

As soon as father felt better he wanted to do the Temple work for his brother. Since they haven't finished building the Salt Lake Temple, mother suggested he go to Logan and do the Temple work there. Father had organized a long list of names of relatives he had collected in Scotland and Australia and had them copied in two large temple books made for this purpose.

He bought this large house here in Logan and set about getting the work done for Daniel and his kindred dead in the Logan Temple. His health was failing but he insisted he was well enough to be baptized for Daniel and he did his Temple work.

Mother couldn't spend all her time here with him and I thought it would be a good time to leave Vernal, take my children and live with father. That was the right decision. I've had a chance to get to know him. He was always gone on a mission or away from home when I was growing up. I found him a very optimistic person and a delight to take care of. All winter he was so sick and now he wants to go home to Salt Lake. I'll miss him.

When Margaret finished reading John bowed his head and shook it in regret and frustration and asked, "Margaret, how could Elizabeth and John end up so miserably? What did we do wrong?"

"I feel we have done everything we know how to do. We've offered countless prayers, talked and pleaded with Johnny and Thomas, but it didn't do any good. We must remember they have their free agency and if that is the way they choose to live their lives, we can't force them to change. Sometimes I wish we could."

John said, "Think of Thomas. Remember when he married our Elizabeth what a wonderful outstanding man he was? He was so spiritual and so firm in the Gospel. I expected him to become a leader in the Church—an apostle. But his drinking and gambling has destroyed him, his family, his home and his business. Everything! And our son John - How can we fight this evil destroyer?"

"John, we have done all we can do, so don't upset yourself. Here is your journal. Don't you want to write in it?"

When Margaret left the room he opened his journal. He really must write a last testimony for his children and grandchildren. John sighed and closed his eyes. Maybe later. He would take a nap for just a few minutes.

Margaret came into the room walking softly trying not to disturb her sleeping husband but he looked so uncomfortable. "John," she softly called. When he didn't answer, she touched his hand. She gasped. It was cold to the touch and his stillness. John's spirit had left his body.

.

# Chapter 22

Margaret stood by the train tracks behind the Union Pacific Station in Salt Lake as the train pulled in. She could hardly wait to see her son James Stubbart and her two grandchildren. Would her son look like his father Mathew? Would he stir up those memories again?

The conductor placed a portable step on the ground in front of the exit then quickly sprinted up the steps back into the train. When he reappeared, he was practically carrying this gaunt, sickly looking man who was leaning on him so heavily both were having a hard time walking.

"No, this couldn't be James," Margaret said to herself. He did write he was ill and asked if she would help him take care of his two children since his wife died just a month ago and he didn't know where to turn for help. Of course he is her son James, she decided.

After the men made it down the steps to the ground and before she walked over to greet her son, she saw a young man heavily laden with a sundry of parcels and bags following closely behind the men. He spotted her and called, "Are you my grandma?"

When she smiled at him and nodded, he came over to her and before putting down his bundles exclaimed, "My name is Mitchell, but they all call me "Mitch". Margaret hardly heard him as she went to help the conductor support her son. They walked him to her wagon and with the help of Mitch got him up into his seat.

Looking back towards the train and the place Mitch had left his packages and bags, she saw a pretty ten-year-old girl standing there. She looked hurt and disappointed. Margaret hurried over to her, put her arms around her and said, "You must be my sweet, little granddaughter. I'm so happy to see you at last."

"I'm Ellie," the girl replied as she returned the hug and she started asking many questions. "Where are we going? Is father all right? Is he going to die? Why did we come here? Are you a mean old grandma?"

Margaret didn't reply and laughing to herself decided, this girl will make out all right. She isn't a bit shy. Yes, she will be able to take care of herself.

Her son James started coughing and she hurried over to him but found Mitch was already at his side handing him a hanky to spit into.

"Oh, he has consumption," she thought. "Now what do they call that, Tuberculosis? How can I help him?"

When they reached the house, Margaret got help to carry James up the stairs and put him on the bed. Mitch stayed near him alert to anything he might need or want but Ellie was walking around the parlor taking in every object and piece of furniture that was in the room. When Margaret walked in she exclaimed, "You have a piano. Can I play it? I always wanted to take piano lessons."

Margaret nodded absent-mindedly. She was wondering where she could take her son and get him out of the cold and smoke-filled city. Some place where the weather was dry and sunny. She thought of Deseret, Utah, a place where some of the men had taken her cattle to winter range on occasion. Yes, she decided that Deseret would be the ideal place. So she took out a Homestead of 21 acres and had workers remodel a red brick house she bought on land that was near the Sevier River that passed through the settlement.

As soon as the house was finished, she moved everything she thought she would need including her piano to Deseret.

James had improved some under the care he was given in Salt Lake and in Deseret he seemed to improve daily. Not realizing how contagious TB was, she had Elizabeth send her son Blyth, who was having allergies and shortness of breath, to come live with them. He was just a year younger than Mitch.

The house was close to the school and Deseret had a Church meeting house already built. Margaret was pleased with her choice.

When she mentioned the closeness of the school and church to James he asked "A Mormon Church?"

"Is there any other?" Margaret answered. "Of course a Mormon Church. We are living here where they are all Mormons."

This started a fit of coughing and James had a hard time getting his breath and when he did the first thing he said was "Don't you think of making my children Mormons. Look what joining that terrible church did for you! I know enough about you Mormons and your evil ways. I don't want anything to do with you Mormons." Then he started coughing again.

"Of what religion are you?" Margaret asked.

"I'm an atheist. There is no God or this world wouldn't be in the mess it's in. There is no God or my children's prayers and mine would have been answered when Jane was so ill. Believe in a God who would take a wife and mother from us?"

"Don't you try to stuff your beliefs down them. As members of the Church of Jesus Christ you claim to be Saints. You people desecrate the word! I wouldn't have come here but I had no other place to turn."

Margaret put her arms around him and said, "Oh, my son, my son. You poor, poor boy."

Later she asked "You don't want your children to have any faith in God? No religious teachings? No reading of the Bible?"

"Yes. When they get old enough they can choose the Church they want to belong to. Yes, they can read the scriptures, but don't let me hear of them going to your Mormon Church house." That settled that. She would not go beyond his wishes.

When they started going to school, the three children were looked on with suspicion because they were different. They were not Mormons. Ellie said she was a Methodist the same as her mother. Mitch claimed to be an atheist and Blyth not knowing what an atheist was, mocked Mitchell and said he was an atheist too.

Margaret had the children read from the Bible and later on had them read verses from the Book of Mormon. James had given her permission to let his children read the scriptures. She reasoned this would include the Book of Mormon. It was also scripture.

She taught Ellie to play the piano and found an eager and gifted pupil. Soon she could play any of the music or songs put in front of her. She borrowed a hymnbook she found in the schoolroom, one used by the Sunday school. When she played from this book, her father seemed to relax and enjoy hearing her play. One time he sang the words to a familiar song until he started coughing.

Ellie never wanted for friends. Margaret let her go to her friend's houses but seldom did her girl friends come to her house. "Why?" She asked her grandma.

"Ellie, maybe they feel they would disturb your father. I think everyone knows he is very ill."

"No, that isn't the reason. I think it's because we aren't Mormons. I heard Mrs. Thompson say so. Are Methodists contagious or something terrible?"

"Oh, no, of course not. Mrs. Thompson just doesn't understand any one who believes different than she does. God loves all of his children, Mormons and Methodists alike. You are very precious to Him and precious to me, too."

A little later, Ellie came from her friend Barbara's house. She was out of breath and all excited and when she found her grandma had this story to tell.

"Barbara has a secret room under her house and it isn't a root cellar, either. It's where they put her father and they don't let him out until these men go away. Sometimes he stays down there for days. She said so. You get down there from the hall and go down a ladder from this trap door but its secret and no one knows that it's there unless they move the rag rug. Barbara and I went down there. It was a room with a bed and all. Her mother was mad and made us come up. He doesn't like to go down there, then why do they make him?"

Margaret had seen this situation before and explained to Ellie, "He has more than one wife, which the Government doesn't think is right so they send these men out to catch him and if they do, they will put him in jail. Is there more than one lady living in that house?"

"There's Barbara's Aunt Nora and her children. She says they are her brothers and sisters but they have a different mother. She says her Aunt Martha who lives down the road has three children who are her sisters, too. How can that be?"

"They are really her half-brothers and sisters. They all have the same father. He is married to more than one wife, which he thought was right when he married them, but members of the Mormon Church don't do that any more since the Government said it was wrong. Barbara's father loves each of his wives and his children and wants to take care of all of his families so he had to hide to keep these men from finding him. He can't take care of them if he is in jail, so don't tell anyone about that secret room, even if you are asked."

"That's what Barbara's mother said." Ellie kept this secret from then on.

Flashing lightning and loud thunder accompanied the downpour that thoroughly wet all of Deseret. It rained all night and into the morning before it quit. Margaret was not surprised when she saw the river rising and wondered if they were going to have a flood. She hoped the small plants that had started to grow in her garden wouldn't be washed out. She had Mitch and Blyth go check the ditch head-gate to see if it was closed and asked them to shovel some dirt around it to protect it and keep the water out.

Although the rain had stopped the ground was muddy. It sucked the shoes right off their feet since they hadn't tied them properly and they left then where the mud had claimed them. It was hard work banking the ditch with such heavy soil and when the boys finished they rested sitting by the rising river wiggling their toes in the mud.

"Let's leave our shoes where they are and tell Gram we lost them."

"Naa," Blyth replied, "she would make us go find them."

"Guess we had better go back but we can't carry them in the house like they are. She wouldn't like us dirtying up her floor. You know how particular she is." So they picked up their shoes and went to the river to wash them off.

Mitch reached the water first and was holding one shoe ready to clean it when he lost his footing and fell landing in the water. Seeing this, Blyth dropped his shoes, grabbed the shovel and held the wooden handle out to him but he didn't take hold of it.

"Put it down." Mitch called, "The water's warm. Come on in. It's deep enough for a good swim." Then he threw the shoe he was holding at Blyth who was walking down the bank into the water.

They were enjoying their swim, but it wasn't long before they had to duck the things the current was carrying down the river. Some were boards and branches and chickens floated past them flapping and fluttering their wings as they fought the water, but all of their energy was wasted. Soon the current was carrying the boys down the river too. They were growing weak trying to keep their heads above the swift water. Then a large wooden box came floating down the river heading right at them. This they were able to grab and hold on to and it kept them from drowning.

After their scare was over, Mitch said, "Hey, look what's in here. Are they whiskey bottles?"

"No, I think they are wine bottles," Blyth answered.

"Whiskey or wine, what's the difference." Mitch returned. "As long as this keeps us afloat. We can ride this box to the end of the river!"

While he was talking, a branch hit Blyth on the shoulder and he lost his hold. Mitch was able to catch him without losing his grip and both of them were holding on to the same side of the box. It started tipping from the added weight and the side they were holding on to, sank into the water and they were left without any support. Again, they would have drowned if a small chicken coup hadn't reached them right then. They were able to climb onto its side, which was the only part above water.

When the boys got over the shock of nearly drowning and the pitching of the shed stopped, they laughed at each other for each was holding a full wine bottle in his hand.

It wasn't long before the chicken coup was snagged, held in a maze of debris collected by a dead tree that reached into the river. Unable to get to shore from this position and afraid to get back into the raging river, the boys opened their bottles. By the time they were found and rescued, both bottles were empty and the two young men were so out of it, they didn't remember who found them or who brought them home. Margaret was so glad they were found and alive, she didn't lecture them about drinking the bottles of wine.

By the next spring, James had gained weight and strength. He was coughing less, had a good appetite, was walking around the house and yard and was interested in his children and what they were doing.

Margaret was so glad to see this change and felt that if he kept improving he might get completely better. So it was a shock when she found him in his room lying on the floor, his head in a pool of blood. He was dead.

Her first thought was, "How can I tell his children?" He was too heavy to lift onto his bed so she turned him over on his back, cleaned up all the blood on the floor and washed his face, rinsing and bathed part of his face with her tears. She put a pillow under his head and found the most beautiful quilt she owned and gently covered him and thought as she saw him lying there. He is just sleeping. Sleeping? Yes, his body is sleeping but his Spirit is much alive.

"Are you here in this room?" She asked aloud. The answer came as she felt his presence close by.

She asked again, "Oh, I was so happy to see you getting well. I thought you would be with us a long time. Why did you leave us now?"

She went into the parlor, sat on the couch and had Ellie and Mitch sit, one on each side of her. Mitch knew something was wrong when she put an arm around both of them pulling them close to her.

"Is father worse?" Mitch asked.

"Yes, I found him on the floor. I couldn't wake him."

Then Mitch asked, "Is he dead?" and Ellie asked, "Is he alive?"

"No, he has left us."

Ellie jumped up and ran into his room followed by Mitch and when she saw him, she threw herself on top of him. Patting his cheek she pleaded, "Don't leave me! Oh, Daddy come back, come back!"

Mitch who was trying to hold back his tears picked her up and holding her sat on the bed and they cried together.

When they heard about his death, many neighbors came to express their sympathy, each bringing a dish of food. Baked and fried chicken, potatoes cooked in many ways, carrot and potato salads, cookies, cakes and pies covered the kitchen table. The depressed family ate very little of it.

James funeral was held in the 13th Ward in Salt Lake City where few persons other than family members attended and he was buried in the Blythe Family plot. Margaret took his children back to Deseret to live. Ellie had so many friends there and Mitch said that was where he wanted to be. He seemed to adapt so easily to country living and he would be a big help to her while she proved her homestead.

She had almost lost it last year. Since the help she hired was so slow clearing the land she needed to plant to hold her claim, at the last minute she had potatoes put in furrows on dry land without any chance of them ever growing. When she was claiming this work had been done, one man said, " Mrs. Blythe, you knew those potatoes would just rot on the ground. How can you say you planted a crop?"

Margaret answered, "You take care of your business and Mrs. Blythe will take care of hers."

With Mitchell's help this year she could be honest with her planting.

Knowing Relief Society meeting was held every Tuesday morning in the Deseret Ward building, Margaret thought she would go before meeting and take the dishes and pans that held the food brought at the time of James death so the Sisters could claim their own. She was asked to stay for the meeting, which she did.

How nice it was to be with the Sisters and join in their prayers and sing the old familiar hymns. She felt she had returned home. Yes, she was right when she brought Mitch and Ellie back to Deseret. Living among the Mormons and with her example they might want to join the Church. This she hoped, but she would not push them, just give them the environment and teach them the Gospel.

Her thoughts were interrupted when she heard two Sisters talking about her. "If we work it just right we might baptize Mrs. Blythe yet." The other one answered. "Oh, she would make a good Mormon, wouldn't she?"

# Acknowledgements

The author wants thank her son, Glen Fullmer, who introduced her to the computer and with much patience helped to get her book ready to publish.

Her daughter, Jean McPherron, helped edit it, as did Jean Bradshaw Boyce but the errors they did not catch are strictly her own.

Richard Ira Elkins gave her permission to use some stories from his books "Ira Hatch Indian Missionary, "PU -AM -EY" and the " The Honeymoon Trail". Juanita Brook's two books, "The Mountain Meadow Massacre" and "Emma" have given her research of John D. Lee's life more details. She suggests you read these books.

She thanks her cousins, Rhea Hatch Wride and her sister, Vivian Grindstaff for the encouragement and help they gave her.

www.ingramcontent.com/pod-product-compliance
Lightning Source LLC
Chambersburg PA
CBHW021052090426
42738CB00006B/306